SKY SPY

RAY HOLMES

SKY SPY

FROM SIX MILES HIGH TO HITLER'S BUNKER

Airlife
England

To those who encouraged me to write this book, particularly my dear wife Anne who typed the amended MSS thrice and to my life-long friend Leslie Bibby for his invaluable aid by making those amendments during his painstaking proof-reading of the MSS I extend my sincerest thanks.

The front cover illustration is an original painting by Geoffrey Nutkins showing the author's close encounter with a Dornier bomber over London on 15 September 1940.

Copyright © 1997 Ray Holmes

First published in the UK in 1989
by Airlife Publishing Ltd
This edition published in 1997

British Library Cataloguing in Publication Data
A catalogue record for this book
is available from the British Library

ISBN 1 85310 844 8

Printed in Great Britain by St Edmundsbury Press Limited, Bury St Edmunds, Suffolk

Airlife Publishing Ltd

101 Longden Road, Shrewsbury SY3 9EB, England

CONTENTS

Foreword

Writing this was never my idea.

At a Merseyside Police Fraud Squad Christmas party I was discussing our damp-course problems with John Baragwanath, a surveyor who was another guest there. John readily recognised my problem, and out of the blue suddenly offered: 'I'll call and show you how to fix it if you'll promise to write a book about the war'.

I was staggered. But the damp was a pest, and I agreed. I followed his advice about making a bell-skirting, and the damp went for good.

The book has taken slightly longer — eight years, to be exact. But I've kept to my side of the bargain.

I just hope, John, that my book is not as dry as my house.

Ray Holmes
July 1988

Prologue

GOD HELPS THOSE . . .

Twenty-nine thousand two hundred feet on the altimeter. Just six miles up. Five hundred feet higher, and I would be making a dazzling white trail that would betray my position to every German fighter within twenty miles.

I had almost crossed the North Sea, and was nearing Holland. The visibility was as sharp and clear as only a February sky can make it after rain. The Dutch coastline stood out in fine detail.

I had known loneliness many times in an aeroplane. But to be hurtling alone towards the enemy at 410 mph was more than mere loneliness. It was desolation.

The German radar had plotted me five minutes earlier when the first intermittent howl came over my radio. Gradually the moans merged into a steady note as their scanning beam swept to and fro, searching for my echoes, finding me and finally holding me. It could be demoralising, but this, I chided myself, must never happen. It will take more than the Hun to shake me. I was on my first mission into occupied Europe to bring back photographs of ships in the Rhine at Mannheim, and this I intended to do.

Although operational flying — that is, flying in combat against the enemy — was no new experience after a fighter tour at the start of the war, high altitude photo reconnaissance was. This was my first sortie with 541 Squadron from our PR base at Benson, near Oxford. It was the climax to a two-month course at Dyce, near Aberdeen, on navigation and photography from 30,000 feet. Flying from the north of Scotland to the south of England, pinpointing and photographing targets at that height, had been fun. Now, over enemy-occupied Europe searching for strange foreign place-names on the map while keeping a wary eye open for pouncing Messer-schmitts, would all be very different.

As, with each minute, I probed seven miles further towards enemy territory, England seemed far behind indeed, and the chances of ever returning there grew remote. Guns, radar, aeroplanes — all sought me manned by people with hatred in their hearts. I wondered what Fate held for me in the next hour. Would I be intercepted, shot at, shot down? Would I have to bale out, be mortally wounded, or crash my Spitfire in flames?

Would I die?

How strange to have to accept that, within possibly but as few moments, I may no longer be alive. No longer exist. Where would I be when my soul left my body? What would I be?

The enemy knew that my twin cameras with their powerful 36-inch focal length lenses were the trained eyes for Bomber Command, and the spies for the Allied armies and navies. They knew that the information I took back on my camera films could trigger off a thousand-plus bomber raid, to rain thousands of tons of high explosive on to their oil refineries, or submarine and rocket bases. Or start a commando raid from our submarines, or by glider and parachute.

So they were out to destroy me. Swiftly and utterly.

The steady moan in my headset showed they had me plotted as a bandit approaching their coast. They would now be launching fighters to cover every possible route I might take to a target. My strongest card was that they did not know what my target was, but must guess it from my course.

Land was visible in clear detail now. Black shadows of cliffs thrown by the low sun were stark against the light sandy beaches. At this crucial moment I had two choices. Either I could press on across the coast, fly a new course to Mannheim for 57 minutes and take my pictures, or I could turn tail and scuttle back home to safety and a flying instructor's job. It was at this point that I found myself muttering: 'God helps those who help themselves'.

'Right, God,' I muttered up to the blue expanse of universe where I knew Him to be, 'I'll do my stuff if you'll do yours. Otherwise', I added with grim wit, 'I'll be seeing you.'

I made a rapid check of my instrument panel, searched once again above and below for enemy fighters, and turned 22 degrees to starboard on to 190 degrees Magnetic.

He did his stuff — on that and over twenty subsequent missions, many lasting up to six hours in one of those marvels of design and construction, the single-engined single-seater blue photo-reconnaissance Spitfire.

'Trust in God, and live one day at a time . . .'

That was my faith through five years of war.

Part One
War Clouds

1
'Let's go Flying'

The world-famous Brooklands racing circuit echoed with the roar of the cheering crowd and the snarl of straight-through exhausts belching blue flame and black smoke, leaving in the air the heady smell of Castrol R. By the twelfth lap the little maroon three-wheeled Morgan, sitting as steadily as a ladybird, had established a comfortable lead over its nearest rivals and was already lapping several of the slower cars. It had today, for the year was 1923, become the first three-wheeled car to break through the 100 mph barrier, and the crowd yelled its acclaim for its driver — Edward Bradford Ware ('E.B.'), the brains behind both the racing car and the 1,000cc V twin JAP engine that powered it.

His back tyre burst at 103 mph as he started climbing the banking. Shreds of rubber tangled in the two driving chains and locked the wheel. E.B. slammed shut his hand throttle, and fought with the steering. But the slithering, sliding car went into a broadside roll. Nose and tail cart-wheeled up the track flinging out its driver, and the Morgan finished a crumpled heap of torn metal the other side of the crash barrier, with E.B. a bundle of rags nearby.

The wreckage, being off the track, was no obstruction so the stewards flagged the other drivers to continue. A crash wagon crew took one look at the pile of wreckage and the heap that had been its driver and decided to leave him until the race was over. When they came to lift E.B. on to a stretcher an ambulance attendant heard a moan. E.B's body was a tangle of limbs but he was alive. His hips were dislocated, the thighs fractured round behind his back. Both arms were shattered, the elbows torn away. But his head was miraculously unharmed apart from a gash on his forehead, and his powerful brain had mercifully escaped damage.

That brain produced the will to live while his body was straightened out and mended. Soon after his release from hospital he was back tinkering with his maroon Singer open tourer, tuning it to touch 70 mph, a high speed for a production car in the 1920s. Yet its engine idled like a sewing machine and started at a touch.

About this time my mother's younger sister Violet met E.B. and brought him to our home. He quickly became very close to the family as he had no home ties. He taught me carpentry, helped me to build my own bench and to set up a workshop in our attic. Later he taught me about engines and had me riding his motorbikes and driving his cars before I reached my teens, third party insurance not being compulsory in those days and a driving licence a mere formality.

E.B. was the official Auto Cycle Union and RAC tester for many makes of British motorcycle. He brought from London the prototypes of the Matchless Silver Arrow twin-cylinder machine, their four-cylinder Silver Hawk, and the four square Ariel, and sent me solo on each. When I reached sixteen he persuaded my father that I should have a Morgan instead of the motorbike every boy wanted. 'Safer and less selfish,' he said. He promised to find me one in good condition, most Morgans, being sports cars, having been hammered into the ground. As their designer he knew every nut and bolt in them.

In January 1931, just after I started as a junior reporter on the *Birkenhead Advertiser*, he drove UR4097 up north from Barnet near London. It was a bitter, frosty 200-mile drive for him in the open, unheated aero-sports Morgan. But although he arrived blue with cold and his hands, which never responded properly to the nerve-damaged elbows, were almost dead, he was cheerful, and proud of the prize he had found for me for £69. It was two years old, but immaculate, and maroon, his racing colour.

I never needed to learn to drive that Morgan. We had talked engines and tinkered with cars so often together that to drive it was second nature, even though it had a hand throttle on the steering wheel instead of a foot accelerator.

In September 1936 E.B. informed me that the RAF was starting a new scheme for training pilots. He said it was tailor-made for me. It was to be called the RAF Volunteer Reserve. Pilots under training would sign on for five years and start with a ten-week intensive course of theory and flying. They would then continue their flying at weekends on aerodromes near to their homes. Travelling costs would be met, and a £25 bonus paid annually. It was possible to buy a good second-hand car for £25 in those days. To learn to fly, and be paid enough to buy a car for doing so, sounded too good to be true.

The catch was that all entrants, who would be given the rank of Sergeant-Pilot, would be mobilised automatically into the regular RAF if war broke out. But in those carefree days of cricket and rugger, of swimming and climbing and camping holidays, the thought of war to young RAFVR Sergeant-Pilots, though faintly stirring and exciting, was quite remote.

Our leaders, however, knew better. They had been watching Hitler. Within three years of the formation of the VR, weekend pilots were providing the nucleus for much-needed operational squadrons.

I wrote off to the Air Ministry at E.B.'s suggestion, and by return a buff envelope arrived for me bearing the Adastral House crest. A letter advised me that VR candidates must have a high standard of fitness, British nationality, and give an undertaking never to go abroad without permission. Two months hence, at 10 am I was to attend for interview and medical.

There were three other candidates. For six hours, with an hour's break for lunch, we were pummelled, interrogated, observed and sounded by five different specialists in their own field. We jumped on and off chairs, balanced rods on rulers, did handstands, headstands and pressups. We were swivelled on chairs. In darkened rooms we manipulated switches to join up split lights, focus horizontal and vertical beams, track shooting stars, and segregate jumbled figures and letters. We had knee jerks, pulse readings, breath holdings. We blew columns of mercury up tubes. We listened to clocks, watches, tuning forks and scrambled speech, separately and together.

We said 'Ah-h-h!' and coughed.

I was handed a thick dictionary. 'Open that as near the middle as you can — preferably within twenty pages either way,' he instructed. I judged the middle and opened it. I told him I was at page 387. As he went to his bottom drawer for a notepad I flicked to the back of the book and snatched a glance at the last page.

'How did you do?' he asked, not taking his eye from the small mirror in which he had been watching me.

'Quite well I think,' I answered guiltily. 'Twelve off centre.' To my surprise he told me: 'Don't worry, that's a point in your favour. We want to test your aptitude for checking your own errors.'

Another doctor carried out the respiratory tests. He let me continue holding my breath after the required seventy seconds — probably to see if I would either black out or burst. I had learned the trick of packing the blood with oxygen by a series of deep breaths in advance. At three minutes five seconds, when my eyeballs were ready to explode, his patience give out. 'All right,' he growled, 'that'll do — we can't be here all day.' He reached for a glass U-tube of mercury on a stand with a rubber tube and mouthpiece on one end. There was a graduated scale behind the mercury. 'Blow it up to there', he said, indicating a red line on the scale, 'and hold it there for one minute.'

This really brought the veins out on the forehead.

'Right, rest for a moment then see how high up the tube you can blow the mercury.'

I was ready for this one. With a couple of gentle preliminary puffs, I started the mercury rocking. Then I gave it my bugle top C. The column of mercury shot up the tube like a rocket, and spurted out at the top. The back of his neck was a dull purple with rage as he went round the floor on his knees with two pieces of blotting paper, scooping up his precious quicksilver.

I wished I could have taken *his* blood pressure at that moment, for he had just no sense of humour.

A week after I arrived home, pummelled but proud, another buff envelope arrived. It was addressed to Sergeant 740055 Holmes, R.T., RAFVR.

I was in.

On 1 February 1937 I arrived at Prestwick aerodrome, which was at that time little more than a farmer's field bounded by hedges. By the middle of the war it had become the trans-Atlantic terminal with long tarmac runways for American-built Lockheed Hudson bombers ferried across to us. I finished my ten-week course at Prestwick with 62 flying hours in my logbook.

A few months after I arrived home, E.B. telephoned us at West Kirby from London. Although he was really a friend of my parents, he asked to speak to 'his mate'. I had just come out of Brookfield

Nursing Home after an appendix operation and was barely walking. I struggled to the phone.

'I've called to say goodbye, Ray,' he told me. 'I just wanted to wish you luck with your flying. Keep it up, old son, but don't join an airline and become a taxi-driver.'

I was mystified. 'What do you mean, goodbye? Are you going somewhere?'

'I'm in a nursing home, with cancer of the stomach. They're just going to open me up.' He told me the address, and rang off rather quickly. I was so upset, it was some time before I could tell my parents E.B. was dying. They understood my distress and made no protest when I said next morning I was going to see him, even though my own stitches had been out only a few days.

I set off in our Rover 10 saloon. There had been heavy snow, the roads were icy, and I was still tender around the middle. I was in no state to huddle behind a driving wheel for any length of time. Conditions were so bad that by nightfall, cold and exhausted, I was still far from my destination, and broke my journey to stay with friends.

I made an early start next day, but not early enough, I arrived at the nursing home to be told E.B. had died during his operation. I always felt he had asked them to make sure he did.

The communication I received on 1 February 1937 from Civil Training Schools at Hendon, London, was to alter my life. It was also the start of a chain of events linked with Hendon. The letter read:-

'Dear Sir,' (the last time they ever called me Sir).

'Information has been received from the Air Ministry that you have been selected for enlistment in the RAF Volunteer Reserve. You are hereby instructed to report to the Reserve Flying School of Scottish Aviation Ltd, Prestwick, Scotland at 0900 hrs on 8/2/37 to commence ground and flying training.'

The communication was signed by a Squadron Leader with an undecipherable signature pp Air Commodore, Superintendent of RAF Civil Flying Training Schools.

I boarded the train at Liverpool Exchange a week later with my Notice Paper for the Flying School safely in my wallet, and mixed feelings in my mind. It was hard to believe that next time I arrived home at West Kirby I would be a pilot.

I wore my regulation RAFVR uniform for the journey. Navy blue double-breasted blazer, with VR badge on the breast pocket, and flat silver buttons embossed with RAF wings, a VR tie, blue shirt and collar, grey flannels and black shoes. If we ever won our wings these would be woven in gold wire on the breast pocket badge.

To Carlisle the journey was a reverie. What lay ahead? How would I cope? What would it feel like to look down from the air?

We changed there, and again at Kilmarnock. By the time my taxi had covered two miles from Ayr station to the Orangefield Hotel, on the fringe of Prestwick aerodrome it was dark. Floodlighting had not been thought of then, and the sandstone hotel looked grim and forbidding with its towers on each corner.

The hotel proved to be half-residential, half our RAF Mess. The receptionist was a middle-aged spinster, bun-haired and pince-nezed, whose broad Glaswegian we could scarcely understand. She had obviously shown many couples on a stolen spree to double rooms, never gone herself.

My co-pupils on the course were over a week ahead of me. I had been drafted as a late entrant with instructions to catch up. Even so, my number on the Volunteer Reserve was 740055 — fifty-fifth to join of the many hundreds of thousands of VRs to follow when war came two and a half years later.

Several of the course had already flown solo. One glance across the lounge showed who these were. They were the ones who rode on a cloud in their armchairs. Little groups of admirers had collected round them to catch their every word and watch their every movement as they illustrated their adventures of the day by opening throttles to climb and miss a church spire, pushing control columns violently forward to dive on an unsuspecting enemy, or rolling over the arm of the chair still clutching a pint, to abandon their burning aircraft.

Having never yet even stood near to an aeroplane on the ground, let alone sat in one and gone cloud clipping, I felt I rated poor material beside these intrepid aviators. Things were to change sooner than I dreamed.

Next morning we were on the airfield by seven in rugger shorts, shirt and gym shoes, doing PT in a biting wind straight from the frozen Highlands. We went through the whole routine and finished with a race round the flagstaff and last one to breakfast's a cissie.

Then over to flights. Locker and Lecture rooms were in the same building. I was kitted out with a Sidcot flying suit with a fur fabric collar and lining, a helmet with earphones, fur-lined flying boots, and leather gauntlet gloves with silk inners. I was shown how to fold an Irvin parachute, then made to pack my own and sign that it was my fault if it didn't open. I was promised a new one if it failed and I took it back. The harness was adjusted to be really snug, to stop me sliding out of it when the canopy opened.

Commander Gibb was my next call. Ex-Fleet Air Arm he, as Chief Ground Instructor (CGI) was OC lectures. He was dark, dapper, with short curly hair and always drank pink gin. He outlined for me our ground syllabus (administration, gunnery, bombing, engines, armaments, signals, morse, RT, cyphers, theory of flight, aerodynamics, navigation, instruments, and airmanship). It seemed to me that in the next ten weeks we would be spending precious little time in the air. Not so, as it proved. Our course of 26 split into A and B flights, with thirteen (thirteen!) in each, and on alternate mornings and afternoons, one flight would lecture while the other flew.

This way we must complete fifty hours' flying each, 25 dual and 25 solo, including five hours' instrument or cloud flying. In fact, the weather was so good, for it was freezing hard most of the time and slashing our faces to shreds in open cockpits, that we finished early, and Air Ministry authorised an extra twelve hours per pilot.

I warmed to Flying Officer Douglas Shields at once. He had been in the City of Edinburgh Auxiliary Squadron and was now a civilian flying instructor with Scottish Aviation Limited, who ran this flying training school at Prestwick for the RAF. Shields was slightly chubby with an angelic face which set to Aberdeen granite when roused. His eyes behind his flying goggles were palest ice blue, his jaw, square and firm. I was soon to realise he really could fly, though, ready to place my life in his hands feeling as a patient does about a surgeon from the moment the chloroform mask covers his face.

'Hello, Holmes,' he greeted me, 'I'm your instructor, we'll be flying together all the time. Flying Officer Shields.'

'Hello,' I said, extending my hand.

'-Sir,' he prompted, ice freezing his glance, though his handshake was firm and warm. 'Sir,' I echoed, obediently, adding '-sorry, sir.'

He nodded, not thawing even slightly. Message received and understood. That's how it was to be.

That morning Flying Officer Shields taught me how to sling my parachute over my shoulder, and to carry it without accidentally pulling the ripcord and emptying the silk canopy out all over the ground. When he was satisfied I could do this safely he gave me his own as well to sling over the other shoulder, and together we walked out to our orange coloured Tiger Moth *G-ADWN*.

He explained the petrol system, the danger of being in the arc of even a stationary airscrew, the effect of movement of the control column on the elevators and ailerons, and of the foot pedals on the rudder. He showed me the throttle and mixture control, and explained the dashboard dials and blind flying instruments. Then he helped me into my parachute harness, gave me a leg up into the rear cockpit, checked my Sutton harness was correctly fastened, connected my headphones into his speaking pipe, and climbed into the front.

There were metallic grating noises in my ears as he plugged in his own headset. His voice, loud but rather metallic, came down the tube. 'Can you hear me, Holmes?'

'Yes, sir.'

'Have you ever flown before?'

'Never sir.'

'Drive a car or ride a motorbike?'

'Both sir.'

'Good. Let's go flying.'

There were hand signals, nods and thumbs-up signs, to the fitter standing out front. He gave the propeller a few preliminary turns to suck in rich mixture, and shouted 'Contact'.

'Contact,' repeated Shields. He flipped up twin ignition switches on the outside where the fitter could see them. One more heave and a step back clear of the airscrew as the engine fired. The whole aeroplane trembled to life. Wings, fuselage, and cockpit instruments all vibrated so violently that I felt sure the engine was ready to jump out of its cradle and the airframe collapse in a heap.

A few minutes of warming up saw the oil pressure dropping. Then Shields ran up the engine at full throttle with his control column pulled hard back and an airman lying across the tail to hold it down. He was flattened by the 100 mph slipstream as Shields flipped off each switch separately to test for revs drop. More waving as he throttled back to a tick-over. The chocks were tugged by their ropes from under the wheels and we were taxying out.

My instructor shouted to me through the headset over the engine noise: 'Taxying must always be at walking speed, swinging the nose from side to side to give a clear view ahead, because the engine obscures your vision. Remember you have no brakes — only your tail skid dragging along the ground.'

Having told me this, he thereupon opened the throttle wide, breaking all the rules, and in a moment we were bounding downwind to the take off boundary at the bottom of the field, at a good 40 mph, ostrich fashion with our tail high in the air. In this attitude we both had a clear view ahead over the top of the engine cowling. At the boundary markers he throttled back and the tail dropped. We slithered round through 180 degrees, searching as we came round for any aircraft approaching to land.

He came out of the turn facing exactly parallel to the windsock and opened the throttle fully. The engine roared, and the airscrew spun itself invisible. In a cloud of exhaust smoke and flying grass our tail went up and our Tiger Moth, triggered by its 120 horsepower Gipsy Major engine, was away.

This was it. This was the moment at which for the first time I said farewell to Mother Earth.

The acceleration forced my back against the seat. My cheeks were dragged taut by the slipstream so that I thought they would surely tear. My arms felt heavy and lost their freedom of movement as we gained speed. I adjusted my goggles which had been blown askew, and watched the air speed indicator. Suddenly the bouncing over the rough grass became more gentle and with a final bump we bounded into the air. We flew close to the ground for a hundred yards, then climbed.

The earth fell away. Trees and farm buildings shrunk. My stomach was still on the ground but my heart was soaring. *I was flying!*

Fields became pocket handkerchiefs. The engine quietened as Shields eased back the throttle and stopped climbing. The altimeter read 2,000 feet. Sheep were just dots, hedges lines, roads ribbons. The clouds seemed close enough to touch and ready to crush our tiny craft. The land was now a map of roads, railways and coast line. It was all, I suppose, as I had imagined, except for the noise. Would I ever grow to accept this din?

In front the leather-coated shoulders of my instructor moved forward as he reached for his speaking tube.

'All right, Holmes?'

'Fine sir, thank you.'

Tiger Moths beside the hangar at Prestwick Flying Training School in February 1937. This airfield has developed into the present-day Prestwick Airport.

No. 1 Course of the RAFVR at Prestwick, February 1937.

'See the aerodrome?' He dipped a wing vertically and turned through ninety degrees to indicate the field now down on our left. I saw him noting my reaction to this violent manoeuvre through a small mirror on the centre section. I nodded, trying to look nonchalant, though my stomach felt otherwise.

'Always know where you are, to find your way back. Too easy to lose yourself if the weather clamps,' he bellowed into the tube. He indicated a promontory in the Ayrshire coastline two miles to the left. 'That's Troon Point. Remember it. It's your landmark to find your way back to Prestwick.' He pointed further out to sea over Troon. 'That island is Arran. Keep well away from the hills on it in bad weather. Electrical disturbances in some of the mountains round here will upset your compass. Remember I've warned you.'

His words were reassuring. Here was a man who was cautious, but confident, prepared for the worst if it should happen. That broad back could shoulder responsibility, his jaw confirmed it. His head swung constantly, always on the lookout. I knew my life was safe in this man's hands. Nothing would ever happen to him. If our engine fell out, or the wings fell off he would still cope.

I remembered his warning about electrical disturbances in the mountains whenever I flew on cross-country exercises from Prestwick. I recalled them particularly when I read in a newspaper at home, a few weeks after our course ended, that a mountain rescue team had found a crashed Anson on a Scottish hilltop. The four navigators on a map-reading exercise, and their pilot, Flying Officer Douglas Shields, had all died. He was the first of many good friends I was to lose, and one of the best.

From that day I realised what insecurity was. Until then death had been impossible while Douglas Shields was in charge, and providing I flew the way he taught me. Suddenly my idol had clay feet. If he could not protect himself, how could he protect me? From now on only one person could protect me in an aeroplane. 'God helps those who help themselves,' I decided.

In the years that followed, with the reassurance of that prayer and out of respect for my first flying instructor, I modelled my flying on his, trying to have his enterprise and courage, and to fly as he taught me.

'Yes, *Sir!*'

2
Shades of Hess

Flying became the be-all and end-all of life, and time flashed by. Being able to write shorthand as a young reporter helped me to catch up with ground lectures. We all had large, black stiff-backed notebooks, alternate pages graph paper, labelled Form 620. Everything in the RAF, I was to find, had a Form number. If you went on leave, drew your wages, were sick, got married, serviced an aeroplane, flew one, or got killed, someone signed a Form. The numbers ran on these forms into thousands but one soon developed the habit of asking for a document not by name but simply by its Form number.

Into our 620s (full title: Royal Air Force Notebook for Workshop & Laboratory Records) went our lecture notes. The ground instructors dictated to me a precis of the earlier lectures I had missed, and I transcribed the notes into my 620 at night. Much of the work was straightforward. Engines I already understood, so learning about compression ratios, valve overlap, dry sumps, bonding and the like was no problem.

Signals showed us the link-up by teleprinter between Air Ministry, and Fighter, Training, Coastal, and Bomber Commands, and thence to the Groups in each Command as well as to Civil Aviation, Admiralty, War Office, and the various outposts of the Empire. On the practical side we learned to send and read Morse Code by buzzer and lamp.

The gunnery syllabus dealt with the Vickers .303 machine-gun, then firing 900 rounds a minute, which sounded an incredible rate of firepower from an aircraft. But I would have been dumbfounded had I known then that within four years I would be flying a Hurricane II in Russia with twelve Browning machine-guns each shooting 2,400 rounds a minute or a total of 240 bullets per second.

And we were taught the theory of making safe, fuzing and dropping 20 lb bombs. Little did I know that soon I would be photographing, from 30,000 feet, craters made by ten-ton bombs dropped by Lancasters on Germany.

Meantime Flying Officer Shields was pushing me ahead with my flying. In the short space of a week I had learned to fly straight and level, execute medium turns, climb, glide and stall. The third day I was shown how to take off into wind and land. On the fourth and fifth days we did tight vertical turns with and without engine, and the sixth was devoted to spinning, forced landings and low flying.

Spinning was the frightener. Lurid yarns went round the Mess of aircraft that became fixed in a spin and corkscrewed into the ground from 3,000 feet; of tail units breaking off during recovery, and wings folding back when pulling out of the ensuing dive. There were engines that stalled, and rudders that jammed. But though we went to bed secretly sick with fear, our greatest anxiety was that others should know we were scared. None of these disasters, of course, ever happened. Even so we returned from flights each evening grateful that we had been spared yet another day.

A week to the day that I first flew with him, Shields told me I was ready to go solo. I was to wait for my check-out with the Chief Flying Instructor, Squadron Leader McIntyre, who three years earlier had been second in command in the Marquis of Clydesdale's expedition which flew over and photographed Everest. This was a tremendous achievement in those days of flying, because the extreme cold and lack of pressure and oxygen in open cockpits presented serious problems for machine and pilot alike.

McIntyre was a gentle man. Whilst our instructors bullied, cursed and swore, he coaxed and even praised. His task was not only to check if a pupil pilot was safe for solo, but also to boost his morale to take the plunge.

The pattern for first solo was to fly four sides of a square. Take off into wind, climb straight to 500 feet, turn left through ninety degrees still climbing to 1,000 feet, then flatten out. Fly across wind clear of the airfield boundary, turn ninety degrees downwind, fly past the take-off boundary, and turn across wind. At this point you cut your throttle, trimmed for your gliding speed at 65 mph, lost height to 500 feet, and turned in for your last gliding approach and landing on the airfield. The skill here was in judging your cross wind approach, making it closer to the airfield and counteracting the drift in a strong wind, but keeping further away in still air.

The laugh was on us when we found that our final approach was over a cemetery. This was — if you'll pardon the expression — a grave joke. Those tombstones in the last few seconds of descent before touch-down seemed to stretch up clutching marble fingers, straining to snag a wheel or a wing and drag us headlong into their midst.

'He's safe enough,' the CFI shouted down to Shields when we landed. He climbed out of the front cockpit, and secured his Sutton harness to stop it fouling the control column. He gave me a thumbs-up and a grin. 'Off you go, Holmes. Good luck.'

That was all. The aeroplane seemed very different with an empty cockpit in front. It was the most exhilarating moment of my life, and I sang the whole time at the top of my voice as I taxyed out, took off, flew my circuit and made my first solo landing. Total flying time to solo: six hours fifty minutes. Shields, with pride, told me his pupil had beaten the record for the course by fifteen minutes.

I was a pilot! Or so I thought. Little did I know. Lord, how very, very little!

★　　　★　　　★

All the basics of flying — circuits and landings, spinnings, aerobatics — were learned within sight of base. A glance over the shoulder, along the wing, even upside down while going over a loop, always gave a reassuring glimpse of Prestwick aerodrome. Contemplating one's first cross-country flight was therefore quite exciting.

True, it was to be only 35 minutes' flying north to Abbotsinch, on the Clyde. But at 85 mph an error of course, a change of wind direction, or being blacked out by a sudden rain squall, could take you away from your destination. So reliable map reading was essential.

Our instructor, we were relieved to learn, always accompanied a pupil on his first cross-country flight.

The route from Prestwick to Abbotsinch was scenically intoxicating, but to the pupil pilot's anxious eye intimidating. Scrutiny of the map disclosed that our beloved coastline — such a comfort in

R.H. after first solo.

Flight Lieutenant
McKinley Thompson,
RFC.

getting home — veered sharply north-west at Prestwick, whereas our track lay east of north. The only recognisable feature, apart from a labyrinth of minor roads winding through hilly countryside, was a pair of lakes at Rowbank Reservoir, towards the top end of Locklands Hill golf course. These should turn up on our port side after about 22 minutes if we were correctly on track. But as there were two more lakes near another golf course at Loch Winnock, confusion could easily arise.

Abbotsinch lay four or five miles short of Clydebank. Between us and that airfield, Glasgow kicked out a hefty industrial foot. The prospect of flying over a densely housed area had one worried about the reliability of the Moth's engine.

Our great cross-country adventure started in the Navigation room. Here the four miles to an inch map was spread out, the track ruled in, and the destination measured for miles and degrees magnetic. The course to fly, ground speed and estimated time of arrival (ETA) were worked out from the wind speed and direction supplied by the Met office. By now eight crucial inches of map have themselves photographed in our mind. Let's hope the Isle of Arran, twenty miles long and twenty miles out to sea, stands out clearly to the west as a landmark throughout the trip.

Flying Officer Shields sits, a glum dummy, in the front seat. 'You have control,' he has told me. 'Take me to Abbotsinch and back.' He is obviously not prepared to help. He hunches there in the shabby leather motoring coat he wears in his green Aston Martin Sports car. Now he props one leather sleeved elbow over each side of the open cockpit to show he has no intention of touching the controls even if I fly him to Timbuctoo.

'Shall I start up, sir?'

'I told you Holmes, you have control. Can't you hear me? Haven't you connected your speaking tube?'

He knows damn well I have.

'Sorry, sir.' Then, to the fitter standing by the propeller, waiting for the signal: 'Petrol on, switches off, throttle closed.' He nods. 'Sucking in,' he shouts back, and tugs the airscrew a couple of times to prime the engine.

'Contact!' he yells to me.

'Contact,' I yell back, flipping both switches up, easing the throttle slightly open, and holding the control column hard back to keep the tail down when the engine fires. After a preliminary warm-up I check the magnetos at full throttle on each switch separately. I pity the airman across the tail in that slipstream. There are no rev drops, and I shut the throttle. I wave away the chocks and taxy out.

The trip was uneventful. Lakes came up according to plan. Abbotsinch airfield was hard to find, being surrounded by a built-up area, but the Clyde was just beyond it and I spotted the airfield in a loop of the A8 Glasgow to Greenock main road. The windsock showed that I must land parallel to the river. It was strange landing on a new airfield.

I expected some commendation, however begrudging, from Shields, for what I considered quite an achievement. Instead, as my wheels touched the ground he bellowed: 'I've got her'. He yanked open the throttle and before I had time to examine my new airfield we were skimming tail up across the grass and into the air again. After a steep left-hand climbing turn off the ground he set us into a steady climb at 70 mph.

'Take me back to Prestwick now,' was all he said.

'Yes, sir.'

Hastily I set my compass on to our homeward course. Soon I saw my lakes again, then out of the mist to the right the 2,866-foot summit of Goatfell on the Isle of Arran. This was reassuring. At Prestwick he jumped out without a word. But as we turned to walk together to the control tower he suddenly said 'Oh, Holmes'.

Hope sprang in my heart. Praise at last?

'Sir.'

'Bring my parachute, will you. It's in the cockpit.'

He stumped in alone.

Next week Shields crashed his Aston Martin. I visited him in hospital. He had stitches in his head. I was ready to observe all the formalities of a pupil to his instructor as I approached his bedside.

'Cut out the bullshit,' he told me. 'We're not in an aeroplane now.'

He chatted about his accident, his Aston Martin, and his girlfriend. He was, after all, human. Sadly, I never flew with him again, Flight Lieutenant Thompson becoming my instructor. I visited Shields several times in hospital, and he was home at Edinburgh on sick leave when our course ended. But he had put me through my first forty hours of flying — and during the 2,000 that followed I never forgot what he taught me.

★   ★   ★

About ten flying hours after my Abbotsinch cross-country I was sent on a solo triangular cross-country from Prestwick, which took me due east to Dungavel then north-west to Abbotsinch, and south back to Prestwick. Each leg was 25 to 30 miles. Total flying time about one hour.

The course for Dungavel left Kilmarnock about seven miles to my port side. The coastline, such a wonderful landmark, faded into the distance directly behind me. The town of Kilmarnock was the end of any real habitation. Now the ground climbed steadily with the River Ayr twisting its way through the valleys seeking its outlet into the Firth of Clyde. A double belt of trees each side of the A74 Carlisle to Glasgow road at Douglas was my landmark for Dungavel, five miles ahead and 1,674 feet high.

Shields had told me when he was in hospital to look for the tiny castle on the hilltop. The Marquis of Clydesdale lived there, he said. He had attended a very splendid ball the Marquis held at the castle for the Edinburgh RAF Auxiliary Squadron. Briefed to fly my cross-country at 2,000 feet, I kept strictly to this height on my altimeter, and found myself circling less than 300 feet above Dungavel. This is not much higher than the average factory chimney, so I had an excellent view of the approach roads to the castle, its stately entrance, turrets, courtyard and building. The air was very bumpy so near to the hilltop.

Reluctantly, after two or three circuits when I began to wonder if the Marquis would emerge angrily with his shotgun, I set a north-westerly course for Glasgow and Abbotsinch aerodrome. At that moment, had I been able to see four years and two months into the future, I would have witnessed Hitler's deputy, Rudolph Hess, rolling out of the twin-engined Messerschmitt 110 he had flown from Germany, and parachuting down on to the very spot, with his still undisclosed peace plan for ending our war with Germany.

On the day Hess baled out over Dungavel — 10 May 1941 — I was with 504 Squadron flying convoy patrols in Hurricanes from Exeter off Dartmouth and Portland. By that time my flying hours had grown from 53 to 513.

Our Squadron Intelligence Officer, Flying Officer Plowman — affectionately known to one and all as Plowbags — brought the highly secret news of the Hess incident to our dispersal the following morning, long before it was released to the Press. He told us Hess had demanded to be taken straight to the Marquis of Clydesdale, by now the Duke of Hamilton, whom he had met pre-war at a sports meeting in Germany. Instead, on Churchill's orders, Hess was forbidden to speak with anyone, and was taken as a prisoner-of-war straight to the Tower of London.

Hearing this story from Plowbags took me back to the day I circled that castle in my Tiger Moth. Was Dungavel, then, enshrouded in an intrigue which could somehow end the war?

Churchill, Plowbags imparted in great confidence to us a day or so later, had now talked with Hess at the Tower. The great man did not stay long, and looked grim when he left, his jaws clamped on a freshly lit cigar. The story under the Official Secrets Act was killed dead for the Press from that moment onwards.

Just why Hess adopted this hazardous method of contacting our leaders without his Führer's knowledge has never been made clear, and now he is dead it probably never will be. It was generally believed that it was because he realised Germany must lose her war with Russia if she did not make peace with Britain.

Sadness was tinged with relief when our Prestwick course finished. It was sad to part from friends who had travelled from all parts of the British Isles to meet on this, the first flying course of the RAF Volunteer Reserve.

We would miss the crisp, clear air of the West Coast of Scotland, the Bobbie Burns countryside, the three Troon golf courses, Ayr Race Course with the forced landing practices, and the snow-capped hills inland, their back-cloth of sky verging on indigo.

The flying instructors had stepped down from their pedestals and become human. As the weeks passed, the harshness of their tuition gradually toned down, and we would go away respecting them. We would miss the draughty hangars, with their pungent exhaust fumes, and the swirling dust clouds outside whipped up by taxying Tiger Moths.

We could now catch our trains, take our logbooks home, and proudly show them to our relieved parents. They would tell their friends: 'Our son is a pilot, you know.'

Which, I suppose, fifty years ago, you could forgive them for saying.

Four years later I flew over Prestwick in a Hurricane I was ferrying to Dumfries. Troon Point was still my landmark for the aerodrome. But the tiny field, the hangar, the Orangefield Hotel, and the Kilmarnock road running along one side were all missing. There was no trace of my old flying school. Instead, there were two enormous cross runways, to take the Lockheed Hudsons which were being flown in their hundreds to us from America. Two hangars, each as big as Wembley Stadium, occupied one side, and the administrative block and domestic quarters at the end were a small town on their own.

If war could bring about such improvements, why not peace?

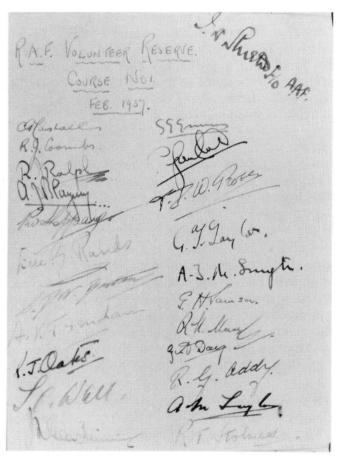

Signatures of the pupil pilots on the course.

3

The Phantom Moth

We were informed on leaving Prestwick that we were to continue our flying training at the VR centre nearest to our home. There were First World War RAF aerodromes at Hooton and Sealand, and a few Service planes occasionally flew out of Speke. All these airfields were within fifteen miles of my home at West Kirby, on the Wirral, and I looked forward hopefully to hearing that I could fly from one of them. But none had any inkling of plans for the VR flying training schools there.

So I wrote to Air Ministry.

My reply advised me that plans were afoot to start a VR centre in October at Barton, which was then Manchester's civil airport. Until then, my nearest centre would be at Desford, near Leicester, and I was accordingly officially posted to that centre! Desford was 137 miles away. Four and a half hours each way in our family 1933 Rover 10 averaging 30 mph, with a couple of hours of flying, it promised to be quite a day. Some compensation was that we could charge for the mileage, and be paid, a shilling (5p) an hour while on duty at the aerodrome.

I was up at 4.30 am one midsummer Sunday, and on the road by five. I arrived at Desford about 10 am. I was told to wait in the crew-room, and an instructor would give me a test for solo flying.

In Prestwick the temperature had always hovered around freezing point, which made flying in open cockpits bitterly cold. Consequently we wore wool-lined flying suits, flying boots and leather gauntlet gloves with silk inner linings. Having never flown in the summer, I assumed that all flying in open cockpits required similar protection against the elements.

I arrived at Desford in a heat wave. When I was told to get ready to fly, I did just that. I put on my full protective clothing, with thick linings inside flying suit and gloves, and wool-lined flying boots. I was sorry for the other pilots who were going to be so cold.

I sat and sweated. I was exhausted after my long drive, with only a flask of coffee and a sandwich in the past seven hours. Just on lunchtime, when only my boots were saving me from melting into two puddles on to the floor, my name was called by an instructor named Lowdell. His pointed black beard gave him an air of ferocity. He sent me to get Moth 'S' (for Sweat?) started up.

I lumbered off with 30 lb of parachute over my shoulder, feeling like a sack of coal already ablaze. Soaking wet inside my flying suit, and with sweat running from under my helmet into my eyes, I buckled on the parachute harness, climbed into the cockpit and fastened my straps. My goggles fogged up the moment I pulled them over my eyes. Two airmen wandered over and put chocks in front of the wheels. I went through the cockpit drill with them, and we started the engine.

After five minutes Flying Officer Lowdell came stamping across. He glowered at me, fastening his parachute harness as if it gave him nettle rash in his crutch. I noted he wore an open-necked, short-sleeved lemon sports shirt. He climbed into the front cockpit, and I heard the metallic scraping as he plugged in his speaking tube.

'All right, Holmes, taxi out and take off into wind, and let's see what they taught you at Prestwick. We'll do some spins for a start.'

This was more a threat that a test, I knew. What right had I, a foreigner from Liverpool, to come crashing in on his peaceful little flying club at Desford?

I was growing hotter every minute. Also, I felt strangely out of place. Not merely unwelcome, but suddenly it seemed that I had learned to fly in another world. I wondered what I was doing here in Leicester in a Tiger Moth, when I should be in Scotland. Could I remember all Shields had taught me four months ago, or was this just a weird dream?

Perhaps I was lightheaded with hunger.

The air, far from being freezing as I had expected swept over me in hot blasts as though somebody kept opening a furnace door. I managed to get the plane off the ground, and felt more assured as I settled down to fly it. We climbed to 3,000 feet.

'Let's see a spin to the right.'

With the throttle shut, I pulled the nose above the horizon to shed our speed. When the wings began to waggle at about 50 on the clock, I pulled the stick fully back into my stomach and held it there. The nose tried to come up still further, failed, and we lurched into a stall. As the nose dropped and my stomach became weightless I kicked on full right rudder.

We were suddenly churning clockwise, spinning vertically down. We could have been bath water swirling down a plug-hole. The aircraft seemed to stay still while the fields and roads all spun round anti-clockwise, far below. When the triangular wood came round for the third time Lowdell (I hated him by now) bellowed: 'All right, come out'.

Full opposite rudder, then stick forward. Whatever happens (echoing Shields) keep that full rudder on. My left foot must surely be bending the rudder bar. No effect. Panic was just mounting as the woods made their fourth appearance, and the spin stopped as suddenly as it started. Centralise rudder — quickly, before we spin the other way — gently back on the stick 'to ease out of the ensuing dive' as they always said. Bring her back straight and level. Throttle open to cruising revs.

If he asks for another I'll be sick down the back of his neck, I vow. Heaven be praised, he just said 'Right, Holmes, go back and land'.

This was easier said than done. Where the hell was Desford? At Prestwick we had that wonderful coastline, with Troon Point jutting out into the sea as the perfect landmark, and crystal clear air. Here there was no coast, a thick heat haze, and nothing but fields. I had noted a slag heap when I took off, and I headed hopefully for it now, trusting it was the only one around. Just beyond, a black dot crawled slowly across the landscape. It seemed to be descending. Sure enough, there was the airfield ahead of him.

Somehow it was a good landing. I think Lowdell was disappointed that it was. I felt he wanted to fail me, and send me back home with 'below average' stamped on my logbook. But sullenly he led me into the crew-room where I signed the authorisation book for an hour of circuits and bumps.

I took the opportunity to discard my flying-suit inner, replace the wool-lined boots with civilian shoes, and pocket my gloves. I felt much better. I grabbed a local map in case I lost the aerodrome, and did half a dozen landings.

Topping up my car tank for the return journey at one shilling and fivepence a gallon (7p!) I had just sufficient money left for a pound of apples to eat on the way home. I rationed them to one every forty miles. It was a slow, weary journey, broken by several cat-naps on the roadside. I arrived about dusk, and toppled into bed.

This was on 2 May. Six weeks later, on 15 June, I made the excursion again. I flew twice, but decided it was not worth the effort, nor was it fair to give the old Rover such a hammering. Regretfully, I struck Desford off my list, postponing any further flying until the VR centre opened at Manchester in October.

★　　★　　★

The day I received the letter from Air Ministry informing me that the Manchester centre was opening at Barton Airport on 15 October, I bought a motorbike. It was a new 350 cc ohv BSA Empire Star, and cost £52.10s. I calculated that with the BSA cruising at 60 mph and doing 60 mpg the saving in time and money would be justified.

Strangely, I found I flew better after riding there. You rode a motorbike as you flew an aeroplane, as part of it. And it had the same open cockpit feeling, too. Quite different from a car.

I arrived at Barton the first day it opened as a VR centre. Not many pupils turned up for flying and as I had already done thirty hours' solo, I was given a ten-minute test of dual, and sent off for an hour. Airwork Ltd were probably delighted to have an aeroplane earning them some money so soon.

Manchester Airport, the predecessor to Ringway, was little more than two fields knocked into one. It was boomerang shaped and very boggy in wet weather. The longest run was 610 yards, with no room to extend. A circular building like a sail-less windmill did point duty in the middle. The aerodrome control pilot had an excellent all-round view of the circuit but the tower was a serious obstruction to any pilot making a cross-wind landing.

The only aircraft using the airfield apart from Gipsy Moths (an older and slower version of the Tiger Moth) were a couple of de Havilland Rapides — pointed winged six-seater biplanes owned by Olly airlines which flew between Manchester, Liverpool, the Isle of Man and Ireland.

My ground lectures at Prestwick stood me in good stead and I was excused these at Barton. By the middle of November I had made eight visits for local flying, practising sideslipping, spinning, aerobatics and local map reading. Then to my joy I was briefed to fly solo to Liverpool, across the Wirral to the Dee, up to Chester and back to Barton. This took me over my home at West Kirby, and it was an experience I shall never forget exploring from the air my own neighbourhood, Calday school and its playing fields, the open air swimming baths in West Kirby lake, and Hilbre Island in the Dee.

Having completed this exercise satisfactorily — in other words, arrived back at Barton in one piece — this qualified me for a cross-country trip actually landing away at a strange aerodrome. None of the airfields in those days had runways and the boundaries were simply natural landmarks, such as ditches or hedges. They could be identified by some sort of hangar and, on a pole, in one corner, a wind-sock. It always helped to see another aeroplane land first. It was essential to watch where he taxied, because often when you were on the ground you found you were in a saucer, or over the brow of a hill, with no visible civilisation in any direction.

Castle Bromwich was our port of call on cross-countries. It was a civil airport with lounge facilities, and served teas. After tea, we booked out at the control tower like real civil airline pilots, and flew back to Barton. Weather was always the snag. Industrial haze would drift quickly up from the iron foundries in the Midlands, or across from Lancashire's cotton mills, making a return journey often a difficult proposition. Our standby on these days was the Manchester Ship Canal running inland from the Mersey past the southern perimeter of Barton Airport. So, when lost, we found the Mersey, then the Canal, and followed it home.

One day in late November, with the light failing and fog settling down, I could not even find the Mersey. I circled and searched until my fuel was very low, and a decision became imperative. I decided to look for a field and lob down. Farmhouse chimneys gave me the wind direction (how cosy and comfortable and safe those farmhouses looked). To my everlasting relief I spotted a long, narrow, pasture free of animals, with a road along one side. I knew it was pasture because new crops do not grow in November, so the ground would be firm.

We had practised dual precautionary landings in a small field at Prestwick; but I had never expected to need to do the real thing solo.

My landing was exciting, but effective. I stopped well short of the far hedge. There were no obstructions such as haystacks, telephone or high-tension wires for taking off again. I taxied back to the take-off end, edging towards the thorn hedge beside the road where a solitary car had pulled up. The inquisitive driver alighted to see what my aeroplane was doing in a farmer's field.

I beckoned him across from my cockpit, and he found a gap in the hedge and approached with obvious apprehension. He was worried about the threshing propeller, which I dare not stop.

'Where's the Ship Canal?' I bawled at the pale, frightened face that stared up at me. He seemed amazed at the question, but pointed behind him, across the road 'A couple of miles over there,' he bellowed back.

'And where's that road go to?'

'Warrington that way, Manchester this.'

'Thanks a lot. Stand clear and hold on to your hat.'

The last warning came too late, and as I sped away to get my longest take-off run I saw him chasing his trilby across the field. By the time I turned into wind he was scrambling through the hedge to his car.

It is an order that a pupil pilot who has forced-landed away from his base shall not attempt to take off again for obvious reasons. Equally, it was an unwritten rule that a pilot did not get himself lost. I reckoned that if I could get airborne again before the police, or any other official busybody could take my number and report me, I was home and dry. No more cars had arrived. My motorist had shown no interest in the Moth's markings. If I was so near the canal, it was easy to get back to Barton. I waved to the car, opened the throttle, bumped across the field, cleared the hedge, and swung right to pick up the canal.

Before my turn was completed, and when I was still less than 300 feet up, I spotted the grey thread of water. Forward visibility was appalling, diminishing by the minute as the daylight faded. I clung to the canal, my lifeline, and flew along it. There was no suggestion of an horizon, just murk. At least there were no hills between Warrington and Barton.

Sure enough, Barton's only hangar soon loomed out of the gloom. Worsley lock gates were just below me. I could discern the outline of the control tower on the left. It looked ghostly and forbidding in the gloom. There were lights in the windows. I made a left-hand circuit, hugging the aerodrome boundary. I was not going to lose it now. I kept a careful lookout for other aircraft. Someone fired a white Very light from the control tower, giving me the signal to land. I came in on the longest stretch, taxied to our line of Moths and parked at the end. No-one came to meet me. No-one seemed to care. No-one knew what I had been up to — or down to. I booked in, changed, threw a leg over my BSA and was through my gears and on my way home within ten minutes of landing.

Next time I went to Barton, a discreet ten days later, there was still talk in the crew room about the 'phantom' aeroplane — no-one knew what type it was, but it was a biplane with RAF markings — reported to have landed in a field east of Warrington. No-one knew where it came from or where it went. It had not been heard of since.

'Very interesting,' I said, and went off on a cross-country for another pot of tea and buttered ice-bun at Castle Bromwich.

At Barton I had an instructor whom I shall call Flying Officer Slawson. He was a fine pilot but a neurotic instructor. Whatever went wrong, whether your fault or his, he flew into a rage.

The most important thing I learned from Slawson was how not to treat a pupil when during the war I became a flying instructor. A young pilot in the early days of his tuition needs careful handling. Firm, yes, but gentle. He is suddenly in a new dimension of powerful and bewildering machines, trying to accustom himself to move above instead of on the earth. If he gets screamed at, blasted and blamed, he will get a mental blockage.

Fortunately I had flown about thirty solo hours before Slawson took me over. Mainly he was authorising me to do solo practice exercises. But what dual I did with him upset my confidence so much that after a year I put in a request for a transfer to a new instructor.

Flight Lieutenant Carr, our CFI, was an understanding man. He was the best possible C.O. He called me into his office.

'Cigarette, Holmes?'

'Don't sir, thank you.'

'Good man.' He lit one himself.

He was fair-haired with a broad forehead, and pale handlebar moustache. He had the bleak, blue eyes of the dedicated RAF officer. He had won the DFC in India. He wore his navy blue VR blazer, with wings on pocket, light grey flannels, and striped VR tie, like a tailor's model.

'Now what about Slawson? You want a change?'

'If possible, sir.'

Almost as though Carr had pressed a switch, there was a knock on the door, and in walked Slawson. I wished the floor would open and swallow me up. It did not, so I stood my ground.

'Oh, Slawson, Holmes is just asking for a change of instructor. He's grown tired of you. Probably had enough of your bloody language. If I give you this new bloke, Henderson, and Holmes goes to Arbuthnott is that OK?'

'Suits me,' said Slawson, throwing me a withering glance. He slumped down in an armchair and lit a cigarette ignoring me from then on.

'Right, Holmes,' said Carr, 'report to Flight Lieutenant Arbuthnott.'

Small world. Three years later Flight Lieutenant Carr, by then a Wing Commander, was posted to 2 FIS at Montrose, for a conversion course on to twins. I was his Flight Commander. He was man enough to accept the transition. Slawson would never have done. But Slawson never had the chance. One day early in the war he was sitting with a pupil in a Tiger Moth waiting to take off when a Rapide came in and landed on top of them. The pupil in the rear cockpit escaped unscathed but Slawson broke both his legs. I can imagine the language he must have loosed at that Rapide pilot.

During my fifteen days' annual training in May 1938, when I was billeted in a house near Barton aerodrome, I flew every day. On 19 May in Gipsy Moth *J9925* my engine packed up and I had to make my first forced landing.

I was flying back from Castle Bromwich across Staffordshire. Beautiful countryside, hilly in places. I was at the required 2,000 feet for cross-country flights. As I flew homewards my mind turned to the landing I made only a couple of hours earlier, at Castle Bromwich aerodrome. A landing on a strange airfield is the most satisfying of all flying manoeuvres. It is always a pleasant experience to recall. I re-lived that last approach, the touch down, taxying in, switching off, and not least afternoon tea in the lounge.

My recollections were rudely disturbed by splutters and coughs from my engine. With each miss-fire, a puff of dirty black smoke from the exhaust was swept away in the slipstream. The rev counter needle was surging erratically. I caught occasional glimpses of the propeller blades when the engine faltered. I cut back to half throttle to help the engine to run more smoothly. The spluttering, though less noisy, persisted. At the reduced revs we were losing height. I would have to put down in a field.

This was hilly terrain. I was much nearer to the ground than the 2,000 feet indicated on my altimeter. The wind blew, I remembered, from the north-west. I turned slightly to port until I was flying into wind. Now, to find a long field with the wind blowing down it which looked smooth, firm, reasonably level, and was clear of trees and telephone or high-tension wires on its down-wind boundary.

The engine grumbled more, but I gave it a trickle of extra power to try and lose as little height as possible while I found my field.

We crossed a quarry with jagged rock teeth. Then came a valley full of trees, and another hill. We only just cleared it. The far side sloped down to farming land. Less than a mile ahead was a farmhouse, on the edge of quite a long rectangular field. The green of the pasture stood out clearly. My guardian angel was working overtime.

This was it. In the field, or in the soup.

The altimeter now read a thousand feet, but I was nearer 600 feet above the ground. There were no obstructions on my approach path, apart from a low, thorn boundary hedge. I throttled right back, and started gliding in an S turn across the downwind end of the field. All was deathly quiet with the engine shut off apart from the low hum of wind through the bracing wires.

I must not be blown too far away from the boundary hedge, or I will undershoot and hit it. Nor must I clear the hedge by too much or I will hit the far boundary and overturn. My last run across wind brought me too close to the hedge. I was going to clear it by fifty feet instead of five. Shields would have had no trouble shedding this height. He would have side-slipped and tail-wagged. He did this on most landings, for the sheer joy of it.

Right, here goes. Swing the nose away from the field to the right, bank vertically to the left, and apply hard top rudder to hold the fuselage up parallel with the ground. The Moth dropped sideways. I felt the wind against my left cheek. Reversing all the controls swung the nose down and across, and put the Moth in an opposite sideslip. The wind hit my face from the other side.

29

The height shed, I was heading for the hedge, well positioned for my wheels to graze through the top twigs. But I was travelling too fast. With the speed gained coming out of the sideslip I would float the length of the field at this speed before touching down. Staying level, I kicked on first left and then right rudder, yawing the aircraft as Shields would have done like a fish in a stream. Each broadside dragged my speed down. The Moth was on a straight course as it brushed over the hedge and sank on three points thirty yards into the field. The tail skid juddered noisily over the turf, dragging us to a halt a hundred yards further on.

I looked round, hardly daring to believe my eyes. Smack in the centre of the field, with not a scratch on the 'plane.

There was no point in moving from here, I might run into rough ground if I taxied. I switched off the engine and the petrol and climbed out. It was not many minutes before the farmer arrived with his dog. He seemed irate, and ready to use his heavy walking stick on me. But when I assured him that I had no option but to land in his field, he mellowed and invited me into his house to meet his wife and daughter. By the time we arrived at his front door we were the best of friends.

I spread my map on his living room table and he located his farm. We were at Gnosall, Staffordshire. I noted the Ordnance Survey map grid reference number to pass to Barton.

His wife quickly produced a tray of tea and buttered scones with strawberry jam from her spotless, red-tiled kitchen. We tucked into these while he made a reverse charge 'phone call to Barton for me. Slawson came on the 'phone, and asked me where I was.

'In a farm at Gnosall in Staffordshire, sir.'

'What in hell's name are you doing there?'

I was tempted to say I was having tea and scones.

'I've had a forced landing, sir,' I replied with some pride.

'What!' he screamed. Typical of the man. Always accusing.

'My engine packed up on the last leg of my cross-country — sir.'

I could hear his disdainful sniff. He never asked if I was hurt or if the aircraft was damaged. Never said I'd done well to get down in one piece. In a seething temper, he demanded 'Grid reference?'

He seemed disappointed that I could supply it, robbing him of any further abuse. I gave him six grid figures that pinpointed my field, together with the farmer's name and telephone number. He could think of nothing more to swear about, so he snarled that I was to wait till I heard from him, and slammed down the phone.

'Seems a nice chap,' murmured the farmer, sliding the plate of scones and a dish of strawberry jam across the table. I grinned my thanks. 'He used to upset me but not any longer. He's sick.'

Within half an hour Slawson's Moth was circling our field low enough for me to recognise Mr Hopkins, our flight engineer and a cheerful fellow, waving from the rear cockpit. Probably he was hoping to get my engine repaired. They flew round several times, finally diving very low over my aeroplane and we saw a map come fluttering from Slawson's machine to the ground. I ran and retrieved it. On the back Slawson had written: 'Field too small to take off again if I land. Will 'phone you in half an hour from Barton.' He wagged farewell with his wings and flew off north. When he 'phoned it was to inform me that an RAF tender was on its way from Tern Hill aerodrome, near Market Drayton, to collect me and my aeroplane.

We were having supper of eggs and bacon when the tender arrived. It was a large grey Bedford with a camouflaged canvas roof over a metal frame. I wondered how the two airmen with it hoped to get my aeroplane away. I soon learnt. Four bolts came from the wing roots, freeing them from the fuselage, the two wings were then lifted off and stowed side by side in the back of the van. A rope was tied round the skid, and the tail section was hoisted up and secured to a towbar on the rear of the truck. The fuselage was now ready for towing backwards on its two landing wheels, the propeller being lashed horizontally to keep the blade tips clear of the ground.

I said goodbye to the farmer and his wife, jumped into the front of the van between the driver and his mate, and we set off for Tern Hill, towing my Moth. I intended to find that farm again some day, and thank them, but I never did.

This was my first visit to a regular RAF aerodrome. It felt as though I was approaching sacred ground. I was in civvies, with little knowledge of Air Force discipline, except that all officers were 'Sir', and that I did not salute as I was not in uniform.

The adjutant, a Flying Officer, came out to greet me. Despite his military moustache he was not my idea of an Air Force type — more like a schoolmaster. I told him I was a VR and a Sergeant, and he said there was a bed for me in the Sergeants' Mess, and that some-one would fly me back to Barton tomorrow. His job was to arrange things, and he did it well. I had supper in the Sergeants' Mess, listened to their radio, read some flying magazines in the ante-room, and turned in.

Next morning a message arrived for me at breakfast to be outside No 2 hangar at 10:00 hours. Squadron Leader Eayres would fly me back to Barton.

I expected to see my Moth in the hangar with engineers working on it but was told the tender had already taken it back to Barton. Why should they waste time mending a strange plane anyway, when they had enough of their ruddy own to mend, the engineer Warrant Officer asked me.

I agreed there was no reason why.

He told me the engine of my Moth had cracked a piston, and probably scored a cylinder wall. No compression. 'That's why it ran so rough and lost power,' he said.

The sound of a heavy aircraft engine being run up drew me to the tarmac. It was a Hawker Hart. The pilot tested his switches then beckoned me over. I hurried across with my parachute and helmet, and clambered on the catwalk.

'Sergeant Holmes?' he queried.

'Yes, sir.' (Sounded strange being called Sergeant.)

'Nice show that forced landing yesterday, Holmes. Heard about it. Neat bit of flying. Climb in.'

'Thank you, sir.'

A fitter helped me into the back seat. I had never been near to a Service aircraft, let alone in one, and was overawed. It smelt of oil and the whole airframe throbbed and rumbled as the powerful engine ticked over. Everywhere I saw wires, gauges, copper pipes and brass fittings. There was a gun firing button on the spade-handle joy-stick. It said 'Safe' and 'Fire'.

Squadron Leader Eayres speeded the engine to a fast tickover to prevent the plugs oiling. The engine sounded throaty and bad tempered. The vibration was now considerable, and the reduction gear of the hefty twin-bladed airscrew clanked and rattled. He waved the chocks away to taxy out. When he opened his throttle it seemed that the engine must surely tear itself out of the frame.

Our take-off was impressive. Acceleration, at full throttle, forced my shoulder blades hard against the metal bucket seat. My cheeks were dragged back towards my ears with the slipstream past the open cockpit. The wheels thumped and thudded over the grass.

The date of this incident, my logbook records, was 20 May 1938. I would have been incredulous had I known that by August of the following year, Hitler's activity in Europe would have caused training to be speeded up so that I would by then be flying Hawker Harts, Hinds and Audax, all solo. I would have been even more amazed to know that by May 1942, I would be back here at the same Tern Hill aerodrome as a flying instructor, following a fighter tour in a Hurricane squadron.

When Squadron Leader Eayres landed at Barton he stayed in his plane while I climbed out. 'Book me in Holmes. I'll shove straight off.' I shouted my thanks. He gave me a nod and a cheery wave, opened his throttle, and took straight off from where he had set me down. Our VR pilots came running out of the crew room to meet me, excitedly watching the silver monster make a steep climbing turn off their airfield.

My welcome back to their midst was warm but to my surprise seemed tempered with a measure of respect. I had, in their eyes, been blooded. I had made a successful forced landing, had spent the night on a regular RAF station, and had been flown home by a Squadron Leader in a Hawker Hart. Not bad, all in 24 hours. At that moment the CFI breezed into the crew room.

'Everyone does an hour's forced landing practice today,' he announced. He spotted me, probably looking slightly complacent.

'You too, Holmes,' he shouted. 'Because you got away with it once, it doesn't mean you'll never need any more practice.'

During my forced landing exercises I could not help feeling how flithery my Moth seemed after that Hawker Hart. I had tasted the dreaded drug, power. There was no looking back.

Shortly afterwards Flight Lieutenant Carr left us to be replaced by Mr Corke as CFI. He was to be called 'Mr' because, despite his long flying experience, he was not commissioned but a Sergeant Pilot, the same as ourselves. All my logbook entries when flying with him list him as 'Mr Corke'. I was to learn that some of the finest air force pilots were Sergeants, who had refused their commission.

It was Corkey, as we referred to him between ourselves, who taught me to land backwards.

As CFI he had no pupils of his own, but gave progress checks to pupils of the other instructors either to ensure that they were up to standard, or in the case of a borderline pupil to decide whether he should be given extra dual or kicked out. His check usually lasted fifteen minutes. If you could keep straight on take-off, climb steadily at 70 mph, do a decent loop or slow roll and recover from a spin, he would then take over and show you something different. It might be an outside spin, which tended to eject you from the cockpit, or a tail-slide which was a perpendicular stall, but backwards, so that when the nose finally did drop you were waiting for the fuselage to snap like a carrot.

He specialised in bunting in a loop — which was looping with the pilot on the outside and the centrifugal force trying to part the pilot from his cockpit. His point was that no enemy pilot could ever outbunt you sufficiently to get the necessary deflection to shoot you down. Which, I had to admit when I progressed to aerial gunnery, was perfectly true.

He knew I enjoyed his demonstrations, and one day informed me he was going to show me a desert sandstorm landing! On that typically dull Manchester day it was hard to imagine trying to land alongside a Sahara oasis in a blinding sandstorm. But I realised what he had in mind when, as were crossing the Manchester Ship Canal at about 100 feet on our final approach, he suddenly stuck his head out of the front cockpit to look backwards past me in the back seat and start watching the ground beneath our tail.

In this attitude, never once looking forward to check our heading, he flattened out our glide, held off for the stall, shut the throttle and landed keeping straight as we rolled to rest. Then he winked back at me through one goggle, took his head back into the cockpit, and taxied in with our tail off the ground at about 40 mph.

Having dutifully praised his effort — and been genuinely sincere in my praise, for it had been no mean feat — I mentioned that I hoped never to be caught in a sandstorm in the desert.

'Probably you won't,' he grinned. 'But what about being forced down in a freak snowstorm here. You'll find you can see quite well backwards when it's snowing, but you'll see sweet Fanny Adams looking ahead. Or,' he went on, warming to his theme, 'suppose a Hun shoots you up, and your engine's on fire, and the flames are fanning your face, and you're too low to bale out?' He left his question unanswered. 'In either case, and in others too if you think about it, you'll be glad if you can get down by your tail instead of your nose.'

I felt he was shooting rather a line, more useful in bringing a cinema audience to the edge of its seat, than in weekend flying. How wrong I was. And how grateful I was to be for Corkey's teaching less than a year later in the summer of 1940 on my first night landing in a Hurricane at Castletown aerodrome on the tip of Scotland.

In June 1939 our flying school moved from Barton to Ringway, now Manchester's new airport. It had only one runway, with an enormous hangar at the east end. The small control tower was near the hangar and had a lounge alongside. An ambulance and crash tender were parked outside the lounge window, while their crews lolled inside drinking tea.

One reason for moving to the larger airfield was to enable us to convert from Moths on to faster Service type aircraft. When we arrived, we were thrilled to find a line of Hawker Hinds and Audax already parked waiting for us outside our hut. Compared to our Moths they were tanks.

The airscrews could have been hewn from a sizeable tree instead of chipped with a penknife. The metal panels around the engines quite obviously housed powerful machinery.

Everything suggested power — even the smell.

Flying Officer Field-Richards gave me my first dual in a Hind. He had been flying Hinds with his Auxiliary Squadron, and knew them well. He did a demonstration circuit and landing. Nothing spectacular. Right out of the book. I was very impressed.

'It's all yours now,' he shouted through the voice pipe.

'Have a go.' He sat back in his seat, the patient passenger. 'Thank you, sir,' I gulped, eager but apprehensive.

I had never driven a bulldozer, but it couldn't have been much different. Instead of pressing the rudder pedals, you stamped on them. You tugged the control column when before you had eased it gently. Opening the throttle did not merely raise the engine revs and speed the swish of the airscrew; it caused everything around you to reverberate, with the airscrew threatening to tug the engine out of its frame.

We roared along the ground, leapt into the air, rocketed to a thousand feet and thundered round the circuit. But by the time we were making our powered approach for the landing the bucking broncho was tamed and responding obediently to every touch. The landing on the runway with a tail wheel was smoother, and more stable than the Moth dragging its tail-skid across the bumpy grass.

After checking me out for a couple more landings, and doing a few aerobatics and a spin, Field-Richards sent me solo. From then on, Moths were kid's stuff. My flying at Ringway was all in a Hind or an Audax, which was the single-seater version with a gun turret at the rear instead of a second pilot's cockpit.

I was in an Audax on 23 August, 1939, during my fifteen days' annual training, when I arrived back at Ringway from a triangular cross-country navigation test round Tamworth and Llanymynech to be given a red Very light. This meant I must not land, usually because someone had pranged, and his kite was blocking the runway. I could see nothing, but there was activity near the enormous hangar. The sliding doors were wide open, and a couple of tractors were slowly towing something out onto the tarmac. At last, out into the daylight emerged the twin tail of quite the biggest aeroplane I had ever seen. As the long fuselage slid from the shadow and the wings finally followed, I realised it was the size of the hangar itself. The building had obviously been tailor-made for it.

I circled several times, growing anxious about my fuel, yet watching in awe as the camouflaged monster was hauled to the runway. Then it was turned and lined up ready for take-off. The wings spanned the width of the runway. What must obviously be two tremendous engines to tug this giant airframe were started up. I saw the propellers start turning almost together, then the trolley starter-batteries were quickly hauled clear. The engines must already have been warmed up inside the hangar, for with the minimum of delay the aircraft trundled along the runway and in a few more seconds the prototype Avro Manchester was making its maiden flight.

The impression I had was that a giant crow, black and menacing, was swooping into the air in search of prey. When it was clear, a white flare gave me permission to land. Back on the ground, I found myself enshrouded in the first of many cloaks of secrecy that I was to encounter during the war years. This, it was whispered, was to be the backbone of our bomber fleet three or four years hence, when Britain would be ready to take the war into the enemy camp.

It was inspiring to realise that somewhere in a back room of our Empire a group of planners were thinking not how we were to repluse the enemy today, but how to hit him tomorrow. Someone realised what sort of a bomber force would be needed to end a war that was not to start for another week. An aeroplane had found its way on to the drawing board years ahead of its time with the bomb-carrying capacity and the range necessary to blast targets in the furthest corner of German occupied Europe.

Over 200 twin-engined Manchesters with Rolls-Royce Vulture engines were delivered to thirteen bomber squadrons and to Coastal Command by November 1941. But following heavy losses on operations and because of technical faults the Manchesters I and II were withdrawn and the Mark III Manchesters were fitted with four Rolls-Royce Merlins and renamed the Lancaster. Seven thousand, three hundred and eighty-seven were built, and it became the best bomber in the world.

We did not really believe, in our hearts, that during that last week of August 1939, we were so near to war. There were all the threats, and promises, and prophecies, but then came the ultimatum. It still seemed like bravado and shadow boxing. But suddenly we, on our VR course, found ourselves flying four or five hours a day instead of two. Someone was pushing hard to get us as good as possible as soon as possible.

On 28 August Corkey called me into his office. 'Holmes, we're flying to Hendon. Pack yourself some overnight kit, in case war is declared and we can't get back. Stow it in the locker compartment of *5515* — here's mine, pack them in together.'

I knew *5515* was his favourite Hind. He always flew it for tests.

'When are we going, sir?' He glanced at his wristwatch. 'Start her up at 10:15 and taxy round here. That'll give me time to make a couple of phone calls to London.'

We put down at Desford to refuel. At Hendon, Corkey disappeared for two or three hours, leaving me to wander around this aerodrome so famous for its pre-war displays. I was blissfully unconscious that within a year I would be flying from this very airfield with a Hurricane fighter squadron at the height of the Battle of Britain.

On the flight back to Ringway we put down at Stoke-on-Trent. Corkey had to see someone connected with his visit to the Air Ministry. He was tired when he rejoined me and glad for me to fly him back to Ringway. I felt very important, bringing my exhausted CFI home.

We landed into a blood-red sunset and parked the Hind by the control tower. It had been a long day. We were both too tired to talk. It was almost dusk when we parted.

'Thanks, sir, I enjoyed that,' I spurred myself to say.

'Good, Holmes, Glad you did. Goodnight.'

It was also goodbye. I never saw Corkey again. I never even heard of him. But I'll bet he did a good job somewhere. He was the sort of man who was the backbone of our Air Force.

The next couple of days we spent dispersing our aircraft to regular RAF stations being hastily prepared as Flying Training Schools. On 2 September I ferried an Audax to Shawbury. A very close friend of the family, Squadron Leader Ed Sullock, AFC, a First World War RFC pilot, was head of Administration at Shawbury. He invited me to lunch when I turned up with the Audax. He lived in quarters off the camp.

'I'm being picked up by one of our instructors in an Anson,' I demurred. 'He's doing a round trip, and collecting us to take back to Ringway.'

'I'll leave word for him to have lunch at the Mess when he arrives,' said Eddie cheerfully, walking me out to his camouflaged RAF Humber Snipe. 'Jump in.'

It was, after all, an order from a very senior officer.

The lunch was home from home with Rene his wife and young daughter Betty. When we arrived back Flight Lieutenant Slawson had the Anson standing at the control tower with both engines running. He, as usual, was fuming and swearing. But Eddie pulled rank to quieten him and I climbed aboard unscathed, though in an atmosphere seething with animosity.

Next day, at 11:00 am, war was declared.

We were listening to the radio in the Ringway lounge when there was a break in the music and the historic speech was broadcast. At that moment, six Fairey Battles which were all leaving for routine delivery to a maintenance unit for storage roared off the ground. It seemed like our first bombing raid on Germany.

That night I slept in the station ambulance. I am glad to say this was the first and last time I went in an ambulance throughout the entire war. The next time was a few days after Germany's surrender, when I was King's Messenger to Churchill while he was at Biarritz preparing his terms for the Potsdam armistice conference. I accompanied two Red Cross nurses in an ambulance from Biarritz to Lourdes to deliver Red Cross parcels. But that is another story, with a whole war in between.

Part Two
Training

4

Seven out of Thirteen

If I was expecting to rush off in an aeroplane and start shooting Germans down the moment war was declared, I was to be disappointed. Our own aeroplanes all having been ferried away from Ringway, my fifteen days' annual course being finished, and a flying instructor's course I was just about to start being nipped in the bud, there was nothing left to do but go home.

We were, of course, by our contract when we first enlisted in the VR, automatically mobilised in the regular armed forces. So one day a letter arrived in the usual long buff envelope that I had now come to know so well, requesting me to attend our lecture centre in Manchester for swearing-in. When we went home after this ceremony we were officially 'on leave'. We were really in 'the mob' with no escape. We were also on full pay as RAF Sergeants.

The next call back to Manchester was for uniforms. If we thought we were to be measured by a tailor, we were too optimistic. There was a church hall full of cardboard crates of RAF tunics, trousers, shirts, ties, sweaters, socks, underwear, boots and forage caps. It was left to us to rummage around and find something to fit. Then we were issued with gasmasks, and identity discs on string to wear round the neck. They gave us each a couple of sets of Sergeant's stripes, pointed out the regulation place on the sleeve, and told us 'Get 'em sewn on'.

On 29 October 1939 I was posted to No 4 Initial Training Wing, Bexhill-on-Sea, Sussex. No 4 ITW proved to be the Sackville Hotel, on the sea front overlooking the English Channel, due north of

Normandy. The hotel had been commandeered for the RAF, stripped of all furnishings, and turned into a suite of drab bareboarded lecture rooms and dormitories. There could certainly be no flying. Wing Commander John Morrison, DFC, who had been a First World War Royal Flying Corps pilot with our old family friend Ed Sullock (they were in Sir Alan Cobham's Flying Circus together after the war) was our commanding officer.

About a hundred Sergeant Pilots had been posted from VR centres all over the country to Bexhill, with an equal number to St Leonards, four miles along the coast. We were the first draft who had passed through the elementary flying training course, and we were here, Wing Commander Morrison told us, to continue ground lectures, concentrating on physical training while plans were made to receive us at intermediate flying training schools. We must, he stressed, be fit to fly. While we were here, he explained, more pupil pilots would be following us through the elementary flying training course we had just completed.

One morning, word came from sea defences that an unexploded mine was washed up on the beach near the hotel. If it had exploded when it ran aground it would certainly have blown all our windows in, and probably the front walls as well. It was decided to sandbag the hotel front as protection against further risk.

Within the hour, a lorry load of potato sacks arrived. Flight Sergeant Nobby Clark marched us on to the beach in three platoons, and split us up into filling, carrying and stacking parties. The real trouble was that there was no sand. The beach was entirely tiny round pebbles, as far down as we could dig. We grinned hopefully at this snag. But too soon.

'All right then,' bawled the Flight Sergeant, 'fill 'em with blasted pebbles.' So we did. We carried them up the beach to the promenade wall, where another party carried them across the promenade to the Sackville. There the 'sandbags' were laid, interlocking them like bricks to form a wall. Throughout the day we toiled, and slowly the wall grew.

We had short breaks for lunch and tea. By dusk the wall was twelve feet high, built around the front of the hotel, with the aid of ladders borrowed from the fire brigade. The last news we heard before we turned in that night was that someone who knew a bit about bombs had said the 'sandbags' if hit would scatter pebbles like shrapnel causing more damage than if we had no sandbags at all.

Next day we carried them all away and emptied them back on the beach.

Inoculations and injections followed. It seemed that sudden death from a German bullet was to be the least of our worries when the medical people listed all the bugs that might kill us.

Gradually we came to accept that we were to remain at Bexhill-on-Sea for the duration of the war. Never again would we see an aeroplane, let alone fly one. Then, suddenly, our postings to FTS came through.

The postings worked down an alphabetical list. G to M, which included all the Hs, went to Sealand, a First World War flying training school. By a happy coincidence it was less than fifteen miles from my home at West Kirby. I wrote off that night to tax and insure my 350 cc BSA which I had put in mothballs for the duration.

Next morning Wing Commander Morrison told us we would all be going home on 48 hours' leave from Bexhill, and that we were to report to our FTS on 12 December. The flying course there would be three months of intermediate training, and three months advanced. From there we would be posted to an operational squadron, the ultimate pinnacle of every pupil pilot's ambition.

The Wing Commander bade us a brief but touching farewell. I took a shorthand note of it. I still have the transcript, dated 8 December 1939, which he kindly countersigned. It reads:

> 'You have been here to try and learn something of the customs and traditions of the Royal Air Force. You are leaving here to take on important work. There is no doubt in my opinion that this war is going on for a very long time. Some of you have grown anxious because you think you won't be in it; I don't think you need have any fears about that.
>
> 'I am quite sure that this war, when it gets toward the end, will be won or lost in the air. We have in this country a great advantage — we have been bombed by Zeppelins and other aircraft in the last war, and the Germans have not; and I am quite sure that the moral effect of bombing will be much worse for Germany that it will be for this country.
>
> 'I wish you all the very best of luck; and I hope I may see you — many of you . . .' [Here the Wing Commander hesitated for some seconds. He seemed to be swallowing hard, and to find difficulty in continuing.] At last he went on: ' . . . I hope to see many of you decorated for doing good work for your King and for your country.'

He gave us a fleeting smile and hurried from the room. There was a hush after he left.

Wing Commander Morrison was followed by Flight Lieutenant P. S. Bett, our Squadron CO, who spoke rather more to the point. He warned us of the fallacy of the argument that this was not a war against the German people but against their leaders. 'War, as war, is a very bloodthirsty business,' he said, 'and the sooner you realise it the better. A famous VC once told me: "The only good German is a dead one".

'I hope when you boys get out of here you will kill as many of them as you can. That sounds a hard thing to say, but sooner or later when you see a few of your pals go west you will agree.'

How right that man was. We might have shrugged off his emotional words as propaganda. But within six months of getting our Wings at Sealand, and being posted to fighter squadrons, seven of our course of thirteen were dead. The other six went on to survive the war. Call it beginners' luck, or what you will. But bit by bit we were growing to realise that when you're up against this sort of situation the only answer is to hang on grimly a day at a time. From somewhere must come that little extra strength when the spirit is flagging and the flesh weakening.

No 5 Flying Training School at Sealand was our first real taste of Service life. RAF Sealand had wide expanses of tarmac around all the hangars, with separate flight offices near each one. Lecture rooms were set well back, clear of the noise, and Messes and sick bay were across the Queensferry Road beyond the main entrance. The airfield was sited where the River Dee suddenly narrows at the rail bridge, a useful position for finding it in bad visibility.

Before we left Bexhill we had the choice of flying bombers or fighters. It was surprising how the temperament of an individual fitted the aircraft he chose to fly. The cool, steady types plumped for bombers, many with an eye to being airline pilots after the war. The 'Let's have a party' types chose fighters. The twin-engined Airspeed Oxfords for bomber training were chosen by 27. The remaining thirteen of us went to 'D' Flight to fly single-engined Miles Masters. Both types were of wooden construction, being lighter, cheaper and quicker to build.

We of 'D' Flight were delighted to find we were to be the first pilots to train on Masters — until news reached us that several test pilots had recently been killed flying them, and also their smaller version, the Magister. Both aircraft were reluctant to pull out of a dive. Test pilots were trying to find out why they were getting killed without knowing the answer.

Eventually — but unfortunately not in our time at Sealand — a very simple modification in the form of two small fins running down the end of fuselage on to the tail planes, of each type, supplied the answer. In the meantime we were to comply with an Air Ministry Order against spinning them (although our instructors always did, and made us too). It was difficult to suppress a sigh of relief every time we pulled safely out of a dive to regain level flight, even after a loop.

Our popular Flight Commander, Flight Lieutenant McKenna, was a peacetime doctor. His three instructors were a Canadian, Flying Officer Howie Marcou, Flying Officer 'Gertie' Lord, and Flight Sergeant Barny Oldfield. Each had taken a course on Masters before we arrived at Sealand, but they were still quite new to them. Their biggest problem was that whereas on Tiger Moths the instructor always flew from the front cockpit which gave much better visibility, he sat in the back of the Master, with the pupil in front. This was because a pilot always sat in the front seat when flying solo.

Converting to Masters was a sobering experience for us. It was the first time we had ever flown a gun-carrying low-wing monoplane, similar to the Hurricanes and Spitfires which were our ultimate aim. We soon found there was more to flying a modern monoplane than just handling a machine 100 mph faster than the Moth. While in the Moth you just opened the throttle and took off, in the Master you had a rigorous cockpit check to complete after starting up the engine.

'Gertie' Lord, always rejoiced in finishing a dual exercise with a beat-up of the ack-ack gun posts at Eaton Hall on the Duke of Westminster's estate, near Chester, where the Prince and Princess of Wales stayed a few weeks after their marriage. At 3,000 feet, 'Gertie' would half-roll then, from the inverted position yank the nose down in the second half of a loop. We screamed vertically on to a nest of gunners, throttle wide open, and he pulled out of the dive practically flying in at one end of their gun-barrel and out through the other. 'Gives them a bit of practice,' 'Gertie' would say, as he headed for home, never risking a second run in case his number was taken.

It was thrilling to be only a thread away from eternity. Many good pilots have met their end over-savouring this thrill, through striving to go just one inch lower.

Sandbagging the Sackville Hotel at Bexhill.

Instructors (sitting) and pupils of 'D' (Masters) Flight. Instructors: Flight Sergeant Barny Oldfield, Flying Officer Howie Marcou, Flight Lieutenant (Dr) J. F. McKenna, Flying Officer Gertie Lord, and the Flight Sergeant. Back, left to right: Sergeant Pilots 'Big' Ingham, Haines, Wag Haw, Denis Helcke, McGregor, Gurteen. Middle: Tony Iveson, Bill Higgins, Holmes, Sid Ireland, Olly Houghton and Gardner.

Peckforton Gap, formed from two hillocks out on the Cheshire plain east of Chester, was a favourite shoot-up site. Peckforton Castle stands on one. With the pink sandstone of the two hills, like buns on a plate blushing in the sun, is it surprising they were known to the pilots of Sealand as 'The Bosom', with the gap between as 'The Cleavage'? To fly up 'The Cleavage' at 200 mph with visitors watching from Peckforton Castle grounds was a rare experience, because they were able to lean over the wall and wave down to us in our cockpits, while we waved up to them. In peacetime, we would never have got away with this sort of flying. It would be straight out of the RAF and back to civvy street. But in wartime it was different. We needed low flying expertise, and knew that with such a demand for trained pilots we would never be kicked out even if we were reported.

There was, however, an exception to the rule, and it led to my arrest and Court Martial.

During one authorised low flying trip up the River Dee to reconnoitre the shipping round Hilbre Island, Sergeant Halton — or Wee Halty as he was affectionately known by us all on the course — was the other pupil sharing the exercise with me. He said he would like to see where I lived so at our regulation 250 feet we circled my home on Grange Hill. Unfortunately we had not allowed for the hill being 200 foot high and when we landed back at Sealand two military policemen met us as we climbed out of our cockpits and informed us we were under open arrest. We accompanied them to the CFI's office.

The CFI was a bumptious, bombastic, dyed-in-the-wool Squadron Leader, with the true-to-type regular RAF blond handlebar moustache. He regarded VRs as an unavoidable wartime evil. His face purple enough for apoplexy, he informed us that a naval Lieutenant Commander home on compassionate leave for the birth of his wife's baby had phoned through direct to our Station Commander. He gave the number of our aircraft — which showed how low we were! — and said the noise had so terrified his wife that she had gone into premature labour. This I later learned was not true.

We were identified and damned even before we landed. We were grounded and confined to quarters for statements of evidence to be taken with a view to Court Martial. When the naval officer learned that the pilot he had reported lived only a few doors away from him, he forlornly 'phoned the Station Commander to say his wife was now fine, that they had a bonny bouncing baby boy and he hoped no action would be taken against the two pilots. Unfortunately he had already dropped his depth charge, which exploded and stirred up a lot of mud. Official complaints of that nature start wheels turning and while his wife was going into labour all the formalities for a Court Martial were going into motion.

Meanwhile Training Command started to ask why Sergeants Holmes and Halton were no longer clocking up their requisite daily flying hours. When Sealand smugly signalled back that we were grounded and awaiting Court Martial for low flying, a snorting reply rebounded from Air Ministry demanding to know if 5 FTS had not heard there was a war on, and that Britain was desperately short of fighter pilots. The signal concluded by ordering our immediate return to flying duties, and demanded that our daily flying time be doubled until we were level with the rest of the course.

As an afterthought, the signal added that the Squadron Leader who had grounded us was posted forthwith to a desk job at Air Ministry. So we never saw him or his blond moustache again.

Matters had now gone too far to stop the Court proceedings but nobody at Sealand wanted any longer even to be remotely connected with it, one head having rolled. In the end, at the suggestion of our defending officer, Flying Officer Penketh, and to get it over quickly, we both pleaded guilty to unauthorised low flying, despite our good defence that we were carrying out an authorised exercise and had inadvertently strayed out of the area. Flight Lieutenant McKenna and Flying Officers Marcou and Lord all went into the witness box and gave us glowing character and work references. The Court Martial announced it would make known its decision in due course, and we resumed our flying, expecting to hear no more of the incident.

But two days later all the pilots on No 45 course were paraded in a hangar. Wee Halty and myself were ordered to step two paces forward out of the ranks while the sentence of the Court was 'promulgated'. We were both given a severe reprimand. This was supposed only to go on our documents as a formality, but in fact lost us both the Commission our Flight Commander had recommended.

As for Wee Halty, his reprimand did not bother him long. For three months to be exact. At the end of our course he was posted to a fighter squadron at Biggin Hill and news reached us in Scotland that his Spitfire had been hit by a bomb while taking off during a Luftwaffe raid on their airfield. He crashed into a petrol tanker, and went up in flames.

★   ★   ★

My most vivid memory of Sealand must, of course, be the night flying.

One evening in April, Flying Officer Lord called to me in 'D' Flight hut: 'Get *7424* started up, Holmes'. I picked up my helmet and rolled off my parachute on which I had been dozing on the floor, and went out on to the tarmac. The hut windows were all blacked out of course, and when I closed the door to cut off any chinks of light, my last link with civilisation seemed to disappear. My eyes were still ten minutes off being adjusted to the gloom, and when a shape loomed up I started as a voice inquired unexpectedly, 'Sergeant Holmes?'

'Yes, that's me.'

'You want *7424*, Sarge? She's over there. Follow me.'

I was grateful for his companionship, and for the comfort from the small circle of yellow warmth his torch made on the ground.

'First bash at night flying, Sarge?'

No good pretending otherwise. 'Yes.'

'You've got a good kite. Good instructor, too. You'll be OK with Flying Officer Lord.'

Great psychologist, this. 'Thanks.'

I was fascinated by the line of flickering yellow paraffin flares stretching across the landing ground. It seemed to go straight towards where I remembered there was a hangar. Surely the fools haven't put the bloody flarepath right in front of a hangar!

'Give you a leg up, Sarge?'

'Thanks. I'll just fasten my 'chute first.' I slung the heavy parachute round my shoulders, fumbled for the side piece with the lock, and clicked the two top straps into place. Then I fished for the loop between my knees, brought the two side straps round and through

47

it, and clicked them home. As I climbed on to the wing the fitter gave me a helpful heave from the back.

The big cockpit lid with its side hinge yawned open, waiting. I climbed in and sat down. The rigger handed me my four Sutton harness straps, and I locked them together over my chest with the split pin. 'Gertie' Lord was being helped into the rear cockpit, which was awkward at the best of times with its tip-up windscreen. There were grating noises in my ears as he connected his intercom.

'Hear me, Holmes?'

'Loud and clear, sir.'

'Good — start her up — switches are tested — taxy out to the taxying post — it's that Christmas tree over there.' I could just see a red, green and white light making a cross on a pole. Someone was waving two torches to me.

Flames which did not show up in daylight spat from the exhaust pipes as the Kestrel sprang to life. I waved the chocks away and started taxying through the darkness towards the torches beckoning me, I felt sure, to my doom.

'Keep going while both torches circle, but if one stops, hold that wing back and turn. If both stop, you stop.'

'Got it, sir.'

At the taxying post, Lord took over.

'I'll do you a circuit first to let you get your bearings,' he said. He was going through his pre-take-off cockpit drill with switches, dials and controls as he spoke. I mumbled my thanks and sat back to watch. How the hell had I ever got myself into this I thought, staring ahead through the perspex windscreen and seeing nothing but blackness stabbed by the Kestrel's exhaust flames.

'Turn down your cockpit light, it's too bright. The switch is top right. Your instruments are luminous and you'll hardly need any extra light.' I adjusted the switch until only the faintest tinge of amber flooded the cockpit. All the instruments now stood out in phosphorescent green. I could now see more outside with the cockpit dark.

Suddenly there was a roar. A flashing green from the taxying post had given us the all-clear for take off, and Lord was pushing open the throttle. I felt a shove in the back as the airscrew bit the air and dragged us forward. Lord lined up with the flarepath and pushed the throttle fully forward, through the gate. The acceleration was exhilarating as the engine took its 5¼ lb of boost.

One flare went past, then the second. Now we were gaining speed fast, bumping across the rough turf, and swinging slightly. Lord kicked on rudder to keep us straight against a slight crosswind. As two more flares quickly dropped behind, the bumping grew less, then stopped. We were airborne! No going back now. A grey streak of road passed under us. I glanced down at my artificial horizon. We were climbing steeply. Speed 135. Lord throttled back to the gate. The Master seemed to sink as he reduced power.

Two heavy clunks told me the wheels had locked up. The green undercarriage lights came on. Funny, I'd never heard the wheels retract into the fuselage in the daytime. The altimeter read 500 feet.

I craned round to look back. As we started a climbing turn to the left, the flarepath came into view below our tail. There was the faint outline of Lord hunched up in his raised rear seat behind his open windscreen. How the hell can the man see a damn thing from there, I wondered. If Lord saw me he gave no sign. He was concentrating on getting round the circuit.

We levelled off at 1,000 feet on the crosswind leg, and almost at once started a further ninety degree turn to the left to fly back down wind parallel to the flarepath. Our landing strip now looked about six yards long, with the winking specks of flares a yard apart.

'Lower wheels on the downwind leg,' came Lord's voice. The dual-controlled undercarriage selector lever moved in my cockpit as he spoke. 'Check green lights are on.' Past the last flare he throttled back slightly, and started to turn on to the third side of our square. He reduced his revs further, and at 120 mph the nose lurched as the flaps came down.

'Bit of crosswind from the left. Watch you don't get blown away from the flarepath. Start your turn in early, and keep your nose into the wind.' Now we were aiming at the flares, losing height rapidly. Everything around us was as black as hell. There was no horizon. At 300 feet Lord seemed to have positioned himself to cross the first gooseneck at an angle instead of flying down the flarepath, but I realised as we approached that he was only counteracting our drift, and that we were making a steady track along the flarepath.

The flares were rushing up at us now. I could see sooty, black smoke curling away from their yellow flames. As we sank lower the flares which had been well separated now seemed to merge into one. There was a crump, a slight bounce, a touch of the throttle from Lord to let us down again, a rumbling of wheels and we had landed, with Lord working at rudder and brakes to keep us straight.

'Feel like having a bash?' We had come to a halt, and I was just debating whether to jump out and kiss the earth. Did I detect relief in his voice? Was he glad to be down too?

'Yes sir, very much,' I lied. I raised the flaps, turned off the flare-path, and headed back towards the taxying post. The port wingtip light of another Master was flying along its downwind leg. That would be Sid Ireland with Flying Officer Marcou. They'd just be about lowering their undercarriage now. Wonder how Sid felt.

The flarepath duty pilot was giving us an impatient green. Obviously wanted me away before Sid landed. Sid was just starting his turn across wind, and starting to lose height. I could see his light dropping. I went through my cockpit drill, and taxied on to the flarepath. As we lined up with the flares I opened the throttle.

'Strange,' I thought, 'if I wasn't being rushed into this I'd never do it for choice.'

'Keep her straight,' yelled Lord, kicking on right rudder. Blast the crosswind.

The tail came up, and I could see the flares better in this position. My eyes were more accustomed to the dark too. I felt more confident. Three flares went past and Lord started prodding at the control column, reminding me to unstick her. I eased it back and the Master responded, climbing into blackness. Eyes down now on to instruments. Must trust them. No good looking out. Can't see a blasted thing outside. Can't tell whether I'm on my arse or my elbow.

My altimeter assured me that I really was climbing steadily. I raised the wheels, throttled back, coarsened the pitch, and started a left hand climbing turn. Gradually the flarepath came into view from behind me. I saw Sid's port light running along the flares and knew he was down. We'd have something to talk about tonight — if we ever got back!

I did three landings with Lord in the back. Then he sent me solo in *7438* while he stayed in *7424* to give dual to Halton. I did three landings solo. After a cup of tea in the flight hut I made three more solo circuits and bumps in *7438*.

That night I crawled into bed with forty minutes' dual and 55 minutes of solo night flying in my logbook. Sid was equally exhausted. There was no talking.

Off to Chester for our 'Wings' party at Bollands. Left to right: Gardner, McGregor, Helcke, Haw, Ireland, Higgins, Houghton.

Bill Hartop smartening up
for Chester.

51

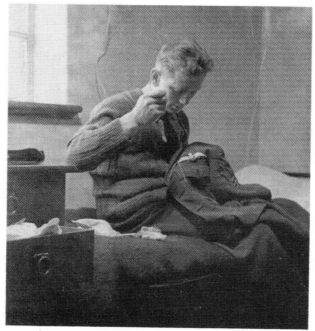

Sid Ireland sewing on his Wings.

Sid Ireland and his guitar.

We were dragged from a heavy sleep by an almighty thud which seemed to be just outside our window. Then the sky lit up as a sheet of flame shot upwards. It had to be a crashed Master. Who was still flying? We hurried to the window. The fire was in the middle of the main Queensferry road, close to the bridge crossing the road from sick quarters. An ambulance and fire tender raced up the road. Neither would be of much use.

Sid pulled a crumpled night flying programme out of his tunic pocket. 'Olly Houghton's the last detail for solo,' he said. 'Wonder if it's him.' It was Olly all right. He had undershot on his approach. We could understand how he would, with visibility so poor and possibly his screen sprayed with hydraulic oil. Poor old — or poor young Olly, for at nineteen he was the baby on the course.

'He wasn't looking forward to night flying,' mused Sid.

Olly was the first to die on our course. The official photograph I have of the forty pupil pilots on No 45 Course bears crosses on the chests of fourteen. Practically one third of our course did not survive the war.

That night, 23 April 1940, we went back to bed and slept, too tired to talk or even think. By 24 April Olly was history.

Off duty at Sealand we caught a bus to Chester. There was a peaceful charm about this old Roman city. Its walk-round walls, quaint coffee bars and drinking snugs in its famous Rows, gave it an atmosphere peculiarly its own. The snag was that during our stay at Sealand, the maintenance unit the other side of the railway, which had its own airfield, was taken over by the Americans, whose lowliest Servicemen were paid over £20 a week compared to our £3-9s (or £3.45p) as Sergeant Pilots.

They bought practically everything in Chester but the Cathedral and the Castle, paying in dollars. Prices in shops and restaurants rocketed when the proprietors realised they were sitting on a gold-mine. By the time we left we could no longer afford to eat out in Chester.

Our most momentous visit there was halfway through the course, when we celebrated our Wings award in Bolland's Oyster Bar. The photo taken as a record, being slightly blurred, captured the atmos-phere of the occasion. About now, Vera Lynn was singing 'If I only had Wings', and we raised the roof at Bollands with our own version.

We spent a very wet winter at Sealand. The waterlogged landing ground made taxying difficult, and lost us valuable flying time. For a few weeks, while our field dried out, we moved to Liverpool airport at Speke, and flew from there. Little did I realise that I was to return there on various missions several times later in the war.

Many an evening Sid Ireland rode the fifteen miles home with me on the pillion of my BSA. Pre-war, a broken ankle had put an end to my rugger career when playing fly-half to Danny Evans, a Welsh international scrum-half. But when I learned that Sid was an Irish international scrum-half, I knew I must play outside-half to him, and took up the game again at Sealand. We enjoyed several games together for the station against local clubs until my ankle broke again. Sid cracked his nose in the same game, so during a few days in sick quarters together we decided to concentrate on flying.

Sid was a man of moods. One moment he was starry-eyed strumming his guitar and crooning about leaving the Emerald Isle. But in his next breath he could be blasting some fellow's soul to eternity, hoping he would die in agony. His pet hate was Jim Gideon. Sid swore by his ancestors of Bally-somewhere-or-other that he would get that creeper Gideon who by ingratiating himself with the instructors had become leader of 45 Course. He loathed this man's high and mighty pride, and vowed many times a day that his last act before leaving Sealand would be to black Gideon's bottom with boot polish.

Nobody took him seriously, but I knew Sid better and had misgivings. Sure enough, after our farewell party on the night before our departure Sid arrived at Gideon's quarters with an ugly glint in his eye and an open tin of Cherry Blossom in his hand. There was a terrible fight. Gideon had a vicious temper and was twice Sid's size. But Sid's Irish blood and natural love of a fight, together with his rugby experience, soon gave him the better of his hefty and by now well-nigh hysterical opponent. In a very short time Gideon's pants were round his ankles, his midriff was bared, and Sid went to work with the blacking.

Unfortunately, due to Sid's determination in the face of Gideon's opposition, the sharp edges of the tin cut Gideon deeply where it hurt his pride most. The fight ended with him being assisted, limping and moaning into sick quarters for antiseptic baths and anti-tetanus injections.

Another very close friend in 'D' Flight was Arthur Ingham. He was affectionately known, for obvious reasons, as 'Big' Ingham. Arthur was without doubt one of the best pilots on our course. A little older than most of us, he had won his Wings pre-war in the RAF class F reserve. He held a science degree, and took our ground lectures in his stride.

Arthur was one of the few members of 'D' Flight not to end up dead. Although he trained with us on fighters, instead of going to a fighter squadron he became a flying instructor, then converted to bombers. The next I heard was that he was CO of the Dambusters' Squadron when it re-formed after their famous Dambuster raid. He rose to the rank of Group Captain. He was the sort of fellow who knew how to get on and how not to get himself killed.

When our course finished on 10 June 1940, we were all sad to part, although eager to get on to operations. We received our postings while on leave. I was posted to 504 County of Nottingham Auxiliary Fighter Squadron, then stationed at Wick in the far north of Scotland. I found 'Wag' Haw, Denis Helcke, Mac McGregor and John Gurteen there when I joined it.

Sid went to 610 at Gravesend, on the south-east coast of England. News came through very soon that he had died when he was shot down in one of the earlier Battle of Britain dogfights. Bill Higgins, another pal in 'D' Flight — a beaming, smiling personality — also posted to Sid's squadron, died the same day. A few days later came the news that Wee Halty had gone up in flames at Biggin Hill.

By now we were beginning to accept that this war was no Sunday School party. The training was over. Battle had commenced. Flying was getting dangerous.

An Oxford makes a night landing!

Part Three
Operations

5
Fighting not Flying

My train journey from Liverpool to Wick to join 504 took 21 hours. We had changes, with long spells in drab unheated waiting rooms, at Carstairs, Edinburgh and Inverness. The last 200 miles from Inverness took nine hours. We spent nearly as much time shunted into wayside halts as travelling. A second engine had had to hitch up to pull our train over Shap. We stopped half an hour in a cutting hiding from a lone raider from Norway looking for a train to machine-gun.

It was hard to understand why so many troops should be travelling to the northern tip of Scotland when the war zone was so far south. Obviously we needed a fighter squadron or two up here to deal with hit-and-run bombers and reconnaissance planes the Germans were sending from Norway. But why a train load of soldiers and sailors? I had not yet appreciated the importance of Scapa Flow to our Fleet, nor the danger from enemy parachutists or glider landings in the flatter areas of Caithness.

At Wick station, lacking both breakfast and sleep, I was met by an RAF van and driven to the aerodrome. Wag and Denis Helcke were waiting at the guardroom to greet me. There was a grand and glorious reunion.

I reported to the Squadron Adjutant in the orderly room and he introduced me to the CO. I expected when I met the commanding officer of an operational fighter squadron to find a granite-jawed character with an oak-tree neck, ice grey eyes, and strong square teeth biting hard on an unlit briar pipe. He would glare at me and expect me to stare back. Squadron Leader John Sample, DFC, was gentle and friendly, almost shy. He stooped slightly. His smile was warm, his voice soft. He inquired about my journey, my previous flying experience, my family and my journalism. He reminisced to me about his own civilian life as an estate agent.

What he did not mention was that as a flight commander with 504 in France when their Squadron Leader was shot down he took over and led the squadron through those dark days before Dunkirk. I later learned he was himself shot down, parachuted to safety and walked twenty miles back to his base, eventually bringing the remnants of 504 back to England when France finally fell. For this, and for shooting down several German aircraft into the bargain, he won his DFC.

That evening in the Sergeants' Mess, and the following morning at Flight Dispersal, I met the rest of our pilots. Half had fought in France. Many still suffered from frayed nerves through being outnumbered in the air by ten to one. We were in Scotland for them to rest and for the squadron to be brought back to strength. Two other new Sergeant Pilots, Bushy and Douggie Haywood, had joined them with our Sealand party. Sergeants Jones (Jaggers) and Spencer (Spaggers) were automatically the senior Sergeant Pilots, both being regular RAF and having been on operations in France.

My flight commander, Flight Lieutenant Joe Royce, also collected his DFC in France. With me in 'B' flight were McGregor and Denis Helcke together with Bushy who became my close pal. Wag Haw went to 'A' flight led by Flight Lieutenant Tony Rook, who later became our CO when John Sample was posted to Group.

One of my most exciting moments of the war was at Wick when I flew my first Hurricane. Before that day I had never even seen one of these wonderful aeroplanes. Joe Royce drove me, with my helmet and parachute, over to the hangar on the morning of 21 June 1940, where *N2705* proudly preened herself on the tarmac. She was a graceful bird, wings outstretched eager to take the air. But heavy cowlings around her nose hid a 1,050 hp Rolls-Royce Merlin motor. Six stubby exhausts sprouted from each side of the powerful V-12 cylinder engine.

Four red patches of canvas doped on the leading edge of each wing protected the barrels of eight evil Browning machine-guns from the elements. Together these guns could spit 160 .303 bullets a second. With one short burst they could rip a thirteen-foot diameter hole in a wall from 250 yards.

I had already spent half an hour studying the Hawker Hurricane handling notes, and memorising the data. Now Joe Royce took me over the controls and instruments, the oxygen bottles, taps and gauges, the gravity and wing fuel tanks. He gave me a few tips about swing on take-off, stall characteristics, and the coarse and fine twin-speed de Havilland airscrew control which was soon to be replaced by the constant speed Rotol propeller that would give a choice of any revs for cruising or combat.

At last came the magic words: 'All right, Sergeant Holmes, if you're quite happy then take her up for thirty minutes and put her through her paces, but keep within sight of the aerodrome.'

I glowed with the triumph of being in a single cockpit aeroplane. I was master of my very own aircraft. The handling notes had listed the speeds for the various aerobatics. I noted with satisfaction that no maximum speed was stated. In other words, this aeroplane would never break in flight.

She handled so beautifully that I was soon at home with all the normal manoeuvres of turns, stalls and spins. The Master had needed force to bank steeply or turn tightly, and to perform a couple of slow rolls was tiring. But to bank the Hurricane was as easy as turning a car's steering wheel. The control column was cunningly geared, and a gentle heave had the aircraft on its side in an instant. Slow rolls, barrel rolls, rolls off the top of a loop all came so easily. The surge from its powerful engine climbed you vertically in fine pitch at 3,000 revs as though heading for outer space. I remembered Joe Royce's warning about the heavy sinking on hold-off for landing. With a little speed in hand she sat on the runway smoothly and steadily at 68 mph and ambled to a docile halt.

The Hurricane and I were going to be good friends.

Back at dispersal with the Form 700 signed for exercise completed I saw the syllabus we had ahead of us. Formation flying, an oxygen climb to 25,000 feet, aerial and air-to-ground gunnery, R/T procedure, sector reconnaissance round the islands and waters of Scapa Flow, flapless landings in case of hydraulics failure, and methods of abandoning the aircraft in emergency.

We had now, Joe stressed, to forget all we had learned about how to fly an aeroplane. Now we must concentrate on learning to use it as a gun platform for shooting down the enemy. The game was getting better every minute.

Wag, Denis and Bushy had flown their first solo the previous day. We were comparing notes on the qualities of this super machine when Flight Lieutenant Royce put his head round the crew room door.

'Oh Homer,' he called, showing by his dropping of the formal 'Sergeant Holmes' that I was now accepted as a squadron pilot, 'Will you sign for "N" again, and take her over to Castletown. Grab a map, it's twenty miles up the coast near Dunnet Head. One runway only, the other's not finished yet, so watch out for bulldozers and lorries. Squadron's just been posted there.'

I was already gathering up my helmet, oxygen mask and parachute as he added: 'When you've landed, taxy to the flight hut. There's no perimeter track but there are ground crews to see you over the rough ground. Your personal kit will follow by road.'

That was my first and last landing at Wick for four years. My next landing there is another story.

Castletown I found was an airfield very much in the making. Circling it I saw that ground was being bulldozed to clear a level track for the second runway. Mounds of clay were piled along each side inviting disaster for any pilot unfortunate enough to swing on landing. The strip ran between a belt of trees and a farmhouse. One end finished on the brink of a shallow valley where a few sheep grazed. It was a picturesque setting with the choppy water of Pentland Firth half a mile to the north. The craggy-cliffed islands of Scapa Flow made a natural harbour for our fleet across the Firth.

There was a windsock on a pole beside a small wooden building the size of a large garden shed. This was the aerodrome control pilot's hut, from which the arrival and departure of all aircraft would be handled. I parked my aircraft and walked across to it. Inside was an Aldis signalling lamp, a Very pistol, a few red and green cartridges and a folding chair. I was to guide the other aircraft down from here.

The windsock hung limply in practically still air. I yelled to a couple or airmen to bring white boards to make a landing 'T'. They set these out at the end of the runway indicating the direction for landing. A fitter lent me his *Picture Post* magazine, and I squatted on the grass in the sunshine, browsing through it until the other pilots showed up.

Quite soon Hurricane *TM-B* zoomed across the airfield from the Wick direction. He flew over my landing 'T', noted its position, and made a couple of circuits of the field. I could visualise Flying Officer Barnes, cautious and benevolent, examining the unfinished runway as I had done and spotting my parked Hurricane to which he would taxy in due course.

I almost lost sight of him as he sank into the heat haze on his final approach. Then in a sudden rush he was over the end of the runway, holding off at ninety for a gentle three-point touch-down after a hundred yards. It was when the Hurricane started swinging violently from side to side that I realised Barney's brakes were giving trouble. Air pressure probably gone — a nuisance on earlier Hurricanes. He was having to give bursts of engine to keep the tail straight which was lengthening his landing run. He was too far along the runway now to open up and take off again, and was fighting to get some air pressure into his brakes by rough left and right rudder.

There was no wind to slow him down. Barney was speeding towards the sudden drop at the end of the tarmac onto rough, tractor-pitted earth and down the valley where the sheep grazed. 'B' would certainly tip on its nose down that slope, and probably turn upside-down.

I set off towards the runway as if heading off a wing three-quarter streaking for our line. I saw Barney's look of frustration and annoyance change to incredulity when he saw me running at him. He was obviously asking himself 'What in hell does Holmes think he's doing?'

In fact Holmes had just the slender hope in his heart that if he could grab Barney's wingtip he may somehow swing a ton of Hurricane towards the edge of the runway and save it from tipping over the end. The interception was well-timed. The Hurricane was still travelling faster than I could sprint, but I grabbed the wingtip at its leading edge as it went past and dragged both feet on the ground to heave the wing back. The nose swung slightly to its left. Barney realised what I was attempting and kicked on full left rudder to help me.

Another jab into the ground with my feet, another heave, and the nose came further round. The end of the runway was near now, but the Hurricane was slowing down. I tugged lustily at the wing. The heat was coming through the soles of my flying boots from the friction. Twenty yards from the end I forsook the wing, ran to the tail, and gave it an almighty sideways shove. The aircraft slewed round and skidded broadside on protesting tyres. It ran at right angles off the runway on to stony but level ground.

Barney wiped imaginary sweat (or was it real?) from his forehead, and gave me a grateful grin. 'That'll cost you a pint,' I shouted above the engine noise. 'Look at my bloody boots. I've only had 'em an hour.' The new soles were scored and torn.

Barney grinned and switched off. It was impossible to taxy over the rough ground from where he had finished, and 'B' would need to be towed away with a tractor. 'Cheap at the price,' he yelled back, 'compared with a new airscrew — and probably an undercart too.'

Suddenly I saw him cast a horrified glance over my head along the runway on which he had just landed. 'Good God,' he yelled, 'Wendell's in trouble too.'

Sure enough, *TM-D* had joined the circuit while we were wrestling to save 'B'. Wendell, seeing Barney landing along the 'T', had taken a short turn down onto the runway. Now he was bumping along the tarmac, still far too fast, and yawing from side to side as Barney had done to try to get pressure into his brakes. I sprinted back to head him off, and grabbed Wendell's wingtip at almost the same spot as I had grabbed Barney's. I went through the same routine of tugging his wing back, jamming my feet into the ground, sliding along and heaving at the wing. My boots, having earlier reached the smoking stage, now seemed ready to burst into flames. My feet felt sore.

I ran again from the wing to the tail and shoved it round. 'D' swung obediently off the runway just past 'B'. But unhappily the ground here dropped away in a steeper slope and as 'D' came to a halt its tail slowly reared up, as I lay across it. It hovered half way then carried on upwards, sliding me off on to my back under the fuselage as 'D' settled on her nose. The metal airscrew blades bit the ground, bending them into hockey sticks, and stalling the engine.

I lay in this undignified attitude with the wind knocked out of me, while Wendell, looking even more undignified and cursing heartily climbed out of his cockpit and slithered down the wing to the ground.

My main concern now was for my beautiful new flying boots. The second slide had worn them through to my socks, through which oozed blobs of blood. 'Look at my boots,' I moaned. 'Why didn't you go round again?' Wendell was in no chatty mood. 'Bugger your bloody boots,' was all he said. He swung his parachute over his shoulder, lit a cigarette, and stumped off towards the nissen huts.

Two overshoots that cost me a pair of flying boots.

Barney winked at me. After all, his aeroplane was not bent like Wendell's.

I stayed long enough to take a quick photo, then phoned Wick to stop any more aircraft landing at Castletown until 'D' and 'B' were towed clear.

Barney's Hurricane ('B') and my boots (soled and heeled) shared yet another experience three months later. I baled out of 'B' and it buried itself fifteen feet down in Ebury Bridge Road, Chelsea, bursting a water main. The jerk of my parachute opening caused both boots to fly off my feet and they fell somewhere near Victoria Station. I never saw either 'B' or my boots again.

Castletown was the ideal base to re-form a shot-up squadron. The north-east coast Scottish weather in June was sunny and warm, always clear, rarely hot. Had we gone to an established RAF aerodrome with its modern equipment, furnished messes, orderly rooms, parade square, squash courts and cricket pitches, we would have become submerged in the routine of normal Service life and missed the most important feature of all, the comradeship that bred team-spirit.

At Castletown everything started from scratch. Everyone mucked in to get the jobs done. No unions screamed about demarcation of trades. The pilots went out during stand-down and drove tipper-trucks of clay for dumping, or took vans to Thurso to collect goods arriving by train. We hacked with spades and pickaxes to dig ditches for drains, and carted furniture from lorries into dispersal huts and offices.

The Sergeant Pilots had probably the best time of all organising their own mess. This was a white private house on the tip of Dunnet Head, without doubt the last residence in Scotland, when the RAF took it over. It stood on its own having been for the coastguards. It was empty, and we set up iron bedsteads with biscuit mattresses and blankets, installed lockers, linked up the house wiring to a petrol-driven generator and arranged the lounge with easy chairs around the walls, books and magazines on shelves and the poker table in the middle. We were soon a family of friends instead of members of a mess.

Two airmen cleaned and tidied around when we went over to the main camp for breakfast. Meals were always eaten in the dining room on the camp, or if on readiness at dispersal. But we stocked up our house with grub and beer to enjoy in the evening while we listened to records on our HMV portable, hand-wound gramophone, read, or played a few rounds of whiskey-poker.

An old church and graveyard separated our house on Dunnet Head from the road to the camp. When a 'panic' was on we raced between the ancient graves with scant respect for their peaceful occupants, and scrambled into the waiting brake that rushed us to dispersal.

Our routine on arrival there was straightforward, although the hours on duty were long with the light June nights so far north. 'A' and 'B' Flights had nine aircraft and nine pilots each. One flight of six aircraft had always to be at readiness, prepared to put all six up into the air within three minutes. The other flight, meantime, was available to come to readiness if required within either fifteen or thirty minutes, according to the time allowed by Group.

The 'available' flight never left the aerodrome. The officers could stay in their Mess and the Sergeant Pilots could go to their house, to be called to readiness if required. Only when a flight was 'Released' was it free — until dawn next day, about 3 am. This meant always sleeping in camp beds at dispersal.

Operational commitments at Castletown were small, enabling the new pilots to train. The established fliers would help them with their training by leading the 'Sprogs' on formation practice or taking them on sector recces along the coast, or round the Orkney Isles with the naval base in Scapa Flow behind the Island of Hoy.

Scapa itself was the only area forbidden to us. The Germans captured many British aeroplanes when they drove the Allies out of Europe, and they were flying them over here as spy planes from Norway on photographic or bombing missions. The Navy did not intend to have their ships either photographed or bombed by aeroplanes posing as British, and made it abundantly clear from the outset that any aircraft — repeat *any* — that ventured over the waters of Scapa Flow would be instantly fired upon by the guns of all ships. Our squadron must not even chase an enemy aircraft across that area. We kept well clear of Scapa, giving it the code name of 'The Circus'.

Our maps, four miles to the inch, showed all the kinks in coastlines, together with rivers, harbours, roads and railways which made them all recognisable from the air. Prominent features such as a headland, estuary, island, large lake or high hill would be identified by code letters in alphabetical order round the area. Thus we could be quickly directed to any point on the map, such as six miles north of 'B' instead of having first to identify the name of a town or river before we could find our way there.

Now that we were flying real fighter aircraft with radio and guns, it was imperative to know in advance how it felt to fire those guns while in flight, instead of waiting for our first taste of action to find out. So one of our first exercises was to fly to a quiet stretch of sea, make a low search to be certain it was clear of small fishing boats, then fly over a second time at about 100 feet and blast away with the eight Brownings.

The experience was a sobering one. With your reflector sight switched on you would keep your bead on the white of a wave crest, pretending it was a Hun, then FIRE! The racket as each gun hammered out its twenty shells a second was deafening, even above your engine noise and with your helmet covering your ears. The second burst was not so bad, as you were ready for the din. The third was music to your ears because you were now, you felt, a hardened fighter pilot living by gun-law.

The effect of the shooting on the controls of the aeroplane was unexpected. When a single round is fired from a rifle the recoil as the bullet leaves the barrel jerks back the butt into the marksman's shoulder. This recoil is used in the machine-gun to throw back the breech block and eject the spent cartridge case. On the way forward again it grabs a new round from the ammunition belt, rams it into the barrel and fires it. This process is repeated twenty times a second on each of the eight guns, until the pressure is removed from the firing button. This recoil, although absorbed to some extent in the gun itself, still gives a pronounced braking effect to the aeroplane, slowing it down noticeably and making the nose sink. The sinking effect, when only 100 feet above the water, can be disturbing.

The most lasting impression, however, is the dreadful effects those bullets have on impact even with water. After the guns are fired, nothing at all appears to happen. Then, after a lull of perhaps a second while the bullets are speeding to their target there is a seething and frothing of the water ahead as though a school of enraged sharks has suddenly surfaced. A second later you have skimmed over the maelstrom.

We were fortunate to have in 504 two expert formation fliers in Flying Officers Jack Hardacre and Trevor Parsons. If you were leading them, they would close in on either side of your aircraft until the trailing edges of your two wings were within six inches of the leading edges of theirs. Their wings would overlap yours until their propeller tips would be threshing a foot from your wingtips. A sneeze could now bring disaster all round. Was it preferable, you wondered, to try a gentle turn, or should your keep straight on towards Norway until you ran out of petrol?

Finally you signalled and banked to port. The one on the inside dropped down and the other climbed so the three aircraft always kept in the same relative position even in a vertical turn. Gradually, as you gained confidence, your manoeuvres became more daring. An exercise always ended with a shoot-up of the flight hut. Then, climbing steeply, the leader waves his two aircraft away in a Prince of Wales feathers while he does a climbing roll straight ahead.

Having such skilful exponents of the art to copy as Hardacre and Parsons, our own formation flying improved quickly. When the day came that we suddenly had to climb as a squadron through cloud all twelve aircraft tucked in and followed the leader through the thick fog until we emerged at the top. Cloud piercing is one of the most exhilarating experiences in an aeroplane.

There are thrills in aerobatics. There is satisfaction about a successful forced landing. Tight formation flying tests concentration. An exhausting night sortie earns the blessed relief of relaxation. All these experiences merge to make the overall fun of flying. But the sheer joy of having control of an aeroplane in, above, around and through an ocean of frothing, champagne bubble clouds, brings its own particularly heady intoxication.

When 'A' Flight was on readiness and we of 'B' Flight were at thirty minutes' availability, Flight Lieutenant Royce would mark our blue and green sections of three aircraft each for an hour of 'formaggers'.

Pilots took turns to lead so that we all gained experience as a section leader, but on operational trips the senior pilot was always number one. Flight Lieutenant Royce would stroll in stroking his chin. Finally, marking the readiness board accordingly: 'You lead Green section today Bushy; Homer number two (on Bushy's starboard), McGregor number three (on his port)'.

Out at his aeroplane the pilot's parachute lies on his wingtip.

504's Sergeants' Mess on Dunnet Head, five miles from John O'Groats.

Aeroplane modelling at the Mess — Jones and Spencer (left) and Spencer's wife, who travelled up to visit him.

A friendly game of whisky-poker.

The route through the graveyard to readiness from the Sergeants' Mess (back left). Wag takes a breather.

On the reflector sight behind the windscreen hangs his helmet, with oxygen mask and radio headset attached and connected up.

The fitter has plugged the trolley battery into the aircraft. 'Contact' is a thumbs-up to the fitter. The airscrew slowly turns. If the engine is too cold to fire, the pilot injects rich mixture into the carburetter with the booster pump. The engine continues turning, then fires. The pilot 'catches' it and sets it to a fast tickover. The fitter disconnects the trolley battery and pulls it clear.

On practice trips the engine runs for a few moments at a fast tickover until the correct oil pressure and coolant temperature are reached. On operational scrambles this formality is unnecessary, the ground crews having run engines periodically to keep them warm.

Bushy, who leads today, calls ground control for permission to take off. Blue section files out in order of take-off. The three aircraft race down the runway in single file but staggered slightly to avoid slipstreams ahead. Bushy climbs gently straight ahead for a thousand feet before turning left. Numbers two and three follow at full bore, turning low and steeply to head him off and tuck in neatly beside him on the down wind leg of the airfield.

Bushy pushes his radio control to transmit. 'Hello Crocodile, Green section airborne, over.'

'Crocodile receiving Green One strength nine. OK. Listening out.' The exercise has now started.

We head first for the coast, making a left-hand circuit of our recent base at Wick. Mac and I steal a quick glance down at Wick airfield. Then we race north to Dunnet Head, and swing left for our present base at Castletown.

Bushy taps the back of his head with one hand. Instantly two slides behind and below him and three throttles back slightly to take up the same position behind two. In line astern we dive at the house that is our Sergeants' Mess, roaring in succession 100 feet above the roof. The leader must be careful not to go too low because two and three are below him, dodging his slipstream.

The Mess is empty. Everyone is at flights, or flying. It is simply a salute to absent friends. The din brings our two batmen rushing out in alarm, but they are waving after we have gone. Into a steep climbing turn Bushy, banked vertically, wags his wings, calling the others to re-form. We slide back into Vic.

Now there is a run round the Orkneys, carefully avoiding 'The Circus'. The Navy have no sense of humour when it comes to shoot-ups. They are too trigger-happy. High cliffs fringe some of the islands. It is exhilarating to fly down to the waves below the cliff tops. At this height you realise how fast 300 mph really is.

An occasional cormorant, with his long neck and fast beating wings, skims a few feet above the sapphire sea, searching for the herring shoals. He turns away in alarm at the approach of the Hurricanes. Seagulls voice their indignation with yellow wide-open beaks as the three aircraft flash past them. One bird chopped by an airscrew, explodes against the windscreen. But the bullet-proof glass two inches thick and inclined backwards thirty degrees glances the bird off and its carcase drops into the sea.

Returning over the Pentland Firth, Bushy points upwards, nodding his head forwards. Open the throttle, we are going to climb. He calls us into tight Vic with me on his right and Mac on his left. Then he opens up to 4½ lb of boost at 2,850 revs and eases up his nose till we have settled into a steady 160 mph climb into the first cloud.

It is very bumpy inside the cumulus cloud, with its strong up-currents. I give my straps a yank to tighten them and hold me more firmly in my seat. I try to make my bumps match Bushy's, following his wings when they bounce. We still get occasional glimpses of the ground. First a green pasture with a few trees, then a few seconds of cloud and then only blue water with no hint of land.

By 9,000 feet the cloud is solid. For the next thousand feet it grows steadily darker. Occasionally I glimpse Mac over the top of Bushy's fuselage. His face is a mask of concentration. He is staring at Bushy as though hoping to mesmerise him. He is determined not to lose him. We suddenly emerge into sunshine and I see Mac is sweating. He's not the only one.

The sunlight, broken by wisps of cloud, is a series of brilliant diamond flashes. Rainbows, their colours startlingly clear, surround some of the cloud tips. Then, suddenly, we are rushing out of a mattress of cotton wool and climbing steeply away from it up into endless blue. Bushy breaks us up. It is playtime. This is what we have all been waiting for. We are going cloud clipping.

One of Deanna Durbin's most popular records was about waltzing high in the clouds. She must have been cloud clipping. I swayed in my cockpit humming her tune, lilting her words into action as I scaled a precipitous snow mountain, then stall-turned to dive into a valley of feathery cliffs.

A gap has opened below me, and I can see the ground. A half-roll and a vertical dive takes me down the 3,000 foot long tunnel. Pulling out and swinging to return the same way I find the gap had already closed. So I yank back with the stick, open up to full throttle, and fully fine pitch, and go rocketing back into the cloud and out at the top in a matter of seconds.

Bushy has been watching, and is waiting to jump me. From behind a hillock of froth he streaks in a vertical turn and sits under my tail as I climb vertically, losing my speed and in a very vulnerable attitude from which there's no escape in combat. At that moment I spot Mac, chasing his own shadow through a rainbow that's racing him across the clouds. I roll over and swoop on to him to make a dummy quarter attack from his left. As he breaks to the right to evade me Bushy hems him in from that side, and he's our prisoner. We disperse again for a few more mad moments, breasting the peaks, swooping into the valleys.

Finally Bushy calls up Mac, passes over the leadership to him, and he leads us back home. Playtime over. We re-form and Mac takes us down from 10,000 to 2,000 feet in a screaming dive that sets our eardrums popping. We pinch our noses and blow and swallow to relieve the pressure. Then back to base for a shoot-up of dispersal, a Prince of Wales feathers, a break into line astern, wheels down, flaps down and on to the runway one, two, three . . . We arrive back in the crew room all grins.

Life was good. It was exhilarating. In those days we got high on our own adrenalin. No drugs. And no hangover.

6
Thirty Plus

As the peaceful summer days of July in Scotland slipped slowly by, war was warming up in the south. And we of 504 were growing restless at missing the fun. Intelligence reports revealed more than the public were reading in the daily newspapers and we followed with interest the game of aerial chess being played out between the Luftwaffe and RAF.

The Germans were making high-altitude daylight raids on south coast ports as decoys for second and bigger attacks at low level on our airfields. The Hun was probing for our weaknesses, to find how we would shape in an all-out death struggle. Our radar infuriated them, for every wave of aircraft they sent was plotted and intercepted by fighters before it crossed our coast. So they went for our radar stations and masts. Being so scattered on high ground along our coast these were hard to defend. When the enemy scored a hit, it did not take them long to find our blind spot and through the gap came a bomber stream.

Eight hundred miles north at Castletown we were furious and frustrated at missing all this action. While we were chasing lone Heinkels the boys down there were mixing it with raids of sixty-plus. There was always the slender hope, of course, that any day we'd find ourselves in the middle of a German invasion from Norway and for this reason the CO decided we must practise flying in flights of six aircraft, instead of in sections of three. As soon as possible, the CO urged, we must get both flights airborne together and operate as a squadron!

That day came sooner than we expected.

Without warning one morning the Tannoy suddenly blared out: '504 Squadron — repeat, the entire squadron — airborne, and climb to angels 12 over base.' Wag came running towards his aeroplane, rubbing his hands in glee. 'This is it Arty. The real McCoy! Wizard! We'll show the bastards.'

Bushy, sniffing nonchalantly, exaggerated the artificial twitch of the mouth we had all cultivated when excitement loomed ahead. He quietly remarked: 'Good-eh!' as he grabbed his parachute. But there was nothing nonchalant about the manner in which he started up and taxied out.

Though hearts really were racing, this being our first squadron scramble, there was surprisingly little panic. The odd lighted cigarette may have been flung into a chair, or poker dice scattered around the floor in the rush to get out of dispersal, but nobody lost his head. The ground crews were superb. From all directions came the splutter and roar of Merlins leaping to life. How those boys had got to the aircraft ahead of us was a mystery. The din mounted as twelve engines thundered their eagerness to be away. Dust clouds, and the occasional forage cap or empty oil tin caught in the slipstreams, went swirling across the airfield. Each pilot, goggles pulled down, peered through the dust storm to follow his leader as the twelve raced to the runway.

The CO led 'A' Flight, with Joe Royce and his boys of 'B' Flight right at their tails. The last aircraft was off the deck in under three minutes. We never did it so fast again.

In the air each man linked up with his section leader. 'A' Flight, and Blue section of 'B' made a Vic of nine aircraft. Green section tucked into the box, below and behind, ready to weave if attack was threatened. We were all on the same radio frequency, but R/T silence was imperative to leave the air clear for communication between the squadron leader and Ground Control.

As we climbed, circling the airfield, Crocodile came in: 'Thirty plus bandits, angels 15 flying due west, heading for Point D. Climb 065 degrees.'

'Wilco,' John Sample acknowledged, swinging left.

Two minutes later: 'Vector 090 now. What are your angels?'

'Angels 9.'

'Roger. Keep climbing. Out.'

We were now crossing the coast, heading towards the emerald

vastness of the North Sea. The air was crystal clear, and cloudless. Diamonds glittered on the water where the waves broke two miles below. What invasion weather for the Hun! All eyes strained, searching for the cluster of black specks that were to give us our first taste of real war.

At 12,000 feet the CO started a gentle zig-zag. He was not keen to engage the enemy too far out to sea. Any of our aircraft that were hit must have a chance to limp back to land.

Crocodile's transmitter clicked on again.

'Pancake,' was all he said. There was a full five seconds' silence from Sample. Heads were swivelling inquiringly in cockpits, seeking a reason for this incredible message.

Sample's voice, puzzled, 'Please say again, Crocodile'.

'I say again, pancake! And again, Pancake!' Crocodile sounded very angry.

'Wilco.' Sample obediently led us back to Castletown. There were no shoot-ups this time. We landed sedately. We set down by sections, and taxied in to be met by our loyal ground crews. They had not heard the radio exchanges and were rushing out to see whose aeroplane had blown the patches off the wing leading edges, showing their pilot had fired his guns in combat. None. Big anti-climax.

Back in the crew room the CO was already on the scrambler phone to ops. He listened intently, then smiled. 'Bloody Observer Corps,' he grunted, as he slammed down the phone. We waited expectantly, hanging on his words.

'The Observer Corps reported thirty-plus Heinkels. Quite positive identification. Definitely Heinkels, flying in at a great height from the sea. Strange thing was, our radar had not plotted them.'

'Why not, sir?' It was Joe Royce asking.

'Because they have just been identified as bloody seagulls flying at about 500 feet. Migrating or something, I suppose.'

That little false alarm cost us close on 500 gallons of precious petrol and it seemed about the same amount of sweat. But the false alarm had its good points. First it demonstrated to us quite clearly that we were not manoeuvrable as a squadron. We were clumsy and unwieldy in sections of three. Fine for a spectacular fly-past but futile in a fight. It was impossible to make sudden turns without first signalling a warning and that all took time. Secondly, it had pilots concentrating too much on formating with their leader, leaving them little chance for individual enterprise and aggression.

It was decided after long discussion that we would scrap the traditional four Vics of three, and instead have six pairs. Each pair would be in line astern because a number two could always follow his leader through any manoeuvres while sitting under his tail. The CO would of course, lead with his number two behind him. Out to his left and his right, and well back so that he could turn suddenly without colliding with them, would be two more pairs, with two more behind them. Finally, the last pair would weave at the back, one 500 feet above the squadron, and the other 500 below. These two arse-end Charlies would be the eyes in the back of the head, searching the sky all round to spot any surprise attacks by Messerschmitts.

This formation, thought up one evening over a tankard of ale, proved highly successful when we put it into practice at Castletown, and even more so when operating against the enemy over London a week or so later.

We spent our days making dummy attacks on each other, trying out evasive tactics in mock air battles, or flying low and fast over land and water. We made flapless landings at 120 mph instead of 90, pretending our hydraulics had been shot away in action and that we could not lower our flaps. We learned how, if our hydraulics were gone, to unlock our undercarriage and drop the wheels by gravity, then skid the aircraft violently from side to side to throw the legs out sideways until the green lights showed they had locked.

Occasionally a lone raider, probably a photographic Junkers 88 from its height and speed, would come on the board and a pair of Hurricanes would go off to intercept. The Germans carried wireless operators who tuned to our frequencies, rather as we can pick up police cars today on our transistors. When they heard us being sent off to intercept they would quickly turn tail for home.

I had still to do my oxygen climb. Extra oxygen is necessary for comfort and a clear brain after about 15,000 feet, and essential for survival above 20,000. The oxygen is stored in a pressurised cylinder and a tube takes it into the face-mask which also houses the radio microphone. Two gauges on the dashboard indicate the supply being fed to the pilot and amount remaining in the cylinder.

I was alone, and levelling out at 25,000 feet on my oxygen climb test when my R/T crackled. Control's transmitter had switched on, I waited for the message.

'Hello Green One, Crocodile here. Are you receiving?'

'Strength nine, Crocodile. Over.' Reception was perfect at that height.

'There's a bogey on the board, Green One. He's twenty miles east of point A, heading due west at Angels 12. Vector 165 degrees, and investigate.'

I acknowledged, and turned on to the course he gave, fishing for my map. It had to be on the crease of course. Point A was at the entrance to Moray Firth, the wide estuary which fifty miles inland becomes the famous Loch Ness. I reckoned my bogey was at this moment near Banff, and that if he held his present course I would intercept him about sixty miles away at Lossie-mouth.

I was twice his height, so I eased my nose down to dive gently and lose altitude at 1,000 feet per minute. This pushed my cruising speed up to just over 300 mph. I should be at his height and position in twelve minutes.

Control crackled through again. 'Vector 160 now, Green One. Look for him to port.'

This was better than cruising round for half an hour at 25,000 feet sucking oxygen out of a bottle. It was a glorious day, as brilliantly clear as it so often is in this part of Scotland. From five miles up I could look back across the Pentland Firth and over the Orkney Islands, to the Shetlands. Caithness, immediately below, was surprisingly green and flat, with its three lochs and three rivers, but I was already approaching the foothills of the Highlands which become the spine of Scotland and run south to Ben Nevis at Fort William. The view to the west was equally dramatic, over the coast line to the Isle of Lewis and the Atlantic Ocean.

I crossed the east coast where it bends inland to Helmsdale and the Moray Firth. There were sixty miles of sea to the other side of the Firth. I had never flown over so much sea and found myself listening attentively to my engine. Its song was sweet. Down at 15,000 feet I spotted my bogey. He was a tiny speck creeping along the coastline towards Lossiemouth. As I drew nearer I made him out to be a black twin engined bomber.

I called Crocodile, and gave him the 'Tallyho'. He came straight back with 'Good show and good luck'. I marvelled at the accuracy of the radar that had plotted the height and course of this aircraft so exactly, almost bringing us onto a collision course.

First I must identify him. If he proved to be German I must cut off his escape back to sea. He was very slow, and taking no evasive action. He must surely have seen me bearing down on him from this clear sky. At three times his speed, I had no difficulty in manoeuvring to his starboard beam, for a dummy quarter attack.

My reflector sight was switched on, its red neon graticule glowing. I adjusted the range for a sixty-foot wingspan target. My gun button on the control column was on 'Fire'. To my disappointment I quickly recognised him as an old RAF Whitley night bomber, making less than 100 mph. He wagged his wings in a friendly gesture as I approached.

That was all very well, but it did not prove his crew were British. Where had he come from? Why was he here? Ground control seemed to have no knowledge of his movements. Was he taking photos as he flew over the airfield at Kinloss?

I called up Crocodile, reported my bogey was a Whitley, and gave him its squadron markings. He thanked me, told me to stand by. I was all for firing a warning burst in front of the Whitley's nose and forcing him down at Kinloss. Plenty of time then to find out who he was when he was on the ground. And find out why he was routed through our Sector with Group. While I waited for Crocodile to check if there should be any Whitleys in the area, I closed in on him. He flashed me no recognition letters of the day. Fishy.

I tucked my port wing behind his starboard wing till I felt the slipstream from his engine. I had to lower my flaps to keep down to his speed. The skin of the Whitley was matt black to camouflage him from night fighters in the dark. I could pick out the rivets in the fuselage and the brush marks in the painted roundels. Through the window I could clearly see the pilot's head.

The bastard was waving at me! Bloody cheek! Whether he was a Hun snooping for photos or a British pilot who'd lost his way, it made no difference; he still had a ruddy nerve. Now he's lowering his wheels! Is this to show he's friendly and one of ours, or is he really going down? This will be one for the book if I land back there with a crew of Jerry prisoners!

'Hello, Green One, are you receiving?'

'Go ahead, Crocodile.'

'It's OK. Bogey is believed friendly. Please return to base and pancake. Well done.' The last bit came as an afterthought.

Blast! With all the Whitleys the Germans had captured this could easily be one checking our airfields up here on the Scottish coast. If the Jerries plan a landing, they'll need to know the strength of our defences.

'Wilco, Crocodile.'

I gave the Whitley a friendly waggle of my wings, then as an afterthought a V-sign, peeled off and flew back to Castletown. Flying Officer Plowman, our intelligence officer (Plowbags) was waiting at dispersal for my account of the incident. Squadron Leader Sample came in and read the report Plowbags had written.

'Bad luck, Holmes,' he said.

'Yes sir, it was. I was dying to take a poop at him.'

'Pity you didn't.'

'Control told me to leave him and pancake.'

He grimaced.

'Group have just been on. Your Whitley is at this moment heading balls out for Norway.'

In those days what I said was considered very rude indeed.

Every one of the 26 hours I flew on Hurricanes at Castletown had been spent learning how to put that superb piece of fighting equipment to its best use.

The radio was magic. Having until now used a map to find my way from A to B it was unbelievable that I could suddenly call up ground control for a course to steer either to another place, or back to base. We were shown in the ops room how this miracle happened. On a giant table the size of a squash court, was a large scale map of our sector. The exact position of every aircraft was plotted on this map, and by means of a compass rose the controller could give a pilot a course to fly to bring him home or take him to any other point.

Each Hurricane carried two radios. One automatically transmitted a coded signal for that aircraft and it was this signal that enabled its exact position to be plotted every quarter of a minute. The other radio was a two-way telephone (R/T) for speech contact with the controller. Thus the bogey of straying too far from base in bad weather, or getting lost in cloud above mountains or out of sight of land over the sea was removed.

Each interception proved the usefulness of radio. If a Hun approaching the coast knew fighters were up to intercept him, he would play a cat-and-mouse game in and out of cloud making complicated changes of course. After half an hour of blind man's buff you lost your bearings completely, and were thankful to be told which way to fly home.

It was always fun to chase a Hun. From his changes of course you could read his mind and guess his next move. Ground control aimed to manoeuvre you between him and Norway, cutting off his retreat. But the German reconnaissance pilots were usually very experienced, many having been peacetime commercial airline captains. With an English-speaking radio operator plotting our position for him and passing on our conversations with base, he was able to ensure that he kept within reach of cloud cover when approaching our coast.

It was still good to be able to tell the fellows at dispersal that you'd actually seen a bandit five miles away and had got him cornered until he disappeared into ten-tenths cloud. Although we never shot one down from Castletown, we could at least claim that no German pilot ever saw or photographed the Navy at Scapa Flow.

The radio's greatest comfort came at night. During night flying at Sealand the only lights to be seen anywhere, because of strict wartime blackout conditions, were six paraffin flares marking the runway. We therefore flew circuits and landings only, getting out of sight of the flarepath being the loneliest experience imaginable. Flying through velvet blackness and seeing nothing but the luminous glow of your dashboard instruments and the purple flame from your exhausts was enough to start butterflies in the steadiest of stomachs.

On my first Hurricane night trip I was briefed for a short triangular cross-country, over to Cape Wrath on the north-west tip of Scotland then back to Helmsdale on the east coast climbing to 4,000 feet to clear the foothills, and back home to base. About half an hour.

On the circuit, as I was lowering my wheels to land, the oil seal in my propeller boss blew. My hood was open for the landing and I was looking down to the left at the flarepath, so it was not until I started my final straight approach that I found I could see nothing through my windscreen. It was sprayed with a layer of oil. Forward vision had gone entirely.

My mind went back to Mr Corke, my CFI at Barton, and how he went out of his way to demonstrate a desert sandstorm landing by looking backwards over his tail. He did it in a Gipsy Moth, touching down on grass at 45 mph. Was I going to pull one off in a Hurricane at twice the speed!

I opened my throttle, lifting wheels and flaps and went round again while I thought about it. I advised Crocodile of my dilemma. He told me my message was received and he was wishing me luck and listening out.

I made a curving approach almost on to the runway looking over the left side of the cockpit to the point where I straightened up to hold-off. The flame from the four exhausts glared my vision but through them I could make out the flares. At 100 feet, still banked at 45 degrees as I crossed the boundary I saw two sets of dimmed headlamps speeding across the field towards the runway. Crocodile had called out the fire tender and ambulance to await my arrival.

I unlocked my harness to let me reach forward and put a hand round the windscreen and try to wipe it. The slipstream threatened to blow both my handkerchief and my hand away. The plane lurched as I strained forward, and rubbing only smeared the glass worse.

I aimed to the right side of the runway and kept turning to within a few feet of the ground.

Then, as the first flare flashed past I levelled out and gently eased the stick back to bring the nose up into the hold-off position. I followed that flare with my eyes as it fell behind. My wheels grounded as the second flare came into my side vision. These two flares gave me a line to keep straight while looking backwards, just like Corkey had taught me. As the remaining four flares passed, each one more slowly, I stabbed at the rudder and snatched at the brakes, with an occasional burst of throttle to keep straight until we came to a halt.

'That,' I murmured, whistling softly through my teeth, 'was a real Corker.'

I remembered to raise my flaps before I taxied in, but I did not remember mopping my brow with the back of my hand. I must have done, for there were oil smears from my glove on my forehead when I walked into dispersal.

★   ★   ★

Life had settled itself into a pleasant routine at Castletown. Flying Hurricanes was a joy. The small amount of hostile activity by the

Hun just sufficient to keep us on our toes. We were now up to strength, several more pilots having arrived. Morale was high. We were raring to go, keen for action. Even so, the Scottish weather was superb, the air fresh as champagne and visibility clear to the horizon. What more could a pilot ask?

No dream can last for ever.

'Sergeant Holmes, can you spare me a moment, please?'

When Joe Royce gave me my rank, instead of Homer, I knew it was shop. I grabbed my cap, followed him into his office, and saluted.

'Take a seat, Homer, this is quite informal.'

Back to Homer.

'We're on our way, Homer. Probably finish up at London. If we do there'll be more action than that. We're posted to Catterick in North Yorkshire for starters.'

'When do we go, sir?'

'That's the point. You're not going. Not yet, anyway.'

'Sir?'

He tugged at his streak of black moustache. 'Half a dozen aircraft are still in the middle of radio and airscrew mods and they must be finished before they leave here. It'll take a couple more days.'

'Some of us have to stay back and fly them to Catterick?'

'Right, but they need a leader who can map-read because we are not on Catterick's frequency. The CO wants you to lead them down.'

'Thank you, sir.'

'It's not as simple as that, Homer. Half the pilots you bring with you will be officers who, as you know, don't have your flying time in their logbooks. It's unusual for a Sergeant Pilot to be leading officer pilots. But remember, you'll be the flight commander on that trip, and your word goes.'

'When are you off, sir?'

'Both flights must be airborne at crack of dawn tomorrow. We put down at Drem, twenty miles north-east of Edinburgh — that's about one hour thirty from here — for a refuel and breakfast. Catterick, in North Yorkshire, is another hour and a quarter on from Drem. We'll be there mid-morning. You should follow the same itinerary 48 hours after us.'

He gave me the list of the other pilots staying behind, and their aircraft.

Denis Helcke at Castletown
— killed two weeks later
over London. We all
attended his funeral at
Herne Bay.

'Jaggers' Jones — killed a few
months afterwards as a flying
instructor.

'See you at Catterick on Wednesday, then.'

I replaced my hat, saluted and left. But I didn't see Flight Lieutenant Royce at Catterick.

Our six Hurricanes were delayed at Castletown awaiting spare parts. An Anson trundled in with them mid-morning, and it was late afternoon before we were airborne. Drem knew we were on a tight schedule and gave us a quick refuel and we were away again within the half hour. By the time we landed at Catterick 504 had all left for London. There was a message for me to bring my flight down to Hendon next day, refuelling at Swinderby, a few miles south-west of Lincoln, and Cranfield.

The weather the following morning was hazy. We had exchanged our crisp, clear Castletown visibility for industrial murk. We agreed to fly in close formation if the weather thickened. A couple of new pilots tended to lag behind but they never lost us and we made Swinderby without incident.

The Met forecast further south was for even poorer visibility and showers. It was important to get to Hendon but after half an hour's flying the weather really clamped, just before some hills. I called them in close, and started climbing. The land was rising as the cloud came down and soon we were only five hundred feet above ground and losing sight of it in wisps of cloud. I held my course, but the two laggards were flying erratically and obviously unhappy. While I was wondering whether to return to Catterick or press on to Cranfield, I suddenly spotted Bedford on my left. There was the road running south-west to Cranfield. I swung round to it and in two minutes we were crossing over the landing ground.

It was an elementary flying training school, very small with no runways. There were trees at intervals along the boundary fence. A few Tiger Moths were clustered around the hangar on the north side. The windsock, with a landing 'T' beside it, showed a slight breeze from the west. I called to the others on R/T to space out in line. Dennis Helcke, who was with us at Sealand, was to land first and they were to follow him in. I would land last, when everyone was safely down.

It was then that I noticed one of the sprog pilots had drifted out of line and was heading away from the airfield towards the brighter weather of Catterick. I chased him and led him back to Cranfield where he landed safely. He was looking green when he booked in at the Watch Office. I was relieved to get this far without incident.

That evening the wind freshened, clearing the haze. By eight o'clock we were circling Hendon aerodrome — just a year after my visit there with Corkey from Ringway in a Hawker Hind. Much water had gone under the bridge since.

By the time we landed at Hendon 504 had already been blooded as Battle of Britain pilots, having done two squadron interceptions, with Bushy and Wendell both shot down. Suddenly, we realised there was a war on.

Later that evening Bushy, whose health as 'the last man to die' had already been drunk, 'phoned from somewhere in Kent to say he was OK but his aeroplane was U/S. An Me 109 had jumped him and put a cannon shell through the side of his cockpit hood which passed over his shoulder, shattered his dashboard instruments, finishing in his petrol tank. By great good fortune the shell did not explode and the self-sealing compound on the tank prevented a fuel leak and a fire.

Bushy had done a wheels-up belly landing in a field, writing off the airscrew, but not much else. He was unhurt except for a few splinters of perspex in his neck and cheek from the shattered hood. Next day a salvage squad collected his Hurricane. They sent him the evil-looking 20 mm German cannon shell, with the explosive removed, from his fuel tank. He carried it as his lucky charm for the rest of the war.

Flying Officer Wendell did not come back. Jebb saw him going down in flames off the Isle of Wight.

Despite the losses we were soon to have there, Hendon was a happy station. Partly, perhaps, the happiness was a mild hysteria. Hendon was a regular peacetime RAF station from the First World War, and the site of many peacetime air displays, so it was well fitted-out, with comfortable quarters. It also had WAAFs, a luxury we had not so far enjoyed on any station.

The WAAFs had been hand-picked for Hendon because it was considered one of the top stations in the country. They were some of the first women entrants into the RAF and were keen and intelligent as well as attractive. Many were trained as aircraft plotters for the ops room and did a wonderful job there working with radar under hazardous conditions. They did an even finer job boosting the morale of the pilots as they became war-weary. There were dances most evenings in one of the Messes or the NAAFI; and there were always some WAAFs joining in sing-songs at the local or in an Underground station when an air raid was going on overhead.

I made an early visit to 24 Communications Squadron across the airfield but there was no news there of Corkey. I never heard of him again, but I never forgot him — nor any of my other flying instructors for that matter. I wonder if all the pupils I had when I was instructing later in the war, remember me! I've just counted them up in my logbook — there were 282. Hi, Fellers!

Wag Haw, who received the Order of Lenin in Russia for shooting down three Germans, and later the DFM and DFC.

7

Caterpillar — and That Sort of Girl

Hendon, although famous the world over as an RAF station, was out of date and too small for fast-landing aircraft like Hurricanes. There were no runways, and the grass was bumpy, so that even after a smooth landing a plane might easily bounce airborne again for a few yards.

The airfield was in a completely built-up part of Greater London, quite near a busy shopping centre and an Underground tube station. There were streets of very smart houses all round the aerodrome perimeter, and we had to skim low over their rooftops to avoid overshooting a landing. The Officers' and Sergeants' Messes were palatial. Both had splendid dining rooms with Mess silver and oil paintings of old aeroplanes. WAAFs and airmen waited at table. The flag went up at dawn and down at dusk to the call of the duty bugler.

504 was the only fighter squadron based there.

We had our own brake, an enormous Humber Snipe with heavy duty tyres, which the CO or either flight commander drove. There was always a duty driver available from MT to take over in emergency — which happened quite often, we soon found.

Our duty hours at Hendon were dawn to dusk. In the dark Jerry would do his damndest so far as fighters were concerned, and we left him then to the tender mercies of the balloon barrage and the ack-ack. Our evenings, therefore were our own. If we did not mind being caught in an air raid we could go by tube into the City. Such excursions usually ended in an Underground station huddled up with a horde of strangers. A taxi, a hitch on a lorry or a long walk took us back to camp after the All Clear.

The days were different. We would hear the horn of the Humber brake when it was still dark about 5 am. We would struggle befuddled with sleep into our clothes, and stumble out to the brake, which shot off to the Officers' Mess. The journey round the perimeter track to dispersal would usually be spent listening to one of the officers (who was half French, although I don't know if that had anything to do with it) being slanged because he had once again got up in the middle of the night and peed into someone else's shoe. The main theme of the protest was if he had to do that why couldn't he use his own bloody shoe? Which was fair enough.

By the time we arrived at dispersal we were awake. It was check helmet, parachute and map, and don Mae West. Then sign Form 700 certifying that your aircraft is serviceable for fuel, guns, radio and airframe. Out and into it to start and warm up the engine. After a check for rev drop on either magneto, and a test of hydraulics and electrics, it was back to dispersal where tea would be made and the poker dice brought out for those who did not wish to resume their broken sleep on biscuit mattresses on the crew room floor.

The CO would report to Group on the scrambler phone that 504 was at readiness, and Group would tell him if any raids were expected. Group received their information, always reliable, from the French underground when Luftwaffe planes were circling their aerodromes and forming up for a raid. This gave us a few minutes' extra warning before their bomber force actually set out across the Channel for Britain.

One day became like another. The Hurricane squadrons would take on the Dorniers and Heinkels at about 17,000 feet. The Spitfires would go for the Me 109s which accompanied their bombers.

Being based close to London, 504 were playing back-stop to head off any bombers which managed to pierce our fighter screen between the south coast and the City. Two other Hurricane squadrons, one from Northolt, would rendezvous with us, usually over the nearby Welsh Harp, an enormous lake so named from its shape. Although the Dorniers never arrived in waves of less than sixty, our wing of 36 Hurricanes provided formidable opposition, as the Jerries found to their cost.

It was at Hendon that we adopted the William Tell Overture as our 'Scramble Song'. The record happened to be blaring out one day when Group sent us off. Everyone went rushing out to the aeroplanes to a rousing 'Diddle-um, diddle-um, diddle-um-tum-tum . . . Diddle umpty-umpty-umpty-um tum tum . . .' The music was so inspiring that it was set aside for squadron scrambles only. The first task of the flight duty telephone operator after receiving a scramble call was to put Bill Tell on the turntable, and turn up the volume full blast.

We got the message. William Tell, run like hell.

Gone were the days of practising squadron take-offs. Now it was the real thing. A mad rush out of the flight hut across a stretch of grass to the aircraft. There being no runway, you taxied at high speed across the turf alongside your section leader who was following the flight commander who in turn was shadowing the CO. When we opened up we roared off in roughly the same direction, looking right and left at the same time to see who you were going to ram, and who looked like ramming you. Somehow we always managed to get airborne without mishap, our Castletown training standing us in good stead as we went into our Hendon Formaggers with six pairs in line astern instead of the traditional four sections in Vic.

There were not more than two raids in any one day, and sometimes only one. This was because Göring was using heavy hammer tactics, trying to swamp us with his enormous bomber force. It worked the wrong way for him. London was at the limit of the range of the escorting Me 109s which had insufficient fuel for their return journey if they were in a dogfight over England. In addition, the big waves of bombers were very vulnerable if our fighters could get amongst them and break up their formation, for they lacked the protection of bulletproof shields for their crews. Hence, one long machine-gun burst into the stern of a Dornier or Heinkel would pass along the length of its fuselage, killing the entire crew.

As a result, the more bombers Göring sent, the more were shot down. This was possible mainly because of our newly invented, and at that time highly secret, radio direction finding equipment which not only enabled approaching aircraft to be plotted, but also estimated the number in a formation, their height, speed, position and their course. Interceptions were thus repeatedly made to the consternation of Luftwaffe air crews even before they had crossed our coast. This gave them the impression that an endless stream of RAF fighters awaited their arrival whereas we were in fact sending up every available Hurricane and Spitfire every day.

Our squadrons stationed in Kent, Sussex and Hampshire did a wonderful job, but paid dearly in losses. Many of 504's scrambles led to nothing because those boys had turned the enemy back before London. Or, if any managed to get through, they turned tail and ran for home when they saw we were intercepting them. As their losses mounted, so their morale slumped.

But we had our fun, and our share of victories, although at a price.

Three days after Flying Officer Jebb reported seeing Wendell shot down, he went down in flames himself. He died three days later in hospital from burns and wounds. Jebb was just my build, and when I was commissioned a month or so later, his parents were kind enough to make me a present of his 'Best Blue' uniform, which he had never worn. Officers had to buy their uniforms.

Pilot Officer Clarke went missing about the same time. Nobody saw what happened to him. He just never came back. His aircraft and his body were found in 1987, when a memorial service was held in his memory.

If anyone thinks these were tense, grim, nerve-wracking days for fighter pilots, they could not be more wrong. The flying was always fun, and the prospect of combat exhilarating. If a chap scored a victory there was a party in celebration. When a pal 'had it' there was a party of consolation. In quieter moments, given time for thought, the other side of the coin came up. This was when one began to wonder how one came to be mixed up in this sort of thing anyway, and what had happened to John Gurteen, and Sid Ireland, and Dennis Helcke, and Bill Higgins, and Wendell and Jebb and the rest, who had all been nipped in the bud.

How it affected the others I never knew. Only two actually admitted their qualms, but their nerve had gone and they were grounded.

In times of stress we used 'the twitch!' This was a sideways jerk of the head with a pulling down of one side of the mouth — indicating that we were pretending to be terrified and hiding the fact that we probably really were. Morale was always high. We were young and fit, stretched taut with excitement, living a day at a time and not thinking about tomorrow.

One illustration of this was when Bushy sang his solo to 504 as we flew into battle. It must be appreciated that the strictest possible R/T silence had always to be observed. Only in very exceptional circumstances must anyone break it, the air being kept clear for messages between the CO and ground control. Every pilot could hear both sides of these conversations and know exactly what was happening.

Bushy had a girlfriend named Winifred. Her photo was taped to his dashboard and her name was printed on the outside of his cockpit so that it was always the last thing he saw as he climbed into his aeroplane. Bushy also had a favourite song called 'Imagination'. He would lie down and writhe on the ground, calling plaintively for Winifred each time Vera Lynn's catchy rendering came over the radio. Everyone accepted that 'Imagination' was Bushy's song.

Judge, therefore, how we felt when the squadron had just reached operational height, and the CO was waiting for a course to steer to intercept the enemy when the strains of 'Imagination, is silly — you go around willy-nilly . . .' unmistakably in Bushy's love-struck tones smote the ears of every pilot in the squadron.

At first it was funny. We thought this was just Bushy fooling.

Wings started waggling in time to his tune. But he went on, and on . . . 'Imagination is funny, it makes cloudy days sunny . . .' Then followed the second verse — 'Have you ever felt a gentle touch, and then a kiss — and then — and then . . . Find it's only your imagination again. One thing was certain, this was no imagination again . . .' This was Bushy crooning himself into a Court Martial.

The explanation was simple. When a radio was switched to transmit, a peculiarity was that as you spoke your voice echoed clearly to you through your own headphones. Obviously, Bushy did not realise he was on transmit, and was revelling in his rendering of Winifred's special song rather as though singing it to himself in his bath.

'Imagination is crazy — your whole perspective gets hazy . . .' No one could tell him over their radio to belt up because he had jammed every transmitter. Pilots nearest to him closed in and gave him hand signals to switch off, but he cheerfully gave them rude ones back.

All this time the CO was missing vital messages upon which the safety of London may well have depended. To say he was livid was mild. Everyone but Bushy could picture his cockpit hood steaming up. Finally, in his exasperation, Squadron Leader Sample signalled his number two to hold his course while he peeled away and dropped back alongside the astonished Bushy, just singing, '. . . for example I go around wanting you — and yet I can't imagine that you want me too . . .' He broke off, astonished to find the CO by angry thumb gestures was sending him home.

Bushy, completely mystified, but obedient, turned tail and set course for Hendon. No doubt he was wondering if his aeroplane was on fire, or streaming petrol, or one wheel was dangling down. But land he must, that was the order, and his hand went to the transmit lever to call up base and say he was joining the circuit.

Hell Fire! Horror of horrors, the set was already on send; the awful truth dawned in a flash.

I'll say this for Bushy, little things did not dismay him. He jerked the lever back to receive — we all heard the whine stop with relief — threw his aeroplane round after the squadron, opened up fully, and within minutes had regained formation.

Back at base after the sortie when we next heard Vera Lynn singing 'Imagination' we noticed that Bushy, instead of swooning on his back on the turf, simply sniffed nonchalantly a couple of times, glanced up to the gods for guidance, and ignored her captivating song. Winifred's name, however, stayed on his cockpit, and her photo remained just above his airspeed indicator. He never forgot Winifred, and we never let him forget 'Imagination'.

Fighter Command's best day was Sunday 15 September. This was the day the RAF claimed a record 185 German planes shot down, although revised figures set the number lower. The occasion was marked by a telegram to our CO from the Air Minister, Sir Archibald Sinclair, reading: '504 Squadron, congratulations on yesterday's score. A splendid piece of work.' Another, from the head of Fighter Command, read: 'Well done, 504. Your success yesterday is an outstanding example of the hard fighting which is frustrating the enemy's action. Keep it up.' These telegrams were good for our morale, too. A pat on the back when the going is hard never comes amiss.

That day, 15 September 1940, marked the end of the Battle of Britain for the Germans. They knew the air supremacy they needed over the Channel if their armies were to invade England, was lost.

It was also the end of the Battle of Britain for me.

I have the very kind permission of Ralph Barker, who wrote the following article, and of the *Sunday Express* who published it, to reproduce this story which appeared under the title 'Scramble to glory' in their issue of 7 September 1980, on the occasion of the 40th anniversary of the Battle of Britain.

★   ★   ★

'SCRAMBLE TO GLORY'
By
Ralph Barker

' "The hottest tip", cabled London correspondent H. R. Knicker-bocker to his New York newspaper, "is that the German invasion of England is coming tomorrow, Friday."

'Friday the 13th. Friday 13th September 1940. He added that there was no place on earth where he would rather be.

'He was not alone in that. Almost every Londoner wanted to be at the centre of the excitement.

'One homesick evacuee child wrote this imaginative appeal: "Dear Mum, we had an air raid yesterday and the village is wiped out. I am the only evacuee still living. Will you let me come home?"

'Also drawn toward London were the men of the fighter squadrons the pilots whose task it was to defend it. One such Merseysider was Ray Holmes, Sergeant R. T. Holmes. With his Hurricane squadron, No 504, he had been moved south from Scotland to Hendon as a replacement for one of the tired and depleted squadrons that were being withdrawn.

' "Arty" Holmes, as he was nicknamed because of his initials, had joined the RAF Volunteer Reserve — the VR — when it was first formed in 1936.

'He was entrant number 55. Fair-haired and blue eyed, and 5ft 7in tall, he had a strong athletic frame which disguised his lack of inches.

'At weekends, when not playing cricket or tinkering with his three-wheeler sports car he was learning to fly. Mobilised at the outbreak of war, he was eventually posted to 504 Squadron. Operating from Hendon their task was to back up the forward squadrons who were intercepting the raiders nearer the coast.

'They were to challenge any bombers that got through. They made their first interception when London's dockland was set ablaze.

'After helping to break up several large bomber formations Holmes's squadron was released at dusk on Saturday September 14th and that evening he visited London's West End.

'Londoners took little notice of the sirens during the day, work continuing in office and factory until roof spotters sounded an urgent warning. Buses continued to run until bombs actually fell.

'But at night it was different. Arriving by Underground on the Northern Line, Holmes and his companions found women and children sprawled on the platforms, selecting pitches for the night. Children were doing their homework on tables fashioned from luggage, men played cards and acrobats entertained.

'On Sunday September 15, Holmes's flight was brought to readiness at dawn. The cloud of the previous day had dispersed and it promised to be a fine late-summer day. Yet the radar stations were reporting no activity and the squadron was stood down.

'Feeling scruffy after the early call and the long wait at dispersal, Holmes took a bath. He was luxuriating in it when someone banged on the door.

' "Quick, Arty, there's a flap on — we're on readiness!"

'There was no question of saying "I'll be down in a minute", he leapt out of the bath, and with no time to towel himself properly, slipped into a blue open-necked sports shirt with no badges of rank, pulled on his blue RAF trousers, and ran out to the transport, socks in hand. Someone pulled up the tailboard after him and the truck moved off.

'Pulling his socks over his wet feet was a struggle as the Humber brake bumped and swerved round the perimeter track, at the northern end of the field. As they piled out, the loudspeakers were already ordering them to scramble.

'Holmes ran shoeless to his locker in the dispersal hut, grabbed his flying boots and his Mae West lifejacket, and chased out to the plane, where the ground crew were waiting.

'They had already started the Merlin engine and put his parachute harness in position in the cockpit and they helped him on with his safety straps as he climbed in.

'His helmet, already connected to the oxygen supply and the radio, was hanging on the reflector sight, and he grabbed it and rammed it over his head, covering his bedraggled unkempt hair. It had been a breathtaking flurry of activity, and he was still wringing wet.

'Ahead of him he saw the Squadron Leader, John Sample, taxying towards the far end of the field for the take-off into wind. He waved "chocks away" and tucked in behind the other Hurricanes as they flattened the grass with their slipstream.

'Hendon was a small airfield with no runways and they would be taking off over houses. They needed a good take-off run. There were twelve Hurricanes altogether, six from "A" Flight and six from

"B" Flight, and once airborne they would form up into two parallel lines, each line in three sections of two. This was the formation they had found gave them most room to manoeuvre. Holmes was leading Green section in "B" Flight — the weavers — keeping a look-out astern.

'The take-off itself was a shambles, each pilot ramming his throttle fully open to keep up, but as they climbed over the airfield they settled into formation. The orders were to orbit the airfield at 12,000 feet and await instructions. Soon they were climbing in tight formation through banks of cumulus cloud.

'At 8,000 feet they emerged from the cloud into a clear sunlit sky. Orbiting at 12,000 Holmes, drying out rapidly, shivered with cold.

'The airfield itself, camouflaged and partly obscured by cloud, was impossible to keep in view, but Holmes picked out the silvery expanse of the Welsh Harp. Then they were ordered to climb to 17,000 feet and given a course to steer to the south-east to intercept a raid of thirty-plus Dornier bombers heading for London.

"Tally-ho!"

'From the rear of the formation, flying straight into the sun, Holmes could see very little ahead. High above the Dorniers would be their fighter escort of Messerschmitt 109s. But the tactical plan was to leave the enemy fighters to the Spitfire squadrons, which were much better equipped in terms of speed, ceiling and rate of climb to deal with them. The Hurricanes would go for the bombers. For the moment it was still Holmes's job to guard the squadron from the rear.

'Ahead and slightly to the right, crossing their track diagonally, he saw what might have been a flock of seagulls, until they loomed incredibly quickly into focus and he felt the familiar leap of the heart that was not exactly fear yet was horribly near it. He recognised all too readily the bulbous nose, like a festering blister, the pencil-like fuselage, tapering to the delicate, toy-like twin tail.

'As predicted, they were Dornier 215s and there were thirty-plus all right. They formed a disciplined, symmetrical horde heading for Central London that it was the job of the Hurricane pilots to break up. It was at moments like this that Holmes looked to the leader. John Sample, the squadron commander, was an auxiliary. He had already won a DFC as a flight commander in France before Dunkirk, and he inspired confidence.

'On this wing of the bombers there were twelve Dorniers in close formation in four sections of three. Sample turned so that he appeared to be approaching at right angles, but he allowed the bombers to pass ahead of him so that he led the squadron into a quarter attack, with the Hurricanes nicely placed at an oblique angle slightly astern.

'The swarm of Dorniers occupied a sizable area of sky. As the Hurricanes wheeled in, skidding and sliding as they jostled for position, the pilots in the leading sections picked their targets. One after another they said to themselves "That one's mine."

'The Dorniers became ragged, but they put down a fierce barrage for the Hurricanes to fly through. By the time Holmes, the last one to attack, had fired his first burst, the scene ahead of him was kaleidoscopic and he was uncomfortably aware of a blistering return fire.

'Now the break away without exposing the Hurricane's belly to the Dornier's guns. As the Dornier disappeared from his sights to the right he did a vertical bank to the left and used bottom rudder to skid away before closing the throttle and diving steeply to complete his escape.

'So far as he knew he had not been hit. He eased the Hurricane out of the dive, then climbed steeply, intent on rejoining his squadron for another attack.

'As he looked round the sky was bewilderingly empty. The squadron it seemed, had disappeared. So had the Dorniers.

'Breathing deeply to settle his diaphragm, he scanned the sky above him, then glanced westwards, wondering how many of the Dorniers had got through. All he could see was a tightly-formed section of three, probably the original leaders, still on course for London.

'There was no one about to intercept them but him. These, he said to himself, are mine. He hoped there were no '109s to interfere.

'A last searching look round and he opened the throttle, aiming to overtake the Dorniers on the port side, keeping for the moment out of range of their guns. A lone attack from astern was out — he would be exposed to the guns of all three bombers. Instead he picked the wingman on the port side and angled his approach so that as he came within range the other two Dorniers could not fire at him without hitting their own man.

'He started firing at 400 yards range and was closing in steadily when a cloud of smoke from the Dornier blackened his windscreen.

He was so nonplussed that for a moment he just sat there not knowing what to do next, but instinctively he shut the throttle. It wasn't smoke on his windscreen it was oil, a treacly deposit that must have gushed from the Dornier.

'As the airstream dispersed it he was aware of a monstrous shape right in front of him, filling his windscreen, blotting out the sky. It was the Dornier, slowing down rapidly, and he was about to collide with its tail.

'He rammed the stick forward and felt the shoulder straps of his safety harness cutting into his collarbone. Without them he would have gone straight through the cockpit hood. As he grazed under the Dornier's belly he thought he would hit the propellers. Then he realised with a shock that they were stationary. For the moment at least, he had put both its engines out of action, which was why the Dornier had slowed down so suddenly.

'When he looked back the Dornier was gliding earthwards. But the other two were still sticking close together, holding grimly to their course.

'He would try the same attack on the other wingman. Crossing over to the starboard side he opened the throttle to draw level. Judging the angle as before, he crabbed in for a quarter attack. His first burst was right on target, and a tongue of flame licked back from the Dornier.

'Someone was trying to get out of the back of the plane, presumably the gunner. Holmes was aware of a white flicker of silk in front of him, but then he almost lost control. Correcting hurriedly he realised that the German gunner's parachute canopy had draped itself over his starboard wing, leaving the gunner trailing helplessly behind.

'He had not stopped to think, before this moment, of the men in the Dorniers. His attitude was entirely impersonal, and he was concentrating on avoiding their gunfire and preventing them from getting through to central London. Now, he thought only of the poor devil suspended under his wing.

'He jerked the stick from side to side, but nothing happened. The chap was still there. Using hard right rudder he yawed the Hurricane in a skidding movement to starboard. He saw the canopy billow slightly, then it flattened briefly, slid along the leading edge to the wingtip and was gone.

'The third Dornier — the leader — was still pressing on towards

Hendon aerodrome, photographed at midnight by the light of the Thameshaven fires.

Two of my loyal ground crew at Hendon.

At Hendon — loading the four port-wing Brownings.

Parts of my wrecked Dornier at Victoria Station.

central London, apparently undeterred, height 17,000 feet, speed unchanged. A flash of involuntary admiration turned quickly to anger. The pilot must be hell-bent on some suicidal mission, like bombing St Paul's or even Buckingham Palace. Both had been hit in the last few days.

'He felt as though he was facing some resolute wing three-quarter on the rugger field, legging it for the line, with himself the last hope for the defence. He might be concussed himself in the tackle but he had to bring his man down.

'Oil was seeping over his windscreen now but it was not outside. It was coming up inside from his own engine. Someone in the previous attacks must have hit him.

'That, with no one else about to help him, made the destruction of the Dornier all the more urgent. His engine was running rough and the rev-counter was starting to surge.

'His ammunition too, must be almost exhausted. He would have to bring the Dornier down with no more than a two- or three-second burst.

'He could not avoid the Dornier's return fire, but he could mini-mise it by making a head-on attack. That would give him a point-blank shot into the pilot's glass-fronted cockpit.

'Overtaking the lone Dornier, he turned to make his frontal attack, not quite from head-on, but slightly to port, offset about twenty degrees. That would give him a chance to break away before there was any risk of collision.

'The closing speed must be something like 500 miles an hour. He had only seconds left, and his thumb felt for the firing button. As the bomber came fully into focus he pressed it. He had reached lethal range when his guns sputtered to a stop.

'He was hurtling straight for the Dornier. In a moment he must break away. But the German pilot had not deviated one inch from his course. There was only one way to stop him now. Hit him for six.

'It was something he had never so much as dreamt of before, a split second revelation, quite unpremeditated. But in the heat of battle, with his own machine crippled, and in a desperate bid to smash this inexorable invader before it broke through to his target — he was more than ever convinced now that some deadly precision attack was intended — he shunned the instinct which bawled at him to turn away before it was too late and held his course.

'How flimsy the tailplane looked as it filled his windscreen, as fragile as glass; the tough little Hurricane would splinter it like balsa wood.

'He no longer felt cold. As he aimed his port wing at the nearside fin of the Dornier's twin tail, he was sweating.

'He felt only the slightest jar as the wing of the Hurricane sliced through. Incredibly, he was getting away with it.

'The Hurricane was turning slightly to the left, and diving a little.

'He applied a gentle correction. Nothing happened. The dive steepened, and he shut the throttle. He jerked the stick violently now, forwards and sideways, but he still had no control. The angle increased to the vertical.

'Suddenly he was conscious as the cloud tops rushed to meet him, of his speed in the dive, four to five hundred miles an hour, 8,000 feet; already he was halfway down.

'He unlocked and slid back the hood. The cloud thickened around him, blindingly white, hurting his eyes and the screech of the dive was deafening. He undid his safety harness and tried to climb out.

'The buffeting was so violent that for a moment he thought his head was caught in the propeller. Yet something in the cockpit was holding him back. He had forgotten to unplug the radio lead to his helmet.

'He climbed back in to release it, and this time, as he struggled blindly out, eyelids clenched against the blast, the airstream caught him with renewed savagery and draped him with arched back over the hump of the Hurricane fuselage. In doing so it snagged his seat type parachute somewhere inside the cockpit.

'The Hurricane was diving vertically now. He could still see nothing, but time must be short. Kicking frantically, he thudded his boots against the control column. As the Hurricane lurched into a spin he was catapulted out by centrifugal force.

'Immediately behind him was the tail fin of the Hurricane and as he was blown backwards it struck his right shoulder. He was scarcely aware of it at first, but the shoulder went dead.

'The sudden cessation of sound and the curious hush, told him he was out. He felt for the D-ring of his parachute, but he sought it in vain.

' "Where is it? Where is it?"

'At last his fingers closed around it. But when he tried to pull it, he could exert no pressure. His right arm, paralysed by the bruised shoulder, was useless.

'He was talking to himself now, desperately, urging himself to act.

'He was still clutching the rip-cord ring in his right hand, unable to move it, and the ground must be terrifyingly close. What could he do?

'He grabbed his right wrist with his left hand and tried to tug his arm across his body. There was a sudden explosion above him. For a moment he thought that with the speed of his fall his chute had collapsed. Then he found himself spinning like a top and swinging like a pendulum, all in one motion.

'He reached up and grabbed the rigging lines, and that stopped the spin. He was still swinging as if on a trapeze.

'Gyrating above him, in lazy slow-motion, but uncomfortably close, was the Dornier. Twisting and turning like a falling leaf, it was exuding a bright jet of flame. Its wingtips were severed, and its tailplane had snapped where it joined the fuselage and was falling separately. Below him, nose-down and diving vertically, was the Hurricane.

'He did not know it, but his scrap with the stricken Dornier had been witnessed by hundreds of Londoners through a break in the cloud, smack over Hyde Park Corner. Knots of people were pointing excitedly upwards as Dornier, parachute and Hurricane, in reverse order came tumbling out of the sky.

'Holmes had seen nothing of the ground since the start of the scrap. Now, as he looked down, he saw that he was swinging back and forth across a vast expanse of railway lines. They were less than 300 feet below him. Each set of parallel lines had a third line beside it. The tracks were electrified.

'He was drifting over the junction approaches to Victoria Station.

'To the right of his lateral swing was a three-storey block. They were flats, facing Ebury Bridge Road, and their roofs were steeply raked. If he could only control his drift he might just manage to clear those flats on his next sideways swing and drop down in the road.

'Within a few seconds he could see that he was not going to make it. He hit the roof, and he looked for some handhold or foothold. It was better than being electrocuted.

'For a moment, as he slid down the roof, the parachute supported his weight and he tip-toed on the slates in his stockinged feet like a marionette, for his flying boots had both jerked off when the parachute opened. The air began to spill out of the canopy.

'Clawing desperately with nothing to grip, he started to slide and roll down the slates. Snatching in vain at the gutter, he recoiled from the dizzy drop below. After all he had gone through he was going to break his neck falling off a roof.

'A terrific jolt jerked him to a halt. He had both legs inside an empty dustbin and his toes puppet-like again were just touching the bottom. His parachute had wrapped itself round the top of a drainpipe and arrested his fall.

'He freed himself from his harness and stepped out of the dustbin. Around him the silent stillness of London on a Sunday seemed undisturbed. He was in a garden at the back of the flats. Two girls appeared in a garden next door and he vaulted the fence to greet them. Elated at his succession of escapes, from the plane, from electrocution and from falling off the roof, he embraced and kissed them both. "I hope you don't mind," he said, "I'm so pleased to see you." They seemed equally pleased to see him.

'Inside the flats he telephoned his squadron to say where he was, then turned to see a Home Guard Sergeant, middle-aged but almost twice his size approaching with an iron bar.

' "Hold it," Holmes called. "I'm on your side!"
' "Would you like to see your aeroplane?"
' "Yes, where is it?"
' "Just up the road."

'The Hurricane had come down at a crossroads and missed all the buildings. It had plunged fifteen feet into the ground and was scarcely visible.

'He collected a souvenir of his Hurricane by scrambling down the crater — a piece of the Merlin's valve cover bearing the S of Rolls and the R of Royce.

'Bits of the Dornier had meanwhile landed in the forecourt of Victoria Station. Two of its bombs had fallen on Buckingham Palace, one on the Queen's apartments and one in the grounds, more than justifying Holmes's anger and his readiness for personal sacrifice.

'The Dornier was the first German aircraft brought down over central London. The crew, baling out at a much greater height, drifted down on Kennington Oval.

'A crowd gathered where the Hurricane had gone in, and they gave Holmes a spontaneous cheer, patting him on the back and pumping his hand. Then the Home Guard Sergeant, seeing that he had hurt his shoulder and strained his side, walked him to Chelsea Barracks to see a doctor. It was his second excursion that day in his socks.

'After he had seen the doctor they opened the bar in the Sergeants' Mess and it was drinks all round. "Do you always fly dressed like that?", the CO asked.

'Someone came in with a message "There's a lady outside wants to see you."

'They found him a pair of brown Army plimsolls, and he walked across the parade ground to the gate. A frail woman in her thirties was waiting for him.

' "Was it you that came down in that plane?"

' "Yes."

'She held out a flat-fifty tin of cigarettes. "Will you take these as a present?"

' "No really — I couldn't possibly." She did not look as if she could afford them.

' "Please do. My baby was outside in his pram. They're for making your plane miss my baby."

'He could not tell her that at 17,000 feet and all the way down the last thing in his thoughts had been missing her baby.

'Nor had he the heart to tell her he was a non-smoker . . .'

There were two interesting and unexpected sequels to this incident, 44 years later.

The first was a letter from Alfred Price, the author of *September 15*, telling me he had interviewed the pilot of my Dornier (now a doctor) who after baling out was taken prisoner at Sevenoaks in Kent. He had said his plane was fitted with an experimental flame-thrower, for burning up attacking fighters.

He had also said that when giving a demonstration to high-ranking Luftwaffe officers of the new invention while flying low over an airfield, the diesel failed to ignite when he switched on the flame-thrower. The smart uniforms of the German officers were drenched with the black oil — rather as my windscreen was when I thought I had shot the Dornier oil tank, and nearly collided with his tail because my vision was blotted out.

The second reference to the Dornier flame-thrower came in a letter in October 1984 from Geoffrey Nutkins, the Area Co-ordinator of the Shoreham Aircraft Preservation Society 1940-45 who wrote to tell me he had obtained a small identity label from 'my' Dornier that crashed on Victoria Station. He kindly enclosed a photo of the label.

He ended his letter by saying he had corresponded with two of the crew members in Germany who had told him their Dornier had been carrying an experimental flame-thrower in the tail. It had been switched on to fire at my Hurricane when I was making a stern attack but fortunately for me the fuel failed to ignite. The result was that I was deluged with oil instead of being, as was intended, fried to a crisp.

The Army sent me back to Hendon from Chelsea Barracks by taxi. Apart from two enforced stops due to the beer at the Sergeants' Mess, we arrived without incident. It was several miles, and I was concerned about the cost, but the cabby assured me the Army had already footed the bill, so I sat back and enjoyed the journey.

We had some trouble getting the taxi past the guardroom until I explained that I was a shot-down pilot from 504 returning to base. It was my driver's first visit to an RAF airfield and he was excited to be directed between the hangars along the perimeter track, and round it to our dispersal. He dropped me there, and had a quick look round at all our aircraft. He was suddenly in the middle of the Battle of Britain. We wished each other luck, and he set off back to the city. He would have a tale to tell.

It was now mid-afternoon, warm and sunny and still. 'B' Flight sat around in deckchairs or dozed on groundsheets. Over the radio Vera Lynn was singing 'In Room Five hundred and four' which we all confidently assumed she must have dedicated to us. We always thought that, after radio direction-finding, the glamorous Vera Lynn was England's next-best secret weapon. Her singing could make strong men's eyes fill-up. She was the best morale booster of the war.

I was warmly welcomed back at the flight. They bombarded me with questions about how many I'd bagged, what it was like to bale out, where I'd landed, and what happened to my plane. Then

Plowbags, the squadron intelligence officer, took me off for debriefing.

I asked Joe Royce for another aeroplane to go back on readiness, but he spotted that my shoulder was stiffening from the bump on the tailplane and packed me off to sick-quarters. The MO diagnosed a chipped shoulder bone, which X-ray confirmed, and he grounded me for a week. I was bitterly disappointed, protesting that it was good enough to fly. At which the doctor countered: 'And if you had to bale out again?'

The CO cheered me up with the news from Intelligence that Jerry was packing in after today's pasting, so there'd be little flying for any of us.

Suddenly I found myself involved in a whirl of Press publicity. The newspapers, dying to find new angles to the Battle, had started it when an enterprising young reporter tagged along as I was walking with the Home Guard Sergeant towards Victoria Station in my stockinged feet, to see my aeroplane in its crater.

'Excuse me,' he said, falling into step, 'I'm a reporter.'

'Snap,' I said cheerfully.

'Pardon?'

'I said "snap." I'm a reporter, too. But off duty at present.'

'No, honest, are you really! I'm from the Press Association.'

'We cover the Law Courts at Liverpool for PA. My father has a news agency there — say, perhaps you could get a message to him?'

'Sure, what do you want to tell him.'

'Well, he may hear I've been shot down, and think I've had it. Just tell Dad I'm OK, will you?'

'Of course, with pleasure.' I gave him our home phone number as it was a Sunday.

He rushed off. He was a live reporter. He had got his story. From the phone number he obtained my address. That night I was named with my West Kirby address on the radio as the pilot who shot down the Dornier on Victoria Station 'in a three to one dogfight'. The Dornier was dubbed the Buckingham Palace raider.

Headlines in Monday's morning papers were almost without exception. 'Tell Dad I'm OK.'

During the afternoon the CO called me over to the Officers' Mess and said the BBC wanted to interview me. 'But sir, what about Official Secrets?'

'To hell with secrecy — give them the lot. The censor will cut out what they mustn't use, and the public, bless'em, are panting for something to cheer them up.'

A couple of days later the BBC sent me the script of what went over the radio. This broadcast, and the stories in the newspapers brought me 132 letters, from relatives and friends, from old school pals and masters I had not seen for years, from team-mates in the cricket and rugger clubs, from girls I scarcely knew and from colleagues on newspapers in Liverpool and Birkenhead. I wrote a separate reply to each but it took me three weeks, and cost me three days' pay in postage stamps.

About this time, a van called at dispersal with a metal airscrew blade from one of the Dornier's engines which had been found on the roof of Victoria Station, together with my parachute harness I had left hanging from the drainpipe. There was no sign of the nylon canopy — this had gone for ladies' underwear.

A parcel arrived by post with a card on which was hand printed: 'With the thanks of the Residents of Ebury Bridge Court'. The parcel contained a handsome shaving and toilet set in a leather zip case, which I still treasure.

The CO gave me a week's sick leave when the MO grounded me. An hour later it was cancelled when he showed me a signal from Group which read: 'Her Majesty the Queen has graciously commanded an audience at Buckingham Palace with Sergeant Pilot R. T. Holmes'. An order accompanied the signal saying I must be kitted out smartly, and stand by to await the Royal Command.

I was sent to stores and issued with a new uniform. The camp tailor sewed on Sergeant's stripes and wings, making alterations for the off-the-peg tunic to fit like a glove. I bought new black shoes to replace my heavy regulation boots. The camp barber trimmed my hair.

That night London was bombed in one of the heaviest blitzes yet. Group caught a packet, and word reached us that the Royal family had been moved to safety from the Palace, probably to Windsor.

It was about this time that I met Dorothy.

She was pert, pretty, and worked in the ops room at Group. Sixty feet underground, with a handful of other carefully picked members of the Women's Auxiliary Air Force all in their teens or twenties, she helped to plot enemy bomber raids as they crossed the English Channel and Kent towards London. Numbers on flags indicated the strength of the attacking force, and their progress.

Different coloured flags showed our squadrons of fighters getting airborne along the route of the raiders and inching their way across the map to intercept. They were flying courses transmitted by the Ground Controller, up in his balcony with a bird's eye view of the battle.

From time to time the lights flickered as the thump of bombs shook the operations room. This was a reminder that the war was not just a game being fought out on the ops room table, but a life and death struggle.

One stick of bombs, exploding at exactly three second intervals, came steadily nearer and louder, until it seemed that the next must surely be a direct hit on their room. Outside, later, they found the nearest bomb had thrown up a fifty-feet deep crater in a garden a hundred yards away, uprooting a 200 years old oak, but no other damage.

The girls, concentrating on their task, ignored these dangers. If they felt fear they never showed it. This was partly their training but mainly their spirit in carrying on to help the fellows up there whose progress they were plotting on the table.

Dorothy turned up at our Mess in a party from Group. The MO had put my arm in a sling but I discarded it on the dance floor as being too conspicuous and instead casually tucked my right hand into my tunic belt. The shoulder still ached, and I preferred not to dance; so I sat watching on the stairs that ran down into the ante-room. I found Dorothy was sitting nearby.

She was nineteen and shy, but thawed out to tell me about her work at Hendon and her home, and how she quit secretarial college to join the WAAF.

I found I wanted to dance after all.

There were waltzes and slow foxtrots in dimmed lights. The saxophone moaned dreamily. My arm felt much easier round her waist. We stayed together all evening. When I found she was off duty next day it was only natural to arrange another meeting. We decided to have a walk in the country, the weather being warm and settled. Dorothy said she would bring a picnic lunch, as cafes were all closed.

She looked trim and sprightly as she walked to meet me at the guardroom next morning. I admired her fast-stepping shiny black shoes, her slim ankles and shapely calves in non-regulation nylon grey stockings. I knew they were specially for her date with me. Her hat was just far enough back for a wave of fair hair to sweep up over the peak. Her pony tail was held in place with a thin sky blue ribbon.

Our picnic was in her haversack. She would have been on a charge if the military police had found that her gasmask, which must be carried at all times, was replaced by a flask of coffee and a packet of tinned salmon sandwiches.

As she approached I realised with a start that she was frowning.

'Hello Dorothy, everything all right? Not on duty or anything?'

'No, Ray, but you know you made a bit of a fool of me last night.'

'I did? How?'

'The girls all knew who you were but I didn't and you never told me. They were mad that I monopolised you all evening.'

I was genuinely perplexed.

'You didn't tell me it was you who parachuted down near Victoria Station on Sunday. We all heard about it on the wireless.'

When she saw she was embarrassing me, she pecked me on the cheek and told me I was forgiven. This pleased the MP Corporal at the guardroom window, nearly as much as it pleased me. Certainly it took his mind off her gasmask case.

'Have a good day, Sarge,' he called, winking at us as we strolled through the main gate.

'Thanks, Corporal, will do,' I called back.

We ended up at Elstree, wandering round the film sets. The production people and cameramen were very friendly to a couple in uniform, invited us in and showed us round. We ate our picnic sprawled on a hillock in the hot sun, watching cowboys shooting Red Indians and seeing their horses go sprawling. The sky was ruffled with cumulus cloud, but there were no aeroplanes. At last, reluctantly, as the September sun started to sink we made our way back to the bus route. Dorothy was on late roster.

I kissed her goodbye in fading light near the transport taking her back to the Ops room. As I strolled back into the Mess, Bushy came hurrying across the lounge, careful not to spill two pewter pots of beer. He held one out to me. 'Where the hell have you been Arty? The CO's been asking for you all afternoon. Sink this beer, then breeze over to the Officers' Mess. He said he'd wait for you there.'

'What's cooking?'

He shrugged as he swigged his beer.

'Don't know. Been up to anything — what?'

They tannoyed for Squadron Leader Sample, when I reported at the Officers' Mess. He came briskly out of the ante-room to the hall.

'Thanks for coming up here, Sergeant Holmes,' he began — (strict formality in the Mess). 'Hold on I'll get you a beer.'

When he came back and handed me a mug he went on: 'Group say you can now go on a week's sick leave. Thought you should know as soon as possible, 24 Communications Squadron will fly you to Sealand — that's your nearest airfield to home isn't it? — in a Rapide. The pilot has to stand by at Sealand to bring you back immediately if your call comes to go to the Palace.'

'But, sir, when does my leave start?' I was thinking of another day out with Dorothy.

'Right now. Get cracking at once. You know what Group are. Be away at crack of dawn before they change their mind.'

'What about my leave pass, sir?'

'That's all fixed with the Adjutant. Report at 24 Squadron hut at 08:00 tomorrow, and Flying Officer Clennell will have your pass there waiting. I'll send the brake over to the Sergeants' Mess for you. Good luck, Homer, have a good leave. Sick leave doesn't come off your annual leave, you know. You deserve it, anyway, jolly good show. Cheers!'

I drained my tankard. 'Thanks, sir, for everything — and the beer, too!'

I returned somewhat dejectedly to the Sergeants' Mess. There was a touch of nostalgia at the thought of another visit to 24 Squadron, a year almost to the day that I had called there with Corkey in the Hawker Hind. Before the war! But I was sad to have to make a phone call to Ops that night to say goodbye to Dorothy. The call drew a blank. 'Sorry, Sergeant, personal calls not permitted to WAAF personnel on duty in the operations room,' the switchboard haughtily informed me.

Dorothy was due off duty at 2 am. Orders were that she went straight by MT brake to WAAF quarters. She would sleep in till 10:00. Just about then the communications squadron Rapide carrying me and my Dornier blade touched down at Sealand after a bumpy 200 miles in the old six-seater.

Somehow — I never knew how — the instructors at my recent FTS at Sealand had learned I was due. Gertie Lord and Howie

Filton. Scramble . . . !

Squadron Leader Sample always cycled to his aircraft on a scramble, to save time and breath.

Ground crews of 'B' Flight 504 at Filton.

Me 110 tail and machine guns after 'the Friday'.

Marcou were waiting on the tarmac to greet me when the Rapide taxied in. Flying Officer Frazer who had flown me here parked his aeroplane, organised himself with quarters, and settled in to wait until word came to take me back to Hendon.

My instructors of 'F' Flight wanted my story first-hand of life in a fighter squadron. Hurricanes, parachute jumps, Germans — the lot — what was it like? They were all brassed off with Training Command and dying to get on to ops.

Pupil pilots unashamedly stared at a real live fighter pilot back from the battle zone.

Several drinks later someone mentioned that a bus was due to pass the camp bound for its terminus at Heswall, fifteen miles away. They pushed me on to it, wedging the Dornier blade and my kit bag under the stairs. If you ever wish to travel incognito by bus, don't include a Dornier propeller blade, bent and bullet-holed, in your luggage. The conductor will want to know about it, then some passengers who have overheard . . . Finally the driver will stop in a lay-by and come inside and you will have to tell the story all over again.

I hitched a lift from the terminus the last five miles to West Kirby. A kind motorist — for motorists in those days were kind, when they had to make their five gallons of petrol last a month — was very understanding when my propeller blade would not fit into his boot. I am afraid it left an oily smear on the pale blue leather upholstery of his Flying Standard.

That Dornier blade dogged me for years. At home its only place was on the garage floor against one wall. My mother was proud of it but relieved when it went as an exhibit for the Hoylake Spitfire fund. From there it travelled round the country going on show at other Spitfire fund-raising displays. Some months later when I was in Russia I received a letter from father telling me it had arrived home again and was back in the garage.

After the war a souvenir hunter wrote asking for the blade for his war museum. Gladly I put it on a train for him to Basingstoke. Five years later a man wrote from London to say he had a German propeller blade, with my bullet holes in it, from the Dornier 215 I shot down over Victoria Station on 15 September 1940. Would I like it? If so he would be delighted to despatch it to me by train, carriage paid.

I wrote back declining his kind offer, but as an afterthought suggested he might just send me the bullet holes. Some amusing correspondence followed and I was sorry never to have met him. I suppose that blade is still knocking about somewhere — it weighs about 30 lb, and is five feet long, so it is not likely to get mislaid behind a dressing table, down a settee or even at the back of someone's garage.

504 Squadron was posted to Filton, near Bristol, where nine Concordes were many years later assembled from parts built at Weybridge and Toulouse in France. Nine more were assembled in France. I must rejoin the squadron there at the end of my leave. Flying Officer Frazer and his Rapide went back to Hendon. I taxed and insured the family Rover 10 saloon and drove it to Bristol averaging 29 mph for the 160 miles, which was good on those roads, with a top cruising speed of 38.

I never saw Dorothy again. I hoped she would write, but she never did. I could not write to her because I never knew her other name.

Anyway, at Filton I met Tania. War really is hell!

Filton aerodrome had one runway in 1940. It ran due east to west alongside the hangars of the Bristol Aeroplane Company. Here, the famous Bristol Blenheims, Beauforts and Beaufighters were turned out with Mercury, Perseus and Pegasus engines in comparative peace during 1940, while London and the south coast ports of Portsmouth, Plymouth and Southampton were under heavy bombardment.

504 were posted from Hendon to Filton to counter the change of tactics by the German High Command after their crippling losses during the Battle of Britain. They turned their attention to aircraft factories in England, aiming to destroy our aeroplanes before they even flew, and cripple our research.

Filton had its first raid on the morning of Wednesday 25 September, while I was at home enjoying my sick leave from Hendon. It was one of the most enterprising and successful of all the German daylight raids on England. It owed its success to clever diversionary manoeuvres. While a wave of Heinkels made a low-level attack on Portland, two separate wings of Messerschmitt 110 fighter-bombers went to Plymouth and Portsmouth.

All three raids were decoys. Each was escorted by Me 109 fighters whose object was to draw off our intercepting Spitfires and Hurricanes. Simultaneously, three more squadrons of Heinkel bombers crept across the south coast at low level below our radar, climbed to cloud cover at 15,000 feet and flew north towards Bristol. There must have been several hundred German aircraft engaged in this involved plan. It was only when the entire formation of Heinkels was pattern bombing the massed factories of the Bristol Aeroplane Company that Hurricanes of 238 Squadron intercepted them. But calamitous damage had already been done to what was at that time the largest aircraft and aero-engine plant in the world.

In all, 91 factory workers died, many through direct hits on their air raid shelters. More than twice that number were seriously injured. Damage to hangars, test beds, assembly plants, gas and electricity services and nearby railway lines was devastating. The following morning, Thursday 26 September, 504 Squadron was posted from Hendon to Filton. We were to move on the Friday and I was enjoying the last few hours of my leave at home when the telegram arrived posting me direct to Filton to rejoin my squadron there.

The barrage balloons round Bristol were hoisted down to give 504 a clear approach to the runway. The twelve aircraft taxied up to the north-east corner of the field, and refuelling started at the new dispersal.

One large hut, with several rooms inside, was to house the pilots of 'A' and 'B' Flights, and their ground crews. The weather was superb, with blue sky and warm autumn sunshine and just the occasional white cumulus cloud. Loudspeakers played 'Music while you work'.

Suddenly, as Vera Lynn was promising 'We'll meet again', her song crackled off and a stern metallic voice commanded: '504 Squadron — Scramble — repeat Scramble. Thirty-plus bandits approaching from south at 12,000 feet.' Then, in kinder tones: 'Good luck chaps.'

Many of the aircraft had not even been refuelled after their flight from Hendon.

The exhausted ground crews, who had travelled overnight in convoy from London, plugged in starter batteries. Merlin engines rumbled to life, chocks were yanked away and the Hurricanes went bounding down the rough grass slope, not worrying about taxying to the runway, their pilots nudging into position behind their section leaders as they became airborne.

They tucked into tidier formation to circle and climb above the airfield. Those watching from the ground (and there were many) said it was an inspiring sight. Factory workers who had lost friends and colleagues 48 hours earlier stayed out of the shelters, risking their lives to see the action. Soon the tarmac surrounding the factory hangar, despite orders over loudspeakers for all personnel to go to shelters, was black with overalled BAC workers. Practically every shelter was empty.

As the twelve Hurricanes spiralled upwards they met the wave of 36 twin-engined Messerschmitt bombers approaching from the south. Johnny Sample fearlessly took his boys head-on through the cluster of '110s which were just starting their bombing run, hoping to rain destruction on Filton for the second time in three days. The Germans broke up in confusion at the unexpected interception, wheeling away from the fighters, each of whose eight guns spat fire and death. When the Hurricanes broke formation and weaved round for a second attack the Messerschmitts turned for home, dumping their bombs for better speed and manoeuvrability.

A circle of milling aircraft developed directly over Filton aerodrome. The runway 12,000 feet below now seethed with waving and cheering humanity. The aircraft workers were enjoying a grandstand view of the pitched aerial battle directly above their heads. Stray bullets whined to the ground around them and sticks of jettisoned bombs burst near the airfield boundary, but these were ignored. They were determined not to miss a moment of the battle. One bomb blew up a house at Patchway, just north of the airfield, killing the four occupants.

The twin tail shot off one Messerschmitt floated down near 504's dispersal. The fin, with its swastika and its bullet holes, was later to grace the doorway of the crew room.

Out of control, this bomber dived into a wood a mile away, its crew trapped in, and exploded. Three others, trailing smoke and losing height rapidly, headed for Bristol. A Spitfire Squadron finished them off before they reached the coast.

The scream of engines as one Me 110 nosedived in flames drowned even the cheers of the BAC workers. It buried itself in a field behind their hangar. Four German airmen who parachuted from their damaged planes were seen floating down and were quickly captured. Their uniforms had gone for souvenirs before the Military Police took charge.

I arrived at Filton by road an hour after this was all over, blissfully unaware of what had been happening. I was bitterly disappointed to learn what I had missed.

The pilots after debriefing pounced on me with their news. 'Arty, it was bloody wizard, it really was,' 'Wag' Haw blurted at me, white with excitement. Wag was nineteen, and though our youngest pilot, one of our keenest. 'We went slap into the bastards right over the aerodrome,' he went on, simulating the attack with sweeping hand gestures. 'Thirty-six '110s. They were dropping their load all over the bloody place, just to get rid of it and get away while we were attacking them.'

Bushy smoothed his black Brylcreemed hair and sniffed nonchalantly, knowing Simon Templar, his idol 'The Saint', would have played it cool. 'Dreaded shambles, actually, old boy. Everyone shooting at everyone else. Aeroplanes all over the bloody place. No-one had the slightest idea what was happening. Bloody dangerous, actually, if you ask me.'

The first raid on the Wednesday had been triumph for the Germans. Their second, on the Friday, was a disaster. 504's only loss was Pilot Officer Hardacre. He was one of the squadron's best pilots, 'A' Flight's joker but in deadly earnest about the serious business of killing Germans. He already had three enemy aircraft to his credit when he died chasing an Me 110 across the Channel from Plymouth. The German rear gunner hit the Hurricane and another of our pilots saw it nose-dive into the waves and disappear in a plume of foam. Nothing was found.

That night in the Mess we toasted Hardacre, as we sang bawdily, 'Here's to the next man to die'. Heartless, but the only way to stay sane. The alternative was to brood and think: 'It might have been me . . .'

After this, 504 knew no peace, not only from the Bristol Aeroplane Company employees but from the citizens of Bristol generally. If RAF uniforms were seen in a bar, pints of frothing ale would suddenly appear on their tables. We became embarrassed about visiting a pub. A tea chest of cigarettes arrived for the squadron from the BAC factory, bought by the workers, with a cigar about a foot long for the CO.

One day an open invitation came from three houses at numbers 4,

8 and 12 Patchways — the road beside the aerodrome, where the house was demolished and the family killed — for any Sergeant Pilots to be their guests at any time. We were shy of accepting, but afraid of snubbing them. A deputation of four was chosen — of which I was one — to visit our hosts. What a party! There were two pretty teenage daughters at each of the three houses! And the daughters all had friends. The doors of 4, 8 and 12 stayed wide open for us. Parties started that always lasted into the small hours. This hospitality continued throughout our stay at Filton, until one day just before Christmas we reluctantly bade our farewells and flew off to Exeter, for a spell of sweeping over France and a summer of escorting convoys through the Channel.

But I am told they still talk today at Bristol, about the 'Wednesday and the Friday'. We took with us our memories — as those of 504 who are left still have — of the kindness we met at those three houses in Patchway numbered 4, 8 and 12.

My visit to the Palace never materialised. Whether it was because the squadron moved to Bristol, the Queen left London, Group was bombed, my Court Martial reprimand caught up with me, or the *Daily Dispatch* newspaper published the secret of my Royal audience, I shall never know. The present Queen, and her sister Margaret, were both quite small in 1940 and it would have been a wonderful experience to have met them both as child princesses.

I did see Her Majesty, however, twelve years later. It was at the luncheon at Cammell Laird's shipbuilding yard at Birkenhead after she had launched the aircraft carrier *Ark Royal* on 3 May 1953. I was reporting the launch for Lloyds List shipping newspaper, and sat at the Press table immediately opposite her, barely ten feet away. My thoughts, as I stole glances at her and received gracious smiles whenever our eyes met, were never away from the audience she had commanded of me! I wondered what she would say if I leaned across the table and whispered: 'By the way, do you remember back in September 1940 . . .?'

And in September 1980, 27 years on, when she was now the Queen Mother, aged 80, and a very wonderful lady, I was presented to her with other pilots at London's Guildhall, on the 40th Anniversary of the Battle of Britain. She chatted informally to each of us for a while. Again I could not help wondering . . . But, I mean, dammit — after forty years . . .

★　　★　　★

About this time, Göring seemed to be developing a special hatred towards Filton aerodrome. It was as if he had suddenly learned that one of the squadrons that punished his glorious Messerschmitt bombers at Bristol was based here. His night raids on the city always seemed to finish with a grand finale at Filton.

During one such raid, about a hundred of us ran from the Sergeants' Mess dragging the WAAF Sergeants and staff with us, and dived into the nearest underground shelter. There was a good deal of jostling and horseplay as the girls scrambled down the steps in semi-darkness, assisted by hosts of fumbling hands. A few faces were slapped really hard before the girls straightened their uniforms and smoothed their hair, and came to rest on the benches around the shelter walls. We were packed in so tightly that as many stood as sat.

It was always said that you never hear the bomb that hits you. We felt certain this was wrong when a screamer froze us into horrified silence. Its howl grew louder until it hurt our ears, and we were sure it would hit us. In one corner a terrified girl wimpered. Some grabbed their neighbour's arm as they listened, staring at the ceiling, and waiting for the end.

It seemed we must be living our last second before being blown to eternity, when there came a tremendous blast. The earth heaved. Cement showered on us from the roof. Echoes of the noise reverberated for several seconds. Crevices split the walls even though we were twenty feet underground. Debris tumbled down the staircase, blocking our exit. Then followed the thump of what sounded like smaller bombs hitting the ground all around. These must be incendiaries or anti-personnel.

When silence came and willing hands dug us out, we went to find the hole made by the bomb that could only have missed us by inches. It turned out to be, we were amazed to find, over a hundred yards away in a field beyond the perimeter track. We went back next morning to view the damage in daylight. First impressions were of a volcano. Instead of a hole in the ground there was a hill of fresh clay fifty feet high. We climbed to the top of this, and looked down into an enormous crater, thirty feet across. The bottom was full of water. In the soft ground over a wide area were small holes, made when lumps of clay landed after being blown sky-high by our bomb. It was the noise of these lumps, big as buckets, dropping around our shelter that made us think we were being showered with incendiary or anti-personnel bombs.

For this one bomb that exploded, there were five on our airfield that did not. These were the greater nuisance. We did not know whether they were time-bombs, set to go off at intervals, or duds, or slightly defective being fuzed and ready to go off if any slight vibration disturbed the detonator. To our bomb disposal squads they were all UXBs, and were flagged off for vehicles to be re-routed round them. Even though they were unexploded, each had made a hole probably twenty feet into the ground. Fortunately it was possible to get listening devices down to them.

Very gingerly earth was shovelled away until the detonators could be located and removed by Army experts. Our ballistics people recognised these as bombs assembled by slave lavour in Czech factories taken over by the Nazis. The Czechs had skilfully sabotaged the detonators to render them harmless. Many UXBs were dropped round Bristol that night. Those brave Czech saboteurs had saved a large number of British lives at the risk of their own.

★   ★   ★

They were singing about Amy Johnson — 'How can you blame me for loving Amy?' — the world over when I first met her at Lord Leverhulme's Hulme Hall in picturesque Port Sunlight, in the spring of 1931. She was on a lecture tour around the country after her solo flight to Australia which made worldwide headlines.

I was a very junior reporter on the *Birkenhead Advertiser*.

I had not the reporting experience to cover such an important assignment as Amy Johnson's lecture. Wilf Woollett, the deputy editor who was marked for it on the diary, fell ill. As I had a sports Morgan three-wheeler and was the only reporter with wheels to get to Port Sunlight at short notice, I was telephoned at home and sent there.

Amy's lecture was almost over when I arrived. It had been well received by her admiring audience. Afterwards with some hesitation I introduced myself. She was friendly, and glad to get away from all the fuss. She was not much older than I was, and I wrote my article more as an interview than a report of her lecture. I admired her both for her courage in making that hazardous trip and as a person.

She was happy to accept a lift back to The Central hotel in my maroon Morgan. She was an open-air girl with loose fair wavy hair, as much at home in the cockpit of an open sports car as in an aeroplane. When she smiled her eyes were the pale blue of an ocean catching flecks of foam. Her humour was frivolous. She insisted that I call her Amy. My Morgan had no doors and she laughed when I slid one arm under her knees and the other round her waist and lifted her in and out.

I next met Amy nine years later, on 15 October 1940. We had breakfast together at Cardiff airport. 504 were still at Filton, and I had been on a dawn patrol with Flying Officer Blair White. We were after a Ju 88 which was trying to get bomb damage photos of the BAC factory following their Wednesday and Friday raids.

It was a beautiful autumn dawn, still and warm. The grass was grey in the half light. My flying boots were soaked as I trudged through the dewy grass to 'L', my new Hurricane that replaced 'B', lost in London. We climbed steeply off the runway through the narrow lane of barrage balloons, which was cleared for us. The Palethorpes, as they were code-named for R/T messages, nestled just below cloud base at about 6,000 feet, a cluster of silver sausages. Two or three thousand feet higher we nosed through the cloud into a crystal clear sky. It was much lighter now and we had an early sight of the sun peeping over the horizon.

Control sent us south. Our lone bandit was near Yeovil, heading for Bristol. He was keeping the cloud layer handy as a bolt hole. We split up, Blair staying up at 'quilt' and sending me down through cloud to 'mattress'.

The Hun knew where we were. His frequent changes of course showed quite clearly that he carried an English-speaking radio operator who was picking up our R/T messages because the pilot always took avoiding action immediately. Eventually Jerry turned for home, without his photos, and we were told to pancake.

Blair called me up to join him and we enjoyed a bit of formation cloud clipping as we headed north for Filton. The end of a patrol was always the cue to let off steam, on the way home. Banking vertically together round the tips of cumulus cloud or swooping through their foaming canyons was exhilarating after the concentration of the earlier patrol.

What we did not know was in the past hour a heavy ground mist had formed from the strong early sun on the deep dew. The cloud base had lowered, engulfing the balloons, and the airfield was now under a thick grey blanket. Control misled us by saying that forward visibility at ground level was not too bad. They gave us a course to lose height over the Avon. We passed close to two balloons in broken cloud. At 1,000 feet and now in dense cloud I tucked my wing snugly behind Blair's. He flew a succession of courses taking him south and anti-clockwise round Bristol intended to bring us on to Filton's east-west runway.

A quick glance at my altimeter showed we were at 350 feet. The runway should be ahead, but there was still no sign of ground. I hoped there were no hills or tall trees. Blair threw me wry glances, obviously not happy, but he had to follow Control's orders and I had to keep with him.

As I nursed my throttle and controls to maintain station, with my eyes glued on his wing and fuselage, a church spire flashed past his left wing. Blair pointed upwards and nodded his head forward vigorously, indicating that he was opening his throttle fully and climbing. I gave my engine full boost, yanked the nose up and turned slightly to starboard to avoid colliding with Blair. Then I went on to instruments and climbed straight ahead. At 8,000 feet the cockpit brightened. Flashes of sunlight hit the instrument panel through broken cloud. Suddenly we were back in the dazzling blue again. Blair, half a mile to the left, had seen me emerge and was wagging his wings for me to join him.

When I was alongside I saw he was making mock motions of wiping sweat from his brow. I wasn't needing to pretend.

He had his map in his hand and I heard him asking Control for another base to land. After a few moments they gave us a course for Cardiff. Near the coast the cloud broke and it was as clear as a bell to land at the civil airport.

There at breakfast sat Amy Johnson. I recognised her immediately, and when I reminded her of our meeting at Hulme Hall she remembered me and my Morgan at once. I introduced Blair White and she invited us to her table. We had a fun breakfast together.

She was now, she told us, an ATA pilot ferrying aircraft from factories to squadrons. She was here collecting an Avro Anson to fly it to an aerodrome on the south-east coast. During breakfast we had a message that the fog was lifting at Bristol and when we arrived back at Filton it was bathed in sunshine.

Two days later I read in the *Daily Express* that Amy Johnson, with engine trouble in an Anson, had ditched in the Thames. A vessel going to her rescue had somehow caught her up in its propellers. She died what must have been a dreadful death. I never read if they ever recovered the body of Amy — wonderful Amy.

★　　★　　★

Being caught with a woman in Service quarters was akin to high treason. For treason, the punishment was a .303 bullet between the eyes. The other, more scandalous, crime merited a penalty worse than death — disgrace, discharge, and a permanently besmirched character.

The real sin, of course, was breaking the eleventh commandment and being caught. Nevertheless, the risk was not to be taken lightly.

Rose was blonde, vivacious and curvaceous. Although barely out of her teens, yet almost out of her bra, she tended towards the brassy beauty of the heavy drinker, hard smoker and fast liver. Tony, a sweet little Ops room WAAF, had already warned me that Rose openly boasted in their dorm of her conquests with the pilots of 504.

Rose slid into the opposite seat at my table in the Clifton Cafe on the north side of Bristol. I was recovering from a spell of frantic Christmas shopping, a wearying task in those days of empty shelves and utility articles.

Our knees brushed, not accidentally, under the table as she sat down. She told me her oppo, Joyce, had gone back to camp with a headache leaving Rose in town to see a Clark Gable film. We finished in a double back seat at the cinema. I knew by the end of the show the buses would have stopped running in the blackout, so I had booked a taxi to take us back to Filton. It was becoming an expensive evening.

Clark Gable was shooting his way out of a burning caravan, with howling Red Indians spraying him with arrows when the film suddenly moaned to a halt. A hastily hand-printed slide appeared on the screen, reading, 'Air raid alert, RED — repeat RED. Hurry to nearest shelters immediately.' The urgency of the warning was emphasised by the clatter of exit doors as they were flung open. A blast of night air swept in. Rousing music blared from loudspeakers.

With a whine and a crump the first bomb landed a mile away. More followed, getting closer. The fifth almost hit our cinema while we were still struggling to get out. Flakes of ceiling floated down, and a chandelier swung crazily. Slabs of plaster toppled from a wall. The lights went out as a main in the road was hit. Surprisingly there

R.H. on wing of Hurricane 'B' at Filton.

'A' Flight crew room, left to right: Trevor Parsons, John Sample, Tony Rook, Scruffy Royce and Wag Haw.

Our state of readiness on October 26, 1940.

Flying Officer Frisby and the dancing girls.

was no panic. Attendants flashed on torches. Matches spluttered and cigarette lighters sparked and flamed. There were wisecracks from the fellows, and giggles from girls pretending to be molested.

Thankfully Rose and I at last reached fresh air. Being hit by a bomb in the open seems more pleasant than in a building, even if the end result is the same.

Anti-aircraft guns were now working overtime. The crack of shells splitting the sky was more deafening than the exploding bombs. Purple and yellow flashes lit up the heavens in quest of German bombers. Phosphorescent tracer shells climbed eagerly into the firmament in crimson chains, then fell exhausted to the horizon. The sky flickered as bombs dropped on the Avonmouth dock area of the city. Would an unlucky shot bring the famous Clifton suspension bridge crashing into the gorge?

Rose clutched my arm tightly. I felt the soft warmth of her body pressing against me. She was frightened now and as her hand slid down to grip mine I felt her long nails sink into my palm. I gripped her fingers to ease the nails out of my flesh, and pulled her to a shelter.

The west side of the city was now taking the hammering. A warehouse was well ablaze, and the German pilots were trying to bomb the fire to spread their destruction. Three fire engines screamed down the hill past us, heading for the fire, with sirens wailing. Their drivers must have had cats' eyes to follow the road in such conditions. We dived into the shelter. We were in a furniture warehouse basement, where the sole illumination came from candles and paraffin lamps. The ceiling was shored up with crude wooden beams and steel H girders.

Kettles were soon singing on primus stoves. Tea was brewed and handed round free in mugs. An airman strummed his guitar quietly to his friends in a corner, and soon 'We're going to hang up our washing on the Siegfried Line' was taken up by forty or fifty voices all showing their disdain for Hitler, defying the Führer to do his worst.

As quickly as it started the din outside abated, and the singing died out with it. The long continuous wail of the 'all clear' assured us it was safe to come out. A few searchlights fanned the sky, but one by one these went out.

Now all Rose and I had to do was walk four miles back to camp. The roads were awash where mains had been blown up. There was no hope of a taxi on the broken roads. Rose quickly suggested an alternative. She was on 24 hours pass and not due back in camp until midday tomorrow, so what about a hotel — provided I had enough money for us both for bed and breakfast? Bed! My neck hairs bristled! In those days, to be propositioned in such clear terms was barely short of prostitution. Which would hurt more, the slur on one's so far unsullied reputation, or the hotel bill?

Pride, of course came into it. No fighter pilot could tell an undeniably attractive blonde who has just invited him to sleep the night with her, that his mother would not approve. We found a hotel quite soon, by stumbling over its grass verge in the dark. The building was small, and in daylight might have looked romantic, for it was on a stretch of the A38 Gloucester Road which in those days was still open country. We made our way across the car park to the front door, and knocked. A dog barked in the depths, then a light showed dimly in the hallway and a door opened a few inches on a chain.

'Well?' inquired a tired female voice.

'We missed the transport back to camp in the air raid,' I explained. 'Have you a couple of single rooms for the night?'

A shaft of light from a pencil torch lit us each in turn. It travelled up and down Rose twice and hovered uncertainly for a few seconds on my brevet and Sergeant's stripes before it went out.

'Sorry, we're full up,' the voice announced, and the door closed firmly. We heard bolts being shot home. Rose swore lustily, tracing the doubtful ancestry of the lady with the lamp. 'Let's look for another pub,' she said at last, when she had run out of expletives. We found one a mile further on, with walls that came right on to the road edge. Neither light nor sound greeted our knocking. Rose summed up the landlords of Bristol. 'Bastards, the whole sodding lot,' she muttered. 'Now bleeding what?'

I suggested we bleeding well walked the remaining three miles back to the aerodrome.

'I can't, it's after lights out,' she wailed. 'The guard will book me awol. MPs are down on WAAFs being out late — unless you're with an MP that is. That's different. All night's OK then. What about you, anyway?'

'I'm all right,' I admitted. 'The Sergeant Pilots are billeted in an empty private house up a road behind our dispersal.'

'You mean you don't have to go through the guard room to get to bed?'

'No.'

'Well, then we're laughing aren't we? You find me a bed in there, sonny boy. I don't mind sharing.'

Rose was like a bloodhound on the scent. She was already heading up the road, leaving me to follow. I could read her mind. She was preparing her story for her WAAF pals. This one would be a corker. How she was the only girl in bed with six Sergeant Pilots. The mind boggles.

'But Rose,' I pleaded, 'I can't take you into our house. I'd be for the high jump if it ever leaked out.'

'Oh, really Ray,' she mocked, 'you wouldn't leave poor defence-less little me shivering out here in the cold catching double pneumonia while you went to your warm bed alone. Think how cuddly warm I could be beside you.' She squeezed my arm tightly. I waited for the stab of her finger nails again. An hour later we arrived at the street of houses behind the airfield. They were semi-detached, with small front gardens, and ours was the last on the left.

'Now isn't that cute,' Rose exclaimed, standing hands on hips, feet astride, in the small front garden path. 'Which is our room — up or down, front or back?'

At that moment, to my relief, Wag and Bushy arrived on foot from the Mess. They both sucked Dunhill pipes stuffed with Balkan Sobranie and stood in a cloud of smoke. 'Hello, Artie,' said Wag, 'have we got company?'

'We've got problems,' I nodded at Rose. Bushy chortled. He always was unhelpful in situations like this. 'Don't mind us, old boy,' he smirked. 'We've seen nothing — nothing, that is, except what tells us you've got bang-on taste — what, eh? Good show!'

'Good night Artie,' grinned Wag.

'Yes, too true, Have a smashing night, old boy,' said Bushy. 'Whack-ho!' He sniffed his way towards the house, pulling more smoke from his Dunhill, followed by Wag.

Rose looked after them with warm interest.

'Do they sleep in there?' she asked. When I nodded, she added 'Not tonight, they don't'. She made her way through the doorway and into the hall. Resigned, I followed her up the stairs to the room I shared with Bushy. He had already disappeared with his sleeping bag and pillow into Wag's room leaving mine empty.

'You've got no — er nightie,' I said to Rose. 'Shall I borrow some pyjamas?'

'No, I'll sleep in the buff,' she assured me. 'Often do. Let's push the beds together — be warmer won't it?' I grabbed a chair from beneath the window. 'Here, Rose, before you get into bed shut the door and wedge this under the knob. Then no one can get in.'

'Spoilsport,' she mocked, locking me in a lingering kiss. There was no doubt about the warmth of my welcome if I stayed.

'I'm sorry, Rose, but I'm on readiness at 06:00. I really must get some sleep.'

She arched an eyebrow. 'Not on readiness now?' I moved towards the door, holding it ajar.

'Not even available?' She walked over and pressed her body against me, flipping my lower lip with one finger. With a little difficulty and a lot of regret I pushed her gently away, kissing the tip of her nose.

'Good night, sleep tight,' I said, 'The house will be empty when you wake. Let yourself out by the front door and walk down the road as if you own it. Make your way round the aerodrome boundary to the guardroom and come in on your pass.'

'Thanks, Ray for the tea and the cinema. Sure you won't change you mind? You're very welcome.'

'I know that. Thank you Rose.' The door snicked shut and I sighed with relief as I showered and brushed my teeth before joining Waggy and Bushy in their room.

'Not staying to make the dear gal happy, old boy?' said Bushy. 'Why not marry her?'

'Not for me a bed of Rose's,' I assured him.

Before breakfast Bushy and I did an interception together but Jerry turned back over the Isle of Wight. After scrambled egg on toast in the Mess I slipped back to the house. Rose had left her room incredibly tidy, apart from a dusting of talc leaving her footprints on the lino. My bed was made, and the covers turned down. There was a hint of unaccustomed fragrance in the air. Then I saw them above my bed. Pinned to the wall was a pair of frilly pink panties. Propped on them was a note reading 'To Artie, with all my love. PS We don't all wear grey, WAAF issue ones, you know — or maybe you didn't.'

8

Tomahawk

Shortly after 504 was posted from Filton to Exeter I became temporarily attached to the ATA. No civil airlines flew in wartime, their aircrew and the aircraft both being required for military use. Their personnel were therefore formed into the Air Transport Auxiliary. Civilian airline pilots, with many thousands of flying hours in their logbooks, were ideal for flying different types of aircraft, and they were detailed to fly new aeroplanes from the factories either to maintenance units (MUs) for storage, or direct to training schools or squadrons if required immediately. The ATA uniform was navy blue, with gold badges of rank.

Early in 1941 the Luftwaffe changed its tactics and lone bombers were flying from airfields on the north coast of France to make surprise attacks on our convoys which were arriving in increasing numbers from across the Atlantic and passing through the English Channel, bound with precious war materials for southern ports. Our job alongside 263 Squadron, who were based along the coast at Warmwell, flying Whirlwinds, was to keep a constant daylight patrol over these convoys, and send any marauders packing.

However, the winter had been very wet. At this early stage of the war very few of our airfields had concrete runways and the ground had become waterlogged. Some had runways of wire mesh netting pegged to the turf, but even these were under water with the incessant rain. This presented the factories with a real headache, for they were unable to dispose of the valuable new aeroplanes they were building. These brand-new machines, never even test flown, had to be packed like sardines on the tarmac around the hangars. A stick of bombs from a sneak raider could destroy in a minute months of a factory's output.

When drier weather enabled airfields to be made serviceable again, Air Ministry instructed squadrons to post pilots on loan to the ATA for ferrying duties, to help clear this backlog of aircraft, and I was sent from our squadron.

I reported to ATA headquarters at Whitchurch near Bristol on 5 February 1941. Our duties were clear-cut. We would collect an aeroplane from A and fly it to B. The fact we had never even seen that type of aeroplane before, let alone flown one, did not matter. This was the challenge of the job. My first day there I climbed into an Avro Anson with twelve other pilots, clutching a chit authorising me to collect Spitfire II No *P7524* from Yeovilton and deliver it to Llandow. The other pilots were dropped off at different aerodromes to collect their aeroplanes. At the end of the day we were all collected again and flown back to Whitchurch. The fact that an Anson was only designed to carry a crew of four, or in emergency five, was no obstacle to carrying twice that number.

My forms authorising me to collect my Spitfire were in triplicate because I could have been a shot-down Luftwaffe pilot stealing an aircraft to escape back to France.

It was my first introduction to the Spitfire. Basically it was similar to the Hurricane, and half an hour studying the Pilot's Handling Notes sorted out the differences. The Spitfire handled beautifully. It was lighter to loop than the Hurricane, yet heavier to roll. This was a proud moment and would give me the laugh on the boys at 504, none of whom had ever flown a Spit.

The organisation at Whitchurch was remarkable. Within a few minutes of delivering my Spitfire at Llandow I was picked up in a six-seater de Havilland Rapide biplane. We flew to St Athan and Lyneham, collecting three other pilots, and returned to Whitchurch. Shortly afterwards the Anson landed and nine who had left with us in the morning joined us at tea.

My trip the next day was, by a strange coincidence, to 504's aerodrome at Exeter. I had no chance to contact my pals, and it was strange to see our Hurricanes across the aerodrome. I collected a Spitfire and flew it to Kemble. From here I ferried a second Spitfire to Akeman Street, collecting a third for Little Rissington. Why there were shuffling Spitfires around I never knew, but they were probably having modifications for specialised work by different squadrons.

For the next few days I ferried Spitfires and Hurricanes up and down the country. On 21 February Anson *N1339* dropped me at Speke, to collect Tomahawk *AK160*. This was a special assignment because this particular Tomahawk was the first American fighter to arrive in Britain. Being the US equivalent of the Spitfire and Hurricane and designed for similar duties, it was expected to be something special — rather like the luxury American automobile compared with its English counterpart in those days.

When I walked into Speke Control Tower to report my arrival from Whitchurch and to signal the Anson's departure for its next destination, I was greeted with a roar of welcome from a burly man in civilian clothes who had been chatting to the controller.

'Well, I'll go to hell if it's not Ray Holmes,' he said, waving a mug of steaming coffee at me. 'Ray, you old bugger, come over here and meet the boys.'

Normally one enters an aerodrome control tower quietly and respectfully rather as one would a church with a service in progress. But not when Detective Sergeant Bill Prendergast is around, Bill had been a dear trusted friend at Liverpool CID, in my reporting days, together with Tommy Smith who became head of CID, and Dave Dalzell and Bert Balmer, who both ended up as Assistant Chief Constables. Bill Prendergast was to gain fame after the war as police advisor in the famous TV 'Z-Cars' series.

On this particular day he wrung my hand warmly and guided me round the tower, proudly introducing me to all and sundry as 'his fighter-pilot friend hot from the hell over London'. There were no half measures with Bill. When things quietened down and I explained the purpose of my visit, the airport manager became noticeably subdued. He told me that the Tomahawk I was to collect had indeed arrived, and been uncrated and assembled, but not yet test flown.

'That's all right, Ray'll do that, won't you Ray?' I nodded agreement. But there was more. There was a warning from the US Air Force that after installation of all the additional electrical equipment required by the RAF in the way of radar, VHF and radio identification units the generator shaft drive was so heavily over-loaded that its bearing was tending to seize solid at high revs. This stopped the engine dead. It was essential, therefore, to take off at no more that half throttle and never to exceed half throttle in flight until modifications had been made.

I agreed to abide by the ruling. After all, Speke, although having no runways, was big and gave a very long run. I undertook to test-fly the machine at the same time, and make my report at Yeovilton. Accordingly a tractor was detailed to haul the Tomahawk out of its hangar. I was saying my farewells and about to climb in when the airport manager was handed a length of tape from the ticker machine. He glimpsed at it, then called me down off the wing. 'Sorry,' he shrugged. 'Your trip's off. This and all subsequent Tomahawks are grounded until further notice. Air Ministry Order.'

This was a real snag. There was no taxi-plane calling to take me back to Whitchurch, the Anson being scheduled to collect me at Yeovilton after I delivered the Tomahawk. But Bill, with a resource-fulness later to be so admired in 'Z-Cars', came to the rescue.

'Wait a minute,' he said, 'Ray's not seen this signal. He's practically off the ground now. If this AMO is timed in after his take-off there's nothing anyone can do about it — is there?'

I jumped at his suggestion and the airport manager reluctantly agreed. 'But don't you crash that bloody Tomahawk,' he warned me, 'or we're all up the creek. Remember — no more than half throttle.' Ten minutes later I was gingerly opening up and hoping the engine would not die on me.

Taking off in any strange aircraft for the first time is the most difficult part of flying it. But taking off in a strange aircraft at only half throttle was not a pleasant experience. There was no surge of power to get moving, no acceleration, the tail would not come up, the controls stayed floppy. American instruments were quite different from ours, too. Boost, for instance, was in inches of mercury instead of pounds per square inch. But slowly speed did build up and I was airborne as I reached the control tower to see an Aldis lamp frantically flashing Bill Prendergast's farewell.

I set course straight away, turning left away from the city, in case of engine failure. Still climbing I crossed the Mersey, the Wirral and the Dee. Over Moel Fammau, which I had climbed so often on foot for picnics, I levelled out. I would have liked to have done a shoot-up salute to Bill Prendergast, but not with this unpredictable aeroplane, thank you.

At 4,000 feet, allowing some height to force land if the engine cut, I throttled back for the gentlest possible cruising revs. Now that I

was airborne I became really worried about the AMO grounding the
Tomahawk and the mess I would be in if I crashed this rather special
sample aeroplane from Uncle Sam. I knew damn well it should
never be in the air at all.

But all went well. The weather was clear and the engine ran
smoothly. I made a couple of circuits of Yeovilton before starting
my approach. It was a Fleet Air Arm base with RAF testing flights
there. There was only one runway running past the hangars and
administrative block. The foundations for a second landing strip had
already been started. There was a slight crosswind — not enough for
concern in a familiar aircraft, but I did not know if the Tomahawk
had a tendency to swing, or how powerful its brakes were if it did. I
just hoped it did not have one of those castored tailwheels like the
Harvard which suddenly start spinning like a top, set the tail judder-
ing and send you into a ground loop. Most of all I feared a baulked
landing that would call for an overshoot at full boost with my wheels
and flaps down.

The landing in fact proved uneventful. The three wheels kissed
the tarmac together and the aircraft rolled smoothly to a halt.
Rudder effectively counteracted any tendency to weather-cock into
wind. I raised my flaps, received my green light from control, and
taxied to the parking spot indicated by the waiting duty crew. As I
switched off an airman jumped up on the port wing and stuck his
head into the cockpit.

'CO wants to see you straight away Sarge,' he said. 'That office at
the end of the hangar.' He came back a moment later while I was
still unfastening my straps. 'He said "straight away" and that he's
booked you in at Control.'

'Thanks — what's all the hurry?' I had a fair idea. He shrugged his
shoulders and jumped down. The CO was a Squadron Leader. He
had fair hair and a short ginger beard. His face must have been
badly burned to have permission to grow a beard. On his door it
said: 'Testing Flight'.

'Sergeant Holmes?'

'Yes, sir. I've brought a Tomahawk for you from Speke. First the
Yanks have sent over.'

'I know all about that. Why did you bring it?'

A chilly welcome.

'I understood you wanted to make performance tests on it, sir.'

'You know damn well what I mean. Why did you deliberately

defy an Air Ministry signal stating explicitly that this aircraft was grounded?'

'I thought it important that you should have it at the earliest, sir. If the signal had arrived half an hour later I never would have seen it anyway.'

'But you did see it, and you know the penalty for defying an AMO, don't you?'

'Yes, sir, I do.'

'You know you can get booted out of the bloody Air Force for less?'

'Yes, sir.'

'Good. Well, remember it.'

To my amazement, he then held out his hand for me to shake. 'Bullshit over,' he grinned. 'Well done, Holmes. A bit of initiative, what! It's what we need. Glad you made it — damn good show. Draw up that chair. Have a fag. Now, tell me, just how good are these bloody Yankee kites, anyway?'

In the 26 days I was with the ATA I made 56 flights, landed on 43 different aerodromes, and piloted eight types of aeroplane. A great experience. But I was glad to be back with 504 at Exeter.

Honiton Clyst, Exeter's civil airport, was to be our happiest station of the war. Hostilities had not yet reached Devon and Cornwall. The air battles of London and the south-east coast were in another world. We arrived at Exeter in time to see early spring bringing life and colour to the countryside with blossoms in the orchards and wild flowers in the hedgerows. Very soon we were sunbathing at dispersal in open-necked shirts under our Mae Wests. We enjoyed the flying too, and in seven months there our losses were few.

Off duty, life was like a dream. The picturesque city four miles down the road with its splendid old cathedral, was untouched by war or time. There were restaurants with dance bands and at the top of the steep High Street was a first class cinema. Motor cars in those days were not yet streaming in from the industrial Midlands and the north. No high rise flats besmirched the sky line. Rationing had not struck so hard here. There was always a little extra butter, cheese, milk and meat to spare. Sweets, cigarettes and beer were no problem. Nor was petrol.

We had dropped on our feet.

In April when I was preparing to go home on my first leave since Christmas, Squadron Leader Sample sent for me and told me he was recommending me for the Commission my Court Martial had lost me at Sealand. His gentle manner lost none of its dignity in the concrete-floored Nissen hut office with its semi-circular corrugated iron roof and wooden filing cabinets. Perhaps the basic building added atmosphere to the occasion. We were at war, and 'in the field'.

Sample slid a slip of paper across his desk to me. 'That's what I've told Air Ministry about you. You'd better know.' He looked hard at me as he spoke. Still at attention, I glanced down at the paper, and back to him. He grinned. 'Go on, read it. It'll make you blush. Have a seat.'

I took the paper to an easy chair in the corner. It was embarrassing to read your commanding officer's views of you while he sat there watching. It was all about appearance, leadership, flying ability and the rest.

'Thank you, sir,' I said finally. I set the paper down on his desk, and remained standing.

'Relax, Holmes,' he said. 'You're going to be an officer. You'll be joining us in the Officers' Mess. Better get used to the idea.'

'I'm not commissioned yet, sir.'

'You will be. They need experienced pilots as officers. Now drop in on the Adj. He'll fix you up with your train warrant. And good luck at your interview. Oh, by the way,' he added as an afterthought, 'it's tomorrow.' I thanked him, saluted, and was leaving when he called me back.

'Stand up to the Board during your interview, Holmes. They'll try to bullshit you with a string of questions to put you on the spot. Remember, I'm recommending you and so is your Flight Commander. Show them we're right.'

'Wilco, sir.'

Flying Officer Clennell in the adjoining office, handed me an envelope addressed to Sergeant Holmes, tapping it as he did so with one finger. 'Not a Sergeant much longer, eh? Congratulations.' He was a fatherly fellow. I told him I'd be sorry to lose the rank I had held for four years. I would miss the Sergeants' Mess, and Bushy and Wag and Douggie Haywood and the rest.

'You'll make new friends quickly. This is going to be a long war.

You have to grab promotion when it comes.'

The envelope contained a third class train warrant to London, a hotel booking there near Kingsway, and another third class warrant home from London for my leave.

Going before the interview board next day was something of an ordeal. I felt they were going to ask: 'When did you last see your Father?' Half a dozen high-ranking officers, their chests adorned with First World War ribbons, sat behind a long polished mahogany table. There were silver cups on shelves behind them. The President's first question came out of the blue. He asked: 'Why are you not wearing your DFM ribbon, Sergeant Holmes? Your documents say you were decorated last September.'

I could only reply: 'I've had no notification of that, sir,' hoping that perhaps he would be encouraged to investigate the matter for me. But he just grunted, and nodded for the others to ask their questions.

I remembered what John Sample told me, and I looked each questioner squarely in the eye, standing my ground. It comforted me to feel that probably not one of them could fly a Hurricane. All too soon when I was beginning to enjoy it, the President thanked me, pressed a bell beside him and told me I would be notified in due course of the Board's decision. He gave no hint of their finding.

I replaced my forage cap, took two steps back, saluted to six expressionless faces, about-turned and marched out through the door which opened as I approached. When I arrived home, a telegram was already waiting for me. It revealed the result on the envelope, being addressed to Pilot Officer Holmes. 'Congratulations on your commission from all at 504,' it read.

I telephoned the squadron adjutant straight away. He told me to go to Gieves to be measured for my officers' uniform before rejoining the squadron at Exeter. Next morning a train warrant arrived by post for my journey from Liverpool to Exeter — First Class! My new status as an officer.

Settling in at the Officers' Mess was easy. I was with men who were already my fellow pilots and they accepted me warmly. I soon felt at home. Probably the strangest part of the transition was to have my fellow Sergeant Pilots saluting me, and calling me 'sir'. But they took it in their stride, showing their pleasure at my promotion. A month later, Bushy was also commissioned, and joined me in the Officers' Mess.

Part Four
Convoy Protection

9
Sweeps over France

There were two runways at Honiton Clyst. 'A' Flight had their dispersal at the end of one, and 'B' Flight's hut and aircraft were half a mile away at the end of the other. This was good, for it kept us operating as separate units on alternate duty spells.

At first, life followed the pattern of our 1940 summer at Castletown. A section of two aircraft would scramble to intercept a lone reconnaissance raider. The bonus of these trips was the joy of beholding the picturesque Devonshire coastline running south from Exmouth to Torquay, Salcombe and Start Point. If we chased a Hun over the Channel we were thrilled at the splendour of this rugged coastline as we made landfall on our return.

As weather and visibility improved our merchant shipping losses mounted. The Germans had developed the technique of pinpointing a convoy, plotting its progress and sending a single Ju 88 to stalk it in cloud. A sudden dive-bomb attack nearly always sank one or more ships because they were so poorly equipped with anti-aircraft armament. So 504 went on to full-time convoy patrol duty. We were responsible for the sector from Plymouth to Portsmouth, and every convoy passing either way through these waters had two Hurricanes from 504 constantly in attendance.

A dawn patrol joined the convoy of probably twenty ships which always spent the night holed up in a river, screened from submarines by anti-submarine nets across the mouth. We would cover it while the ships emerged into the English Channel and took station. Then we would circle the convoy anti-clockwise once it was under way, always keeping at opposite ends and passing each time at the middle, thus having a continuous lookout for approaching raiders from any direction. We took sixty-minute spells over the convoy before being relieved by the second section. While we were on the ground refuelling, the third section would be on its way to relieve the second.

My flying hours mounted steadily at Exeter from 10¾ hours in January to 51 in April and 66 in May. This was plenty of flying in a single-engined aircraft with an endurance of only 1½ hours for each trip. But the Hurricanes were beautiful to fly, and we were in our element skimming low over the Channel or along the beaches and climbing up over the cliffs. Best of all was to fly at deck height along a line of ships and see the crews waving over the rails as we rocked our wings in salute.

Our battle technique improved steadily. On 3 May Bushy and I chased a Heinkel nearly to France and on 25 May we intercepted three Heinkels off Torbay. A couple of days later 'A' Flight shot down a Ju 88 off Exmouth. The ship sinkings with this protection meanwhile dropped dramatically.

Our responsibility was next extended to escorting ships from Milford Haven down the Bristol Channel, round Land's End and back to Falmouth on the south coast. Flying each day from Exeter across Dartmoor to join the convoys was a waste of fuel and time, so 'B' Flight moved into quarters at Portreath, an aerodrome on the north Cornish coast. Its runway ended at the edge of a sheer 200-foot cliff. It was quite a sensation to shoot off the end of the runway and find nothing but sea below. Our flying times here mounted still more.

It was at Portreath that some backroom boffin had the brainwave for bringing an aeroplane back to base when in hot humid weather coastal fog would suddenly roll off the sea and blot out the runway. His idea was literally to boil off the fog with what must surely have been the father of all flame throwers.

In conditions of practically nil visibility I was sent up and told to orbit base. This was no problem once airborne as the ground mist was never thick, and trees or towers would protrude through it and provide markers. When they were ready for me I was told to land. At 1,000 feet I could make out the runway quite easily looking down through the mist. But at 500 feet it was hazy, and at 200 feet I lost it completely. On instruments I came in on a steady course and rate of descent.

Suddenly there was a flash as though the sun itself had burst. I found myself at the centre of a bubble of dazzling flame. The grey murk boiled and dispersed in a white cloud of steam. The transformation was remarkable. My runway for a hundred yards became crystal clear and I promptly set my aircraft down on it. Even inside the cockpit I felt the heat from igniting hundreds of gallons of petrol, and expected my own tanks to explode any second. Then to my relief, I ran out of the hot fireball, and came to a halt further along the runway, once more in chilly dense fog. They shut off the flame and a station wagon came out and guided me in.

They called this system FIDO, the letters standing for Fog Investigation and Dispersal Operation.

★　　★　　★

We were enjoying the flying here. Although we always made two, and often three ninety-minute trips a day our losses were low because the pilots were gaining experience and the operational hazards were less. Most time was spent circling the convoys, which for safety hugged our coastline, so normally we flew within sight of rugged cliffs, sandy beaches and wooded bays. The pale blue-green water was so clear that the sea bed was still visible through it half a mile from the shore. Occasionally a splendid estate spread over the rolling hillside. Would they ever hunt or shoot across this land again — and if they did, would man be hunting man next time?

It was on convoy patrol that I found myself talking to a German pilot. The Ju 88s that made these recce trips looking for our ships had radio operators with very advanced equipment. We did not realise quite how advanced, or that a German crew would understand our messages in spoken English, even though in code.

On this occasion there was a continuous layer of cloud not more than a couple of thousand feet thick starting eight or nine hundred feet above the sea. We were warned there was a raider on the board. It was going to be very easy for him to dart out of the cloud, drop a couple of bombs, and nip back into cover again before we could get our sights on him.

My first view came after about twenty minutes of Blind Man's Buff. He was quite a small dot, two miles away at the far end of the convoy. He was appearing and disappearing in wisps of low cloud.

He must have seen me when I spotted him for he immediately climbed up into cloud and out of sight.

Ground control were giving us courses to fly to intercept him so I called up Green Two and told him to stay at mattress (under the bedclothes) while I went up to quilt, and to fly the course control gave to me. In this way he would always be immediately below me even though we were blind to each other.

At the end of one message to me from Green Two a new voice, free of any trace of accent and loud enough to have come over my shoulder, cut into over conversation.

'Hello, Green One. Hello, Green One,' it called. 'Are you receiving me? Over.'

'Hello, last caller. Loud and clear. Who are you, please?'

'Hello, Green One,' came the same cultured voice. 'I am sorry to leave you, but I must go home now. Goodbye.'

There was no doubt now who he was. It was a weird experience to be talking to the enemy you were hunting and trying to kill.

'Hell, Jerry, don't go yet, come back and play,' I taunted. I hoped teasing might make him talk some more.

'Good bye, Green One — goodbyeeeeeee,' was all I heard. He was not taking the bait.

'See you tomorrow?' I suggested. There was a click as his transmitter was switched on again. Then came a quiet chuckle. Not mocking. Just enjoying the joke. Then silence. I knew he was on his way home and that at least our convoy was safe from him.

The experience warmed my heart. I stopped hating all Germans. This one spoke perfect English and must have spent half his life here. Probably he had an English parent. Certainly he enjoyed our sort of joke. I flew back to Exeter feeling that at least I had found one good German. I hoped I might meet him after the war.

The following week 263, the Whirlwind squadron now operating from the opposite side of our airfield, came bursting into the Mess ordering drinks all round. One of their flight commanders had shot down a Ju 88 off Dartmouth. I felt unaccountably sad. I knew it had to be my German friend. I raised my glass to him. 'This is Green One, Jerry, goodbye. Goodbye.'

I drained the glass and went for a game of snooker.

★　　　★　　　★

The Germans always had good information about the movements of RAF squadrons, and quite soon after 504 arrived at Exeter a lone raider photographed us there. From that moment we received flattering attention from the Luftwaffe, who attacked us on several consecutive nights.

On the second night a bomb blew a corner off the Officers' Mess and wrote off a Spitfire, and on the third, a determined low-level attack was pressed home by three Heinkels on our sleeping quarters. Bushy, Wag, Douggie Haywood and myself were in bed when a bomb hit the tarmac outside our billets, bounced six feet without exploding and came through the wall. It passed over our beds, and out through the opposite wall, burying itself in open ground where it exploded harmlessly.

Fortunately for us the bomb, having been stowed horizontally on its rack in the Heinkel, was released from too low a height for its nose fuze to hit the ground. It bounced on its belly and the wall offered insufficient resistance to detonate it as it passed through. Had it exploded on first impact six or more of our pilots would have been maimed or killed outright, wiping out almost half the squadron's flying strength.

Group decided there must be no risk of repetition and the next night all the pilots of 504 found themselves billeted in the Bishop of Exeter's Castle, a couple of miles from the aerodrome. This was superb. The Bishop welcomed us to his home, then he left. On our camp beds in the lounge we revelled in the luxurious surroundings, and lush carpets. Tapestry-covered walls made a dramatic backcloth for suits of armour, swords and lances of warriors in another war. We were full of admiration for the quality of their fighting equipment in those days but agreed that we would rather go to war in a Mae West than a steel vest.

On 11 May we went to war in a big way.

We had thought the mass air battles so common in the 1940 blitz were a thing of the past, and that life now consisted of heading off lone reconnaissance spy planes or intercepting convoy marauders. There was no advance warning of the afternoon raid. The squadron was sent up as a precaution simply because radar showed 'Some air activity' off the Brittany coast.

We were over Torquay when Control suddenly told us fifty-plus aircraft were heading our way. They said (heaven be praised!) that some friends would shortly be coming to our aid. There was no immediate sign of any friends, but from out to sea came what looked like a swarm of gnats.

As they drew nearer they stood out clearly as fast-flying aircraft, growing rapidly bigger and heading straight for us. In another half minute they crystallised into single-engined machines, flying very fast indeed. They were Me 109s! This was a real surprise. Where were their bombers? Surely fighters would not arrive on their own. Or was this a red herring — a decoy to keep us busy while their bombers sneaked over the coast further along?

There was still no sign of reinforcements for us. John Sample headed for the Messerschmitts. We tucked tightly into our Hendon formaggers and 504 hurtled like a javelin on a collision course for the '109s.

It was obvious to the Germans that the Hurricanes would not give way, and as we hurtled towards them at a closing speed of 600 mph I was relieved to see their courage failed before ours. The '109s broke away in disarray to avert head-on crashes. Sample had achieved his object. The enemy in an untidy shambles had lost its advantage of superior numbers.

'Every man for himself,' the CO bellowed over the R/T. This was all we wanted to hear, and we each picked our target and went after it.

The sky suddenly became a death trap. Aircraft climbed and dived and turned, flashing across your vision and just as you were getting a bead on what looked like a '109 it turned out to be a Hurricane. At that speed positive recognition was very difficult. It was dangerous to fire unless you were absolutely certain there was no chance of mistaken identity — and too late afterwards if you found you had shot down one of your pals.

There was little shooting by either side, although chains of tracer did drift across the sky occasionally, fading into the white trails left by tightly turning wings. The arrival of a squadron of Spitfires from Warmwell only added to the confusion. But the German pilots had seen the Spitfires arrive and all at once the sky cleared. The Messerschmitts went scurrying for home, their mission — whatever it was — a miserable failure. The Hurricanes and Spitfires started a half-hearted chase after them but were called back by Control and told to land at base independently.

Back on the ground at Exeter I had difficulty opening my cockpit sliding hood. It was catching at the back on the starboard side. My rigger standing on the wing root pulled it back and pointed out the cause. The metal frame holding the perspex window was deeply gouged where a bullet had ricocheted off it. An inch further back and the bullet would have missed the metal and gone through the perspex and my head.

Blair White was not so lucky. He was shot down near Wellington in Somerset and taken to Exeter Hospital. He had not recovered in time to go to Russia with us, but subsequently commanded 185 and 229 Squadrons in Malta where, sadly, he was reported missing in July 1943.

Three of our pilots claimed 'probables' in the dogfight.

*

In the middle of our convoy-patrolling period at Exeter, when we had settled down to a pattern of work that we hoped would last almost indefinitely, 504 suddenly on 10 July received orders to fly to Friston, a satellite landing ground of Tangmere. This airfield had been hastily constructed during the Battle of Britain as an emergency landing ground for fighters whose parent airfield was bombed unserviceable while they were up on a sortie.

We had, of course, heard of the legless legend, Douglas Bader, and were delighted to find this remarkable Squadron Leader buying us beer at the Mess bar there that evening. He was to lead us next day, he told us, with two other squadrons to form a wing, on our first sweep over France. We found Bader a friendly type but a grim and dedicated killer of Germans. He was the ideal man to lead us on sweeps over enemy territory. His jutting jaw suggested ruthless determination. His artificial legs were no problem. He always stood at the bar to drink.

On our sweep, he explained, we were to escort nine Bristol Blenheim twin-engined bombers to Le Havre on the north coast of Normandy. We were to protect them from any intercepting Me 109s while they went in to bomb submarines and shipping. Then we would wait for them coming out, and bring them home. The journey was 110 miles each way, all over water for practically the full limit of our fuel endurance.

We flew in weak mixture with fully coarse airscrews at lowest revs, hoping there would be no combat over the French coast to eat up our precious fuel. The Messerschmitts met us about twenty miles from the coast. We flew with one squadron of Hurricanes each side of the Blenheims, and one squadron behind them in the box.

The '109s were 5,000 feet above us, and south-west. They were difficult to see in the morning sun. Thirty-six pairs of anxious eyes strained to detect their first aggressive move, expecting them at any second to come diving out of the sun. There was no question of going up and mixing it with them. This would have left the Blenheims exposed.

At 10,000 feet we headed into the broad bay towards the beach of Arromanches, where the historic D-Day landings were to be made three years later. The Cherbourg peninsula was down on our right. When the Blenheims peeled away to port in line astern for their dive-bomb attack we kept our height and flew above them to draw some of the flak, and cover them from the Messerschmitts.

When the bomber leader called to Bader that he was going in, Bader wished them luck, and said we would be flying above them to lead them home. It was fascinating to watch from aloft as the Blenheims screamed down in a 45-degree dive. We could see the lines of tracer from their two forward-firing guns, and seconds later the billows of smoke and flame like a flower opening where their bombs exploded.

But the German flak that met them was heavy. Shells exploded all round the Blenheims. The ground defences were obviously prepared for the attack, probably through an early warning leaked to them by a Quisling. The curtain of shrapnel flung at them was sufficient to shake the purpose of the most determined. But the bomber boys bravely pressed on. Half way down one fluttered violently as a wing was hit, and black smoke streamed from an engine.

Almost immediately a second bomber, on his right, exploded in a ball of flame. One of the German guns had got the range and was taking its toll. Bits of the tail trailed behind the fuselage as it fell into the sea. No one got out.

The remaining seven aircraft continued diving headlong for their target through the stream of shells the Germans flung up at them. At the end we lost sight of them in the smoke from the ground guns, but we saw flashes from exploding bombs through the murk. Then one by one we picked out some Blenheims emerging from the target area. They were weaving furiously in a desperate attempt to confuse the gunners who were still shooting after them.

Only five out of the seven emerged. Two fires marked the spot where the gallant crews had gone in with their bombs. Probably the pilots were dead at the controls before they crashed.

Bader brought our Wing round in a diving turn to link up with the five survivors, now climbing up from the sea. One belched smoke. If it was from a fractured fuel line he was in danger of exploding. He was making poor progress, lagging behind his fellows and gaining little height. His smoke trail grew thicker and quite suddenly he dived and flopped on to the water. He sank almost at once. We saw no yellow Mae Wests in the sea. There was nothing we could do but head homewards with the four remaining Blenheims. More than half the bombers were lost. Bader radioed the position of the ditched Blenheim in the hope that Air Sea Rescue Lysanders or their German counterparts would find someone and drop them an inflatable raft.

We escorted the four surviving Blenheims back to our coast, but never met the brave fellows who flew in them. They waved their thanks by rocking their wings, and headed back to their own base while we, thirsty for fuel, landed at Friston. The Mess that night was subdued and people turned in early. To watch five crews die in as many minutes was a sobering experience, for which beer brought no consolation.

Three days later, on 13 July, we found ourselves this time at Merston, a sister aerodrome to Friston. Bader was waiting for us at briefing, and led us to Le Havre again, but this time on a train-strafing trip. These early sweeps, while expensive in both lives and aircraft, were designed to show the Germans that the day of reckoning was approaching. Britain after two years was coming off the defensive, and starting to attack.

The French underground regularly radioed to England when ships were arriving with supplies, or troop trains were in marshalling yards. With these in mind we would confuse the German defences by flying over the Channel as one big formation of three or four fighter squadrons. Then near the French coast we would split up and each squadron would take different targets, strafing goods trains or marshalling yards but under strict instruction to go for military targets only and to avoid French civilians. These were nuisance raids to get the enemy jittery. As more aircraft came off our production lines and more trained pilots arrived from RAF flying schools in Canada and Rhodesia, bigger sweeps were mounted to hit the Hun harder.

One of these came a few days later.

We received orders to fly to Start Point, fifty miles due south of Exeter. There we were to land on the headland on a grass strip made by knocking down a hedge between two fields. This Devon-shire cliff-top was as near to Brittany as it was possible to get, and would keep fuel consumption to the absolute minimum.

Two 3,000-gallon petrol tankers were waiting to refuel us and two other squadrons as we squeezed 36 aircraft down both sides of the two fields. It was remarkable that there was not one mishap on that crowded makeshift landing ground.

At our briefing beside a haystack overlooking the peaceful beauty spot of Salcombe we were given the staggering news that we were about to escort sixty-nine Wellingtons, eighteen Hampdens, eighteen Stirlings and five Flying Fortresses to Brest. We could hardly believe our ears. When we had taken nine Blenheims across the Channel to France, we felt their massed wings were blotting out the sky, and the roar of their engines alone would shake the targets to the ground. But this raid was to be ten times bigger with each air-craft capable of carrying double a Blenheim's bomb load. They would surely blow Europe itself into the sea! What would we have thought had we known that in a couple of years we would be sending thousand-bomber raids to German cities?

The planning, as with all these raids, was as smooth as a carefully considered chess move. The bombers, with fuel to spare, would leave at pre-arranged times from widely separated points as much as 200 miles apart along the south coast between Land's End and Portsmouth. They would fly a variety of courses, all heading for widely spaced destinations in France. But at a pre-arranged moment they would all turn on to a course taking them to Point X due west of the Channel Isles. Our Wing of Hurricanes would in the mean-time have taken off from Start Point, dropping immediately below the cliffs to water level, and flying directly to Point X at nought feet to keep below German radar.

A few miles from our rendezvous, as we spotted the waves of Wimpeys, Hampdens, Stirlings and Flying Forts converging from all sides at 10,000 feet, we climbed above them to 15,000 feet. The bomber force formed up and headed for Brest with a sheltering umbrella of Hurricanes. From our perch we had a grandstand view. It must have been an awe-inspiring spectacle for the German fighter pilots, and not surprisingly not one attacked our bombers while they unloaded several hundred tons of high explosive on the under-ground submarine pens at Brest. We were briefed to leave the bombers while they made their run in, and form a curtain of fighters a few miles north of Brest for them to fly back through. We would then pick off any Messerschmitts attacking them on the way out.

It was during this curtain patrol, while waiting for the last of the bombers to come safely through, that I spotted ten miles to the north of us two Wellingtons on their way home being jumped by a couple of Messerschmitts who had cut behind us from Finisterre. I called up the CO and he sent me with Blue Two to try and break it up.

The '109s saw us approaching and quickly made a diving beeline for their coast. We did not follow, for our job was to cover the Wimpeys. One was making good progress, but the other had suffered badly from the 20 mm cannon fire of the Me 109s. He had his starboard leg hanging down, a smoking engine and part of his tail was shot away. I wondered how the rear gunner had fared and hoped he had escaped from his turret back into the fuselage.

Sergeant 'Avro' Anson and I had just sufficient fuel to stay with him while he limped into our own base at Exeter. He was obviously in trouble, for the pilot dragged the Wimpey over the aerodrome boundary with no preliminary airfield circuit, and flopped on his belly, on the grass alongside the runway like a panting hound exhausted in the chase.

Avro and myself landed down the runway and taxied back to him. The fire tender crew were already hosing what was left of the rear gunner out of his shattered gun-turret. That red mess staining the green grass had been a boy a few minutes earlier. We felt too mad at the bastards who did this even to be sick.

A good deal of suspense always accompanied sweeps, with the long single-engined drag both ways over water and the constant awareness of lurking '109s. But sweeps had their lighter moments.

On a flight to Friston from Exeter we had one of the best laughs. Trevor Parsons was leading 'B' Flight, and all six Hurricanes were tucked into really tight formation over the Isle of Wight when his engine suddenly coughed badly and his speed dropped off. Down went his nose, which is always the drill to maintain flying speed in the event of engine failure. And down went the five other Hurricanes still with him.

Of course we all realised what had happened. Finger trouble! Trevor had forgotten to switch from his gravity tank to his main tank after take-off, and had run his gravity tank dry.

Our dive was heading us straight for Ventnor. We had lost a thousand feet before Trevor switched over tanks and his engine picked up again. He could see by the way we were rocking our wings that we were all laughing at our absent-minded flight commander. His embarrassment was complete when John Sample, came over the radio with 'Pull your finger out Blue One.'

Trevor replied curtly, 'Finger out. Over and out.' He climbed to bring 'B' Flight back into station with 'A' Flight but we could tell by his R/T voice and by his rough handling of his aircraft that he was furious to have been humiliated before the entire squadron.

Strangely enough, the joke rebounded on the CO himself not long afterwards. John Sample had joined us temporarily at 'B' Flight because, having always flown leading 'A' Flight, he felt he was not seeing enough of his other pilots. One morning I went with him as his number two on a dawn interception. The German who was approaching turned back when he knew we were after him; but Control kept us up for a while in case Jerry returned. Sample signalled to me to tuck in close for some cloud clipping.

I had never flown alongside him before so, feeling I was on my mettle, I tucked in *really* close. As we skimmed through the valleys of dazzling white cumulus my port wing was a foot behind his ailerons and our wings overlapped until my airscrew blades were almost gnawing a wingtip. We climbed and dived and stall-turned for several minutes until suddenly he suffered Trevor's humiliating experience.

His engine spluttered, black smoke spurted from his exhausts with the misfiring as his tank ran dry, and his speed dropped as if he had slammed on his brakes. To avoid a disaster I could only leap over his starboard wing and break away to the right. I waited for him to pick up his speed again. He dipped his wings to show he was OK and to call me back.

As I tucked in again I glanced at his cockpit and saw he was grinning sheepishly at me. He had a 'Don't tell Trevor' look on his face. I took off my oxygen mask and let him see I was laughing at him, and he laughed back.

When we returned to base he did not give me the customary signal to break formation, but kept me at his side for a formation landing on to the runway. He was seeing if I fluffed it at the last minute and would have to go round again. This would give him a hold on me if I told the petrol story in the Mess. I didn't fluff it — Corkey saw to that.

I never told Trevor, or anyone else. Sample knew in his heart I would not. I tell it now because it no longer matters. They were both killed in aeroplane crashes within a few months. But not through petrol — or finger — trouble.

On 1 June I landed from a dawn convoy patrol and was told to report to Professor Jones at GRU. I had heard of neither.

I found the Gunnery Research Unit was a small room at the end of a maintenance hangar. Professor Jones was inside working at a bench with slide rules and tracing instruments. I was to be entirely at his disposal. He was far from my idea of a university professor. He was short, chubby, and bald. His baggy flannel bags were held up, or almost, with a knotted tie. But he knew his guns. He was a civilian, of course, which made our relationship a friendly one. He explained to me all his work on what he called his GRU Assessor.

He was synchronising a sighting shot taken by an aircraft camera gun with a ring and bead drawn on a cine screen. When camera gun photographs of a target aircraft were flashed on to this screen it became simple to see exactly where the pilot had been aiming when he fired his camera gun and where his shots would have gone. Knowing the bullet spread was a thirteen foot circle at 250 yards range it could easily be estimated from the size of the target aircraft how many bullets would have hit the target and where. Speed of both aircraft, range, angle of attack, line of flight and deflection, could all be taken into account, on Professor Jones's GRU Assessor.

But this was only one of his brain-children he was showing me. The real reason for my visit was to test his secret gyro sight. He explained that the toy gyroscope or heavy wheel which we all spun by tugging a string as children and balanced on a tightrope had the remarkable characteristic when pushed of moving at right angles to the direction of the push, instead of in the same direction.

He used this phenomenon to invent a gunsight. Its bead, instead of being fixed, was movable and controlled by the gyro. Instead of a pilot having to work out the deflection to allow when firing, the angle from which he was attacking, and the tightness of his turn to follow his target enabled the gyro sight to work out all these factors automatically. It sounded straight from cloud cuckoo land when the Professor first tried to explain it to me. He sensed my scepticism because he said finally, 'All right, let's go try it!' He grabbed a battered old flying helmet off the door knob and tugged it on his head. I looked at him amazed, with his tufts of hair standing out from under the helmet and his shirt hanging untidily out of his baggy flannel trousers below his blue serge waistcoat. He stared back at me through thick, round, rimless glasses with eyes so clear they were hard.

'There's a Defiant on the tarmac,' he said. 'It's on loan to me. You flew Defiants at the Ferry Pool didn't you?' I wondered how he knew, but agreed that I had.

'Good,' he said, 'Let's go.' He slung his parachute over his shoulder and led the way from his office, strapping his helmet under his chin with his free hand as he went. I grabbed my kit and followed him to the Defiant. He climbed into the Boulton Paul gun turret behind the cockpit.

He had everything planned. I was to make dummy attacks on an Anson from different angles as he would direct, using my normal front fixed reflector sight. He would be calibrating his gyro sight on each attack from the gun turret. We were both shooting camera guns and would compare our films afterwards. These were the first live aerial tests to be conducted with his new toy. He was delighted and I was amazed when we saw his results.

We became firm friends and did a series of flights together over the ensuing weeks, while he made modifications to the gyro sight. Finally he expressed himself satisfied with his invention. Production I expected would now be the problem. But shortly after we left Exeter I learned that his sight had been so well received by air gunners testing it in bombers that a gun turret model had already gone into production. He perfected his fixed gyro sight for fighters shortly afterwards, but by then I had finished my fighter tour, and never used one.

Less than half our pilots were passed for operational night flying, the facilities for training having been so limited. On the night of 26

April I teamed up with Trevor Parsons, our flight commander, to go up at dusk after a Heinkel which was showing undue interest in Torquay. We saw him in the distance against the glow of the sinking sun, but as we flew down the Exe, he climbed into cloud and disappeared. That was the last we saw of him.

Group asked us to remain on patrol, as the Heinkel was still circling a few miles out over the Channel, and might return. As the light faded, Trevor's aeroplane became first a hazy shadow, then a dark silhouette, until it was hard to see and even harder to follow. I called him up and asked if I should proceed independently, but he replied to stay with him and avoid any danger of collision. It would only be for a few more minutes, he assured me, and switched on his formation lights. Navigation lights would of course have betrayed our position to the Heinkel.

I had never followed formation lights before. Neither, I am certain, had any other member of the squadron. They consisted of a tiny, very dim, spotlight at the wing root on each side of the fuselage. A faint pencil beam shines out sideways to illuminate the trailing edge of each wing. That is all it does illuminate. The fuselage fades into satin blackness, and the pilot becomes virtually non-existent. There is just one sharp knife-edge of a wing to be seen.

To keep station on this thin line for a few minutes was quite acceptable. Even a quarter of an hour was no undue strain. But the night had grown black as pitch, the sky indistinguishable from the ground, and even the coastline did not show up. To look away from the streak of light and relax for a moment would have brought disaster for us both.

When, after half an hour, Control asked us to stand by for just a few moments longer, I wondered whether the fool in that comfortable, well-lit operations room was deliberately trying to torture me. I had long since lost any sense of attitude or equilibrium. There was no way of knowing whether we were turning, climbing or descending. I could not even tell if we were in cloud. I could receive no signals from Trevor and only knew he was turning by any sudden change of angle between his wing and mine, which I quickly had to copy.

I had terrible neck-ache, and spots before the eyes. I began to wonder how I would fare when I had separated from him, and had to go on to my own instruments, and land. Mercifully, after fifty minutes, Trevor told me to break away and land independently. He put his navigation lights on now, for safety.

I shut my throttle and turned away, allowing him to go ahead and to my left. Then I put my head in my cockpit and flew on instruments for a couple of minutes to orientate myself. Next time I looked out, Trevor's red wingtip light and his white tail light were 500 feet below doing a left hand circuit for his landing approach. I could dimly discern six paraffin goose-neck flares marking the left-hand edge of our runway.

I followed him in. I had a stiff neck for two days.

504 Squadron at Exeter. Left to right, standing: Sergeant Boreham, Pilot Officer Lee, Sergeant Douggie Haywood, Flying Officer Mickey Rook, Pilot Officer Hunt, Flying Officer Salter (the dreaded Salt), Sergeant Ibn Waud, Sergeant Nurse, Sergeant Lewis. Sitting: Sergeant Holmes, the MO, Flying Officer Blair White, Squadron Leader John Sample, Flight Lieutenant Tony Rook, Flight Lieutenant Trevor Parsons, Flying Officer Barnes, Flight Officer Clennell (Adjutant).

10

The French Connection

I was looking for short, dark hair with a fringe. Five feet seven, slim, very early twenties, and moved like a dancer was the description. She'll wear an apple green full-pleated skirt with a white short-sleeved summer blouse, and a small amber cross at her throat, on a fine gold chain.

I saw her sitting alone at one of the glass-topped tables beside the dance floor. Ivy Benson and her girls on the crimson and gold balcony were playing a waltz. Two slowly rotating chandeliers sent rainbows from a spotlight darting round the walls. She was running a red-nailed finger lightly round the rim of her Martini glass, watching me with an amused smile when I caught her eye. Her smile was an invitation to join her.

As I wended my way through the dancing couples I decided she did look French. She was athletic despite her slight build. Jujitsu trained, they had told me. I was glad we were on the same side. For every reason.

'Vivienne?'

She smiled a warm greeting, noting my rank and pilot's brevet with a swift glance. Her handshake was firm and warm.

'I've kept this place for you, Ray.' She removed her handbag from the other chair at her table. This was my first-ever blind date. If they had all been like that, it would have been a good war. She talked about her father in France as we danced, and I listened attentively. She had to leave all too soon. But before she left, we arranged our next meeting. She insisted that she should leave ahead of me, and on her own. I was not to follow her. This was what she had learned in France, she confided, with a rueful smile.

Our meeting had been arranged in this way.

Bushy and I were just down from a dawn patrol, and starting a game of whisky-poker with our enamel mugs of steaming tea beside us on the wooden crew room floor, when the CO strolled in. There was no formality in the crew-room, so it was not necessary to stand for him. We still wore our white high-necked sweaters, battledress blouses, and inflatable Mae Wests, ready to scramble for a flap.

Squadron Leader Sample waited while I paired up two Jacks for a full-house Kings, then tapped my shoulder.

'Spare a minute, Holmes?' As if I could say no. I somehow felt this was shop.

'I'm on readiness, sir,' I reminded him. He smiled thinly. 'I know. But I'd like a word outside. Stavvers will take your cards, and you're on hand if there's a flap.'

Pilot Officer Staverton reluctantly set aside the near-naked girl he was mentally devouring in an old copy of *Picture Post*, and picked up my cards. He gave her a last lingering look as he squatted on my parachute cushion opposite to Bushy.

'You've two lives left,' I called over my shoulder as I followed the CO out of the hut. 'You lose, you pay.' The cushion hit me on the back of the head before I could slam the door shut.

It was a warm sunny morning and Johnny Sample sauntered towards my Hurricane. He sat against the trailing edge of its camouflaged wing. 'Forgive the cloak and dagger stuff, Homer,' he said, 'but this is how Intelligence want it played.'

I waited for him to go on.

'They've picked you out because of the number of different air-craft types you flew with the ATA,' he said. 'They think you could fly one of the new Me 109Fs.'

I felt one eyebrow creeping up, but I didn't speak.

'They've got rounded clipped wingtips, water-methanol power boosting, and a much improved rate of climb,' he went on. 'They want one to test at Yeovilton.'

I still said nothing. I was waiting for the punch line.

'Don't worry,' Sample assured me. 'They're not thinking of smuggling you over to France in a submarine, or dropping you in by parachute.'

'I'm glad.'

'But there's always a fifty-fifty chance that any one of us could be shot down on a sweep. And the French underground is so well organised that a shot-down pilot could be very useful to them over there.'

'For pinching a '109F and flying it back here, for instance?'

'For instance.'

There was silence for a moment, while I pondered what he had said. Somewhere behind us a Hurricane on test started up.

'Small point, sir,' I broke in at last, 'but how and where do I find this 109F?'

'That's what it's all about. A girl and her mother have arrived at Exeter. They came over from Brittany by fishing boat a week ago. The mother is French, but the girl's father is an English engineer. He's posing as a Frenchman and working as a prisoner for the Germans on aircraft maintenance with one of their fighter squadrons on an aerodrome near St Nazaire.'

'A '109F Squadron, I suppose?'

'Right.'

'Another pause.

'I'd never know how to start the bloody engine with all that German gibberish around the cockpit, even if I did get inside one,' I said at last.

'They brought a copy of Pilot's Handling notes with them. We've had it translated.'

'They thought of everything, didn't they? Have we thought they might be fifth column?'

'Don't worry, they've been well vetted. The husband is highly trusted by the French underground. They are prepared to channel a British pilot to him for him to fix the aircraft snatch.'

I grinned ruefully at him. 'It looks as if someone will be delighted to hear I've been shot down.'

'Only if you don't kill yourself. You'll be a dead loss, dead,' he grinned.

'And where does the little French piece at Exeter fit in?'

'Half French,' he corrected. 'Her father's English. She's just twenty,' Sample added, cleverly playing his ace apparently as an afterthought.

'H'm. And what's she going to teach me?'

'Among other things, how to contact the Maquis, identify yourself to them, explain where you want to go and who you want to meet.'

'Sounds easy.'

'When you've talked to Vivienne you'll be surprised how easy it is. I've seen her photo — in her bikini on a beach in Brittany. Very slim, shapely in the right places, dark Peter Pan hairstyle, with a fringe. Personally I think you're on a winner.' The CO grinned. He knew he had won. 'She'll be waiting for you in Dellers Cafe in Exeter High Street at 20:00 hours this evening.' He described her outfit.

'Find her, Homer, then it's over to you.'

At that moment we had to scramble and I went off on an interception with Bushy. There was one thing I had omitted to mention to the CO. I had not the slightest intention of getting shot down over France.

After my first meeting with Vivienne the plan, now listed as top secret, went ahead. It was stressed to me that none of the other pilots of 504, and especially no relatives at home, were to have an inkling of it. This was vital, I was warned. On various pretexts of visiting the clothing store, or the dentist, or to collect mail from the Mess, I made frequent calls at the Intelligence section. Here information on codes for contacting the Maquis was waiting for me. Although I have long since forgotten the codes, they were complicated and kept changing as a safeguard against leakages.

Much of what I needed to know was filed in a safe. I had to lock myself into the office whenever this safe was open, and sign myself in and out. A cypher officer taught me how to identify myself to a French agent, to find an escape route. I could scarcely believe this was real. I was suddenly a character out of Buchan's *Thirty Nine Steps*.

My battledress uniform received special attention. An innocent looking brass button contained a tiny compass. The shoulders were padded with white silk large-scale maps. The cheap looking clip on my HB pencil swung to the north when removed and balanced on its blacklead point. I was warned not to carry a gun or I could be shot on sight.

On my second meeting with Vivienne, I asked her why she had no French accent like her mother. She smiled impishly, fluttered her lashes and in exaggerated tones replied, 'I teech you zee mos' wunndful language in zee world. Zee Francais is zee language of zee amour, and I teech it to you because I love zee fighter peelos of zee RAF.'

I asked whether she was going to teach me the language or the amour. She kissed her own forefinger, laid it across my lips. I caught the fragrance of her lipstick. She held my chin and kissed both my cheeks. Then she took my hand and said, suddenly matter-of-fact: 'Come and meet Mum. You'll love her.'

I did. Vivienne introduced her mother to me as Yvonne. She looked more like an elder sister. Yvonne was as beautiful as she was vivacious. She wore a swirling, crimson and black skirt with a yellow shirt open down almost to her middle. She looked more French than her daughter, as indeed she was.

Their flat, round the corner from Dellers, and in the shadow of Exeter Cathedral, captured the style of its two occupants. It was bright and fresh yet had dignity and atmosphere. Three steps climbed from a cobbled footwalk to the blackened oak panelled porch, recessed in weathered sandstone. There was a brass pull bell. Heavy beams that centuries back, judging by the pieces cut out, were probably boat keels, ran the length of the sitting room ceiling to a smoke-charred brick inglenook fireplace.

Despite her accent, Yvonne's English was good. I could sense the warmth of her welcome from the playful way she teased Vivienne by flirting with me. On the evening fixed for my first official lesson I had to 'phone Vivienne from the Mess to cancel it. I was glad to note her disappointment. She did not ask the reason. She knew all about careless talk on telephones.

In fact, Bushy and myself, with Micky Rook who was now our Flight Commander, had been called to a briefing. We were to try out a new system for night interception of German bombers. Group had signalled that the Germans were to bomb Plymouth that night. They had rumbled the Luftwaffe's new technique for night bombing, of directing radio beams from two points on the north coast of France a couple of hundred miles apart to intersect exactly above the target for that night.

Tonight the beams crossed at Plymouth.

German bomber squadrons based along the entire length of the north coast of Brittany and France would be flying out across the Channel until they struck one of the radio beams, then turn and follow it until they hit the intersecting beam above Plymouth. With a large target, such as a city or a port, the system was foolproof. Bombs jettisoned at this point made a pattern that would cause dense damage over a wide area.

The RAF, unknown to the Luftwaffe, had two answers to this beam bombing. The first was to bend both the beams so that they crossed over wild, open moorland instead of the target city. At this point enormous fires were deliberately started from oil and old tyres, to mislead the German bomber crews when they arrived into thinking their earlier pilots had set a city alight, and unload their bombs harmlessly in open country.

The second answer was the brainchild of a back-room boffin at Fighter Command. His crazy idea was that with a clear full moon, such as was expected tonight, a fighter pilot, aided by the light from fires on the ground, could make something approaching a daylight interception over the target area. It was only necessary, this genius reasoned, for a fighter to keep criss-crossing the enemy flight path at the height of the bomber stream and sooner or later he would see a bomber, get on its tail, and shoot it down.

That was providing he did not collide with it head on!

It had not occurred to him that the closing speed of the bomber and the fighter would be in the region of 500 mph, and that a collision would be inevitable before either pilot could even start to take avoiding action. We of 'B' Flight 504 were to be guinea pigs for this foolhardy night interception exercise. So, instead of keeping my cosy rendezvous with Vivienne, I was briefed as the pilot to go in first, followed by Bushy, and then by Micky Rook at fifteen-minute intervals. Only one fighter was allowed over the target at a time, for fear two RAF planes might collide, or even shoot each other down.

Before take-off we zeroed our dashboard clocks with ops-room time. I was briefed that exactly three minutes after I reached Plymouth, all ground anti-aircraft fire would cease and simultaneously searchlights would be extinguished. I would then fly into the target area over the city with no fear of being blown out of the sky by our own guns.

I took off and climbed to 15,000 feet from Exeter. It was a superb night. The coastline was clear, waves breaking foaming white on the beaches. I reached my altitude by Torquay harbour and levelled out. It looked peaceful down there, and took me back to childhood holidays I enjoyed there with my parents. Further south, past picturesque Salcombe, was Start Point — or Starters, as we called it — a craggy landmark jutting its chin defiantly into the Channel and proudly propping up an enormous radar mast.

I reduced the brilliance of my reflector sight until I could barely see the thin red graticule. It could dazzle when trying to draw a bead on a Heinkel's black belly. With the sight set for a range of 250 yards for a bomber with a sixty-foot wingspan, I twisted the control column gun button from Safe to Fire. My thumb hovered longingly over the button, keen to squirt lead into a Hun.

The automatic radio in my Hurricane's tail was morsing out code letters of the day on a secret frequency, for our operations room to fix my position and single me out as friendly amongst all the bandits on their board.

Quite soon ground control called. 'Crocodile to Blue One synchronise in fifteen seconds . . . ten seconds . . . five, four, three, two, one, zero.'

'Pipped in, Crocodile,' I sent back.

'You're on your own, three minutes from now Blue One . . . good hunting.' His transmitter clicked off and the air went silent. It was just me and the Hun now, in the moonlight at 15,000 feet.

I cruised in weak mixture at 1,800 revs to conserve petrol. I watched my clock. Our beam bending had not worked tonight. The moon showed our coastline so clearly any fool could map-read to Plymouth. A mile to the south fires flared up as sticks of bombs fell on the quayside. The water in the docks picked up the fires and became pools of blood, as though the explosions had ripped an artery. Searchlight beams fingered the sky, reaching for raiders. When one was located, a dozen lights raced across the heavens searching for him until he became a moth in a candle flame. Then all hell was flung at him by the ack-ack guns.

I had a grandstand view of a Heinkel being hit. Fire suddenly spurted from him, leaving an orange trail in his wake. He dived seawards, twisting and turning in his desperate effort to dodge out of the lights and head for home. White smoke from burning glycol trailed behind him. Seconds later the entire aircraft exploded. Burning chunks cascaded into the sea, and he was gone except for a few vertical smoke spirals and a trail of sparks, marking his journey to hell. A flick of foam was his tombstone.

I was excited to see this happen, yet sorry. There were three or four young men in that crew. True, they were Germans who, minutes before were raining death and destruction on our helpless women and children. But they were airmen, like me, doing the job they were trained and ordered to do. Mothers and wives would mourn, but I was the only one who could have told them what happened to their men. They were the enemy and this was a fight to the death. With luck, I pondered, I would soon have the satisfaction of sending another Heinkel into the sea, just like that.

There was now only a quarter of a minute left. The large luminous second hand crept round the last quadrant. As the needle reached zero I turned as planned towards the burning, battle-scarred city. An invisible hand pulled a master switch and all the guns suddenly stopped hurling their chains of glowing tracer shells into the sky, and the searchlight beams all blacked out.

I felt a thrill of pride at the co-ordination behind this operation. They had stopped just for me. This was battle orders with a vengeance. This was the way to win a war. Now the path was clear to go in and have my crack. The stage was set. I went with a light heart.

I pushed my revs up to 2,400 and my mixture to rich. Starting on the east side of the fires, I turned west until I was flying directly over Plymouth, parallel to the coast, and across the path of any approaching bombers. My eyes bored the sky to the south, willing the outline of a twin-engined monster to materialise from the gloom. Nothing. I swung left through 180 degrees and re-traced my tracks. Almost at once I saw it. Slower than I had expected. Ahead and to starboard slightly above, and crossing my path.

The crew were probably taking full advantage of the lull in the gunfire and the doused searchlights to concentrate on careful bomb-aiming. They did not appear to have seen me. It flew on, a couple of hundred feet above, and a quarter of a mile ahead. It was keeping steadily straight and level, perfectly placed for me to make a climbing quarter attack closing into astern. I couldn't miss!

As I banked to attack, it suddenly happened.

A solitary searchlight split the sky. Probably its crew, when the guns went quiet, heard the Heinkel and the Hurricane overhead. Excitement brought panic and someone switched on. Incredibly, the beam picked out the Heinkel first time. I saw its swallow wings suddenly turn into a blinding white ghost aeroplane as I was going in to attack. Simultaneously a score of more searchlights flicked on, fanning the sky to add their brilliance to the first beam, and sickness to my heart.

The effect on my flying was shattering. My carefully positioned quarter attack became a drunken lurch. I was blinded by the diamond dazzle of a million candlepower boring through my skull into my brain. So harsh was the brilliance in contrast to the previous hour of pitch darkness, that even head-down inside the cockpit I was unable to focus on my blind flying instruments. All sense of equilibrium deserted me. With eyelids shut tightly, I was endeavouring to fly the Hurricane by feel rather than vision, and failing miserably. Vertigo took over. I felt sick and lop-sided. The aircraft skidded one way, at a crazy angle, while I lurched the other. Only my harness kept me in my seat, as I swung and swayed.

Now the ack-ack opened up again. They were not going to miss such a sitter. I had sampled anti-aircraft fire in daylight, seeing a few black shell bursts and even feeling the occasional bump. But this barrage of white hot shrapnel bursting about me and splitting the darkness was hell let loose. If I'd had time I'd have prayed. I had scarcely time even to spit out a stream of expletives before I was fighting to check my Hurricane's crazy diving turn. By the time I regained control I had lost 8,000 feet, but I was out of range of the guns and taking a roundabout route for more peaceful skies to the north. I neither knew nor cared what had happened to my Heinkel.

I called up Control. 'What the hell's going on?', I bellowed with scant respect for R/T procedure. 'Over.'

There was dead silence for a full minute. I was about to call again when my deadset crackled and a voice said 'Stand by, Blue One,' and the transmitter clicked off. A moment later Control came on again. 'Sorry, Blue One. There seems to have been some misunderstanding.'

'Misunderstanding! There's been the biggest cock-up of all time. I've nearly had my arse shot off.' My insubordination as a very junior officer to a controller who was probably a Wing Commander was kindly overlooked, for no rebuke came back.

'Please pancake, Blue One,' I was politely requested.

Bushy, who had watched and heard it all while waiting to take his turn, thought it hilarious. His voice came through his laughter into my ears. 'Good show, Blue One, wizard firework display, what!' I could imagine him sniffing and twitching as he switched off. He could not resist another crack, and came on again. 'Dreaded end, what!'

Micky Rook cut in. Sternly: 'R/T silence please, Crocodile aircraft. All pancake as instructed.'

'Wilco,' I smouldered, and set course full boost and diving steeply for Exeter.

At de-briefing it was Micky Rook, so correct in the air, who blew his top. He was protecting his pilots. 'The dreaded Army,' he exploded . . . 'They should all be stuffed into aeroplanes and blown up with their own bloody shells. Then perhaps they'd pull their fingers out! Stupid bastards! The whole bloody regiment should go on charge. Disobeying strict orders.' He could be forgiven for being mad. Shrapnel from one of our own ack-ack shells had hit his aircraft and taken off his little toe.

It was only after receiving my prescribed operational ration of five cigarettes, one shell-egg and two ounces of barley sugar sweets that I heard about the Luftwaffe's latest *Baedaeker* raid that night. The raids bore this name because our people said the Germans were picking their targets haphazard from a guide book. The places were all attractive holiday resorts with no possible military significance, and therefore devoid of defences. A single squadron of attacking bombers could come in low, free of opposition from guns or barrage balloons.

The bombers would make a couple of unhurried practice runs then carefully, ruthlessly and accurately blast a peaceful holiday resort, probably housing children and old people evacuated from a city, to smithereens. Preferably they chose to destroy something architecturally unique. Tonight it was Exeter Cathedral. My god, I thought, Vivienne!

I had no transport, and scorched the four hilly miles from Honiton airfield to Exeter on my batman's push-bike in the dark with no lamp, in just over a quarter of an hour. Panting and sticky, for it was a sultry summer night, I turned left down the top of the High Street into the main shopping centre of the picturesque old city. The road, with fashionable shops on both sides and Dellers cafe on the left, ran steeply down to the River Exe Bridge.

It was no longer picturesque, and firemen were reeling out hoses. Air raid wardens had cordoned off the thoroughfare. The bombers had gone, leaving carnage. Flames licked from buildings where the roofs had caved in and tenders were running up their escapes. Floodlights probed the rubble, searching for bodies. Stretcher crews rushed dead and injured to ambulances.

The German aircrews had done their work well. They had flown low along the wide estuary, then followed the river in the moonlight to Exeter and flown up the High Street at rooftop height. They could not miss. There was only one main street. After one dummy run, the bombs were aimed with deadly accuracy and effect. Shopfronts collapsed, spewing merchandise into the cratered roadway. Burst water mains sent anything that floated cascading down the gutters.

Dellers cafe, my meeting place with Vivienne only a few nights earlier, was a smouldering ruin. Part of the ballroom balcony protruded through the front wall. Mercifully the dancers and Ivy Benson's girls had left an hour before the raid. As if through divine intervention, the bombs, apart from the odd incendiary, had just missed the Cathedral. But the houses around were rubble. Bull-dozers were already at work delving through the mess for bodies. I felt sick thinking of the fate of Vivienne and her mother. There was nothing I could do to help.

As I cycled sadly back to camp, the moon was retreating behind a bank of clouds. It seemed to be saying it had seen enough for one night. I felt the same. The trip back took three times as long. Next day I could not remember going to bed.

I fretted for days about Vivienne and Yvonne. They were to me like a couple of our pilots who had suddenly gone missing. No illness, no warning, no goodbyes. A sick conjuring trick. 'Now you see them, now you don't — and won't ever again.'

I had a great urge to get away from Exeter. My prayers were answered within a week when 504 was posted to Russia. This was to be a change of scene with vengeance.

The sea trip across the Arctic to Archangel took three weeks.

Quite soon we were operating from Murmansk in Hurricane IIs, escorting Russian bombers on raids over snow-covered Finland. I bagged a '109F when six jumped us on one of these raids.

'This one,' I muttered, as the explosive fury of twelve Brownings pumped lead into him, 'is for Vivienne.'

But Russia is another story.

When we first started sleeping in the Bishop of Exeter's Castle, the crocus and daffodils were beginning to peep through a light layer of snow in the parkland. The day we heard the squadron was posted tc Fairwood Common the sun blazed down and the beds were aflame with roses. We had convoy patrolled and swept through two seasons of the year. We were sad to be leaving this happy station but a new and a different life ahead was exciting to contemplate.

No-one had ever even heard of Fairwood Common. When we arrived there this was not surprising. No-one would want to hear of it. It was on the north coast of the Bristol Channel, near a place called Mumbles. The only runway ran through bracken and heather. Several dummy runs low along the runway were necessary to clear it of sheep, before we could land.

Flight huts at dispersal, camouflaged green and brown, were semicircular, corrugated iron buildings with concrete floors. There were a few new steel lockers scattered at random inside. This was obviously an aerodrome thrown together in a hurry.

All our aircraft were down by 8 am. Word went round that Tony Rook wanted the pilots in his office. He was looking slightly harassed, had not shaved before our early take-off and was tugging at his bushy moustache as he invariably did in times of stress.

'Make yourselves comfortable, chaps,' he began. 'I've a few things to tell you.' He rubbed his chin a couple of times, obviously not quite sure where to begin.

'Well, the first thing is that 504 is splitting up,' he said. 'Squadron Leader Sample has been posted to Group and I'm your new CO. Trevor Parsons is taking six pilots and six Hurricanes with him to Aldergrove in Northern Ireland. They will be the future 504 Squadron, with Trevor as its new CO.'

We mumbled our congratulations to Trevor.

'Their strength,' Tony went on 'will be made up with postings from Operational Training Units and presumably one or two officers from other squadrons. They will have a few months' training at Aldergrove to bring them to operational strength, for posting probably to North Africa.'

He read out the names of the six pilots to go to Ireland. They were the last six Sergeant Pilots to join 504 at Exeter. Tony was keeping the most experienced people with him. Why, we wondered.

'The remainder of us,' he continued, answering our unspoken thoughts, 'will become 81 Squadron. We're posted to Leconfield, which was a peacetime station in Yorkshire. I don't know when we go or what will happen to us there — Group is playing very cagey about it. It's not a station for a fighter squadron so to me, it looks like an overseas posting — probably to the Middle East, with 504 to help put an end to Rommel's rampage there. Any questions?'

There were none. What was there to ask? He had told us all he knew. There was a hum of excitement at the prospect of some real combat action against the enemy, and possibly some overseas leave first.

'Right, then,' Tony concluded. 'Good luck to the new 504. Carry on with the tradition. The squadron has been through a few scrapes in its time. And good luck to the new 81 Squadron — whatever Fate has in store for us.'

'Finally,' he stressed, 'no talking. Neither here, nor in the Mess and particularly not in coded letters to girlfriends. Right, then — breakfast.'

We walked a hundred yards from his office to a grey breeze-block building for breakfast. Trestle tables were laid inside. The news had struck us in different ways, we found over the meal. Wag was enthusiastic, and could not wait to go. It was a chance for some action, an opportunity to shoot down 'some of the bastards'. He was all for getting cracking, right now. Bushy could not care less. 'We've got to go somewhere,' he sniffed. 'May as well be the desert. Warm there, anyway, better than bloody England in winter. Can't stand sand between my toes, though. Any popsies in veils around those oases?'

Barney, not long married, had a young child. He was upset for his wife and we were sad for him. Barney was a good family man. Sergeant Randles' wife was due to have a baby any minute. He was all for putting in for a compassionate home posting until the CO told him that a good pilot like him could be more use to his squadron than to his wife at a time like this.

Of course, no-one really knew what Fighter Command had in mind for 81 Squadron. It was sheer speculation when we talked about going to the Middle East. No-one knew anything — for example that within a few weeks Johnny Sample, our beloved CO now at Group, who had led us through the Battle of Britain and on sweeps over France, would be killed when another aircraft flying in formation collided with him and chewed off his tail. I wondered, when I heard this tragic news, whether he had forgotten to switch over from gravity to main tanks once too often — and recalled his sheepish grin that day over Torquay.

No-one could ever know either that Trevor Parsons, who was taking half 504 to re-form in Northern Ireland, would within a matter of weeks meet a similar fate.

They kept us at Fairwood Common for only five days. In that time we did another sweep to Brest, two days of convoy patrols escorting ships round Land's End, and some air-firing practice off Milford Haven. On 29 July we flew to Leconfield. I was glad to learn that Barney was not coming with us after all, but was going to Aldergrove to help Trevor re-form 504. Barney would make as good a Flight Commander as he would a father.

Part Five
Russia

11
Archangel and Murmansk

At Leconfield, which was a traditionally laid out pre-war fighter station, we found much had been going on behind the scenes. Within a few hours of our arrival we were mustered in an empty hangar where we were joined by another Hurricane squadron, No 134, led by Squadron Leader Miller. The two squadrons were to make up 151 Wing under Wing Commander Ramsbottom Isherwood, a New Zealander with a fine reputation both as a test pilot and a rugby player. He was clean-shaven, square-chinned, short and tough. We were not surprised to learn he had been capped for his country as a scrum-half.

We were brought to attention as he walked from a flight office into the hangar and he stood us at ease to address us.

'Now see here, you fellows,' he waded in without preamble, 'we've been brought here to do a special job. I am sworn to secrecy about what it is, but there must be no talking either on or off the camp about what happens to us from this moment on. All leave is cancelled forthwith. Nobody is allowed off the camp. All outgoing mail will be censored. The first thing is inoculations.'

He turned to the Wing Adjutant. 'All right, Griffiths, carry on.'

Flight Lieutenant Hubert Griffiths, a journalist and author of repute, handed us over to a medical team sitting at tables at the back of the hangar. They went into action with hypodermic needles and a sinister assortment of multi-coloured bottles. They scratched smallpox paste on to our biceps and squirted a wide variety of revolting diseases into our buttocks and arms.

The effects, within a short time were catastrophic. Dead arms and bruised bottoms were the least of our worries. Fever, vomiting, dizziness and fainting smote us all. 81 and 134 Squadrons to a man retired to bed cursing their fate and disappeared from the face of Leconfield for 48 hours. There could have been no surer antidote for careless talk. Nobody cared a damn what happened to us or where we went. Certainly nobody wanted to talk about it.

When we surfaced again, each man was issued with a mosquito net, and the officers with a .45 Webley revolver and ammunition. The mosquito nets were a clever ruse to suggest that the Wing was heading for a hot climate. The guns were serious.

A couple of nights later we were roused from our beds in the small hours, mustered in our hangar with full uniform and kitbags packed, loaded into a fleet of waiting motor coaches, and driven to an empty train standing in a siding at Beverley station.

The train journey was a mystery tour. In those days of blackout it was impossible on a train at night to follow your route. We made no stops at stations, but all place names were erased anyway. Everyone quickly became resigned to the situation and settled down to catch up on their broken night's sleep.

It was still dark when, after many stops and much shunting, we pulled up in a siding, We jumped down on to the track and were led across the rails into a large hall, along a covered corridor, and up a gangway on to a ship. We could have been in any port between Scotland and Southampton.

A group of us stood at the ship's rail, waiting to see the dawn. There was no moon, and the night was black velvet. Ashore there were no street lamps, or lighted windows. On the water if there were any ships at anchor they showed no navigation lights. Ashore there could be made out an occasional glow-worm of a car's shielded headlamps, and the growl of its engine as it crawled through the gloom of the landing stage. As the sky gradually lightened, the silhouette of a high spire took shape. I recognised it at once, and could hardly believe my eyes. I was looking up at Liverpool's Liver Building, the port's famous landmark known the world over. I was on a boat on the Mersey! I had crossed this river over and under it, many a hundred times either on the Woodside,

Seacombe or New Brighton ferryboats or through the rail or road tunnels.

The sky was brighter now, and across the river the New Brighton Pier, Tower fairground, and the fort which guarded the estuary against attack by sea in the First World War, took shape. I stood gazing in wonder, as though seeing for the first time scenes I had known since childhood.

Nestling at the foot of the Liver Building was the old original St Nicholas Church, parish church of Liverpool, across the road from that wonder of the world, the Mersey Tunnel dock entrance. My gaze moved round to Toxteth Hill. Silhouetted starkly against the glow of the now rising sun was the Anglican Cathedral, started in 1910 and still far from finished. Its local sandstone was warming in the first flush of sunlight.

Eight miles away, at our home on West Kirby hill, slept my parents. They would be startled to know that I was so near them now, yet going far away quite soon. I turned to tell Martin Pratt, a cypher officer next to me, how I was but a stone's throw from home. I regaled him with the hours I had spent before the war as a young reporter with a special Press pass that allowed me to board all the liners berthing at this very landing stage in search of news stories. I recalled my rides on the Overhead Railway along the eight miles of docks, all packed with ships, looking for one which would be hoisting two locomotives aboard for export to India, and one on which young Richard Attenborough was bringing wild animals from a jungle for London Zoo.

I described the launches across the river at Cammell Lairds' Birkenhead shipyard, famous the world over, where Sir Robert Johnson always had me at his table for the luncheon, as the representative of *Lloyds List* shipping newspaper.

My recollections were cut short by the clatter of the gangways being hauled ashore as the last man came aboard. No chances were being taken that any man ever left that ship again to leak information about our operation. Ropes were cast off, two tugs fussed around pulling us away from the stage, our screws churned white foam under our stern, and we were away under our own steam, moving up channel towards the Bar Lightship, then seawards on a voyage to the unknown.

Our new home, the *Llanstephan Castle*, was a Union Castle prewar luxury cruise liner, now hastily converted into a troop ship specially to move our Wing. RAF officers shared two-berth first class cabins eating with the captain and his officers in the lavish dining saloon. The white pillars, mahogany walls and beautiful murals of this room with its sweeping double staircase leading up to the lounge and through to the gymnasium, squash court and swimming bath, lent a touch of unreality to the knowledge that we were off to war.

Our troops were almost as well blessed. They slept in tourist class cabins, and shared the crew's dining quarters. The kitchens were still victualled on a peacetime scale, with eggs, butter, meat, fish and fresh milk. There was a duty-free bar, promising us a life, however short, in conditions of opulence we would probably never know again.

Quickly I made good friends with the ship's two radio operators, Icke and Vyle. They could have been a music hall act. I spent many happy hours with them, exchanging stories of war in the air and on or under the sea, and playing pontoon and poker in their cabin. It was their job to know exactly where our ship was, so I quickly learned, although in strictest confidence, that we were heading for Iceland. More than that even they did not know. But it was clear we were certainly not on a course for the Middle East.

Iceland was a mountainous island with craggy cliffs and deep fjords. As we edged into Seydisfjordur between precipitous walls of rock, we came after a couple of miles into a vast inland lake with a small town at the far end. Already moored in the black waters was an assortment of merchant and naval ships.

That night, 20 August 1941, the chef put on a special dinner for my birthday. All the officers at my table signed my menu.

It did not take long after sailing from Liverpool to discover that none of the other pilots of 81 Squadron were with me on the *Llanstephan Castle*. At Iceland I was to find out why.

Wing Commander Isherwood mustered all the officers, consisting mainly of engineers, cypher experts and adjutants on deck and broke the news that we were bound for North Russia. He explained that when Hitler had launched his attack on Russia two months earlier, Churchill and Roosevelt had promised Stalin aid in the form of arms and equipment. Britain's contribution was to include shipments of Hawker Hurricanes for Russian pilots who were short of up-to-date fighters.

Our mission would be to deliver to the Russian Air Force the first batch of forty Hurricane IIs, which had a hotted-up Merlin engine and twelve machine-guns instead of the usual eight. We were to teach their pilots to fly the aircraft, and their crews to maintain the engines, radios and guns. Also, until the Russians were operational, we would be escorting Russian bombers over the German lines.

Some of the Hurricanes were in crates in the holds of the cargo ships in the convoy which had preceded us by separate routes to Iceland. The remainder were on the aircraft carrier *Argus* which was also nearby. These would be flown off the *Argus* direct to Vayanga aerodrome at Murmansk, from which we would ultimately operate.

Now I knew what had happened to Bushy and Wag and Mickey Rook and his cousin Tony, our CO, and all my other pals of 81. They were across the water hardly a stone's throw away, on the aircraft carrier anchored there. That night we exchanged greetings in Morse by torch light.

Our convoy, the Wingco told us, would be met by the Russian battleship *October Revolution* in the Arctic Ocean and escorted to Archangel, where the aircraft would be removed from their crates, assembled by our own technicians, and flown across the White Sea to Murmansk.

'And to make sure they've put them together properly,' he grinned at me, 'Pilot Officer Holmes will test fly them. Then he, and pilots on other ships in the convoy, will fly them to Murmansk.'

It transpired that Wing Commander Isherwood was originally intended to test-fly the Hurricanes. But strict instructions came in a signal from Air Ministry that he was never to fly over Russia because his capture if shot down might have enabled the Germans by torture or other means to learn the whole strategy of this and subsequent convoys taking the Arctic route to Russia.

One of my most striking recollections of Iceland was the complete absence of blackout precautions. For two years now we had been accustomed to complete darkness everywhere at night. Yet here, with a war in full swing, all our ships were ablaze with light, seemingly ready for a firework display. The town at the end of the fjord threw diamond reflections into the still water, and car headlights swept along the coastal road and through the shopping streets, showing we were safely far beyond the range of any German bomber. Booms with wire mesh nets were guarding the mouth of the fjord from submarines.

The first morning in Iceland made it quite clear that someone back home was taking Churchill's promises to Russia quite seriously.

The clatter of winches heaving up anchor chains awoke us before dawn. Last night's luxury hotel had suddenly become a fighting ship, off to war. Icke and Vyle were tapping away in their radio compartment, no longer accessible. The ship's officers, each to his own duty, became wheels in a well-oiled machine.

The RAF and the few official civilian passengers who included British Air Attachés to Moscow, Polish and Czech officials visiting Military Missions, and a handful of American journalists bound for Moscow, now became about as useful as ballast. We all stood aside and watched the professionals in action. Our turn was no doubt to come.

The summer's convoy patrols from Exeter suddenly slipped into another world. Now, I was on a convoy myself.

With the alacrity of well-disciplined soldiers the ships fell into station as they left the fjord. Minesweepers led and the destroyers fussed, playing sheepdog. At the maximum speed of the slowest vessel in the convoy, we steamed north leaving in our wake only the shadowy mountainous mound that was Iceland quickly fading into the morning mist.

Once under way, Icke and Vyle came back into circulation. There were drinks that evening in their cabin. They told me we were heading slightly west of north towards Greenland. Next day we crossed latitude 67½ degrees into the Arctic Circle. The weather, which had been surprisingly warm at Iceland, now became steadily colder. Sea and sky were a purple black. The water turned from choppy to rough and the other ships appeared to be sinking below their deck line as they lurched down the wave troughs. There was no birdlife, although we saw several schools of whales.

At latitude 75, now less than the length of the British Isles from the North Pole, signal lamps started flashing from the naval vessels to the merchantmen as the Commodore ordered the convoy to slew ninety degrees to the right and head due east. We were keeping at this latitude in an effort to avoid detection by enemy recce planes and submarines based in Norway and Finland. Icke informed me that if we were torpedoed now, there would be no point in trying to get out of the water, which was so cold we would be dead within two minutes.

Quite the most exhilarating moment of that long drawn-out ten days' voyage was when, having passed north of the Arctic weather station of Bear Island, we met the reinforcements for our naval escort. From the size of the naval armada awaiting us it was obvious we were now approaching dangerous waters.

The horizon was studded with fighting ships. Sitting patiently waiting hundred of miles up the Arctic for us to join them were the cruiser *Shropshire*, the aircraft carrier *Victorious*, five destroyers and two more cruisers. Our six merchantmen carrying fifteen dismantled and crated Hurricanes, transport lorries, Humber Snipe brakes, Commer Vans, wireless tenders, stores, equipment, provisions and spirits for 550 RAF men (beer was too heavy and bulky) were being escorted by no less than 24 naval craft with enough firepower between them to demolish a town. Any German bombers or submarines trying to tackle us were in for a hot reception.

Two days out from Archangel we were due to meet up with the Russian battleship *October Revolution* which was to guide us south through the minefields guarding the entrance to the River Dvina. This would release our escort to head back across the Arctic to Greenland and meet the next convoy, which would this time be loaded almost entirely with Hurricanes.

For days on end we saw nothing from the *Llanstephan Castle* but grey, rolling water and the other ships in our convoy which all ploughed manfully through the waves, keeping station as though tied together on wires. We had long since tired of waving or passing messages with torches and signalling lamps. In the saloons table tennis tournaments and darts competitions were organised. A few played cards, wrote letters or read books. A popular pastime was learning Russian. Flight Lieutenant Hodson, who had spent the earlier years of his life in Russia and was fluent in the language, gave lectures twice a day and we soon mastered the alphabet, counting, and a few everyday words and phrases. But being of Slavonic origin, and all the words quite different from ours or from French or Latin, we found the task very difficult. A few natural linguists kept up their studies, and some who had a smattering before they started, did very well; but most of us were content to be able to drink a toast (first things first), ask for something at table, say please and thank you and, most important of all: 'I am English. I do not understand Russian.'

When the time came for our rendezvous with the *October Revolution*, low cloud was blanketing out both the sky and the horizon. We never knew how near we might be to her when we heard the heavy drone of a twin-engined aircraft — probably a Ju 88

— flying directly over us. The cloud was only a thin layer because occasionally we caught a glimpse of blue through it. It was so low our masts touched it. But it was heaven-sent because the Germans obviously had prior information of our convoy's progress and possibly the exact time and position of our rendezvous with the battleship had been leaked from the Russian side. They certainly knew exactly where to look.

Our radar must have picked up the bomber earlier for the Commodore had ordered all ships' engines to be shut down with no smoke from funnels drifting upwards through the cloud to betray our presence to the German searcher above. Probably the *October Revolution* was somewhere nearby in the murk doing the same. But radio silence was imperative so we could not communicate.

There we lay, the convoy drifting into ragged formation. The suspense was so great it almost seemed dangerous to speak to each other for fear of being overheard by the German airmen. Back and forth those engines droned. We could imagine the aircrew straining for a sight of our ships. But the cloud held, and at long last our radar showed that fuel shortage had driven the disappointed Ju 88 back to its base in Finland.

The Commodore now had a weighty decision to make. Should he keep the Royal Navy with us to fight off the waves of bombers that would undoubtedly attack the moment the weather cleared? Or should he release them and head for Archangel without even the protection of the *October Revolution*, and its guidance through the Russian minefields?

Icke and Vyle came into the saloon looking pale and grim. 'We're going it alone,' Icke announced. 'All personnel to wear lifebelts and warm clothing continually day and night and keep within reach of their own lifeboat. The Commodore says "Good luck all." ' Vyle, whose chubby cheerful countenance always invited a laugh, added: 'And you'll bloody well need it. It's about time the RAF got its feet wet.'

The convoy fell quickly into line astern led by two minesweepers whose job was to clear a narrow path for the rest of the ships to pass safely through. Farewell and Godspeed messages were exchanged by lamp with the naval escort which had brought us here. They turned westwards and quickly disappeared into the gloom. We went at top speed after leaving the naval escort. There was constant tension. Any heavy vibrations from our own straining ship could have been the sound of distant bombers approaching to attack. The water looked cold, black, deep and uninviting. It would have been a comfort to see even enemy-occupied land after so long at sea.

Every mile we now steamed south through the Barents Sea towards Russia brought us also nearer to German-occupied Finland for we were converging on a coastline along which the Luftwaffe had their airfields. We were not much more than a hundred miles east of them as we steamed through the gap into the White Sea, which was no distance for a bomber force. But our luck held. Low cloud persisted, no more recce planes were heard and thanks to our minesweepers finding and destroying two mines, the convoy went through the minefield unscathed.

The White Sea, now called Beloye More, starts as a thirty-mile-wide channel running inland for nearly a hundred miles before opening out left and right into a stretch of water three hundred miles long and reaching westwards to Kandalaksha, almost on the Finland Border, and thirty miles east to the river Dvina, in which lay Archangel, our destination. We knew that once we had left the Barents Sea and entered this narrow channel we no longer had any room to disperse during an air attack.

To the starboard side of the channel the land was low lying, featureless, being mainly bog and lakes from six feet of winter snow thawing each spring, with nowhere to drain away. Across the bog-land, a hundred miles to the west, lay Murmansk. This north Russian port, a few miles up a river of the same name, was vital to the Soviet war strategy because the northern leg of the Gulf Stream ends there, keeping the river clear of ice the year round when all adjoining rivers are frozen solid for four months. It was from Vayanga aerodrome, near Murmansk twenty miles east of the German lines, that 151 RAF Wing was to operate.

We were unmolested during the two anxious days and nights spent negotiating the channel into the White Sea. It was with sighs of relief that we at last turned left into the River Dvina, to start the final fifteen miles of our three weeks' journey up this river to Archangel. Our route wound through a delta. A Russian river pilot came aboard as no visiting mariner could have found his way. The scenery was desolate and depressing. We seemed to be crawling across flooded fields.

Where there were river banks they were stacked high with timber. Pine logs floating down the river from inland forests were nudged along by men with spiked boots who walked casually across the floating wood. Even from the ships we could hear the scream of circular saws, slicing the logs into planks to be stacked for seasoning. The few buildings we passed were primitive in design, entirely of wood, and unpainted. We learned later that the only tools used in their construction were axes, cross-cut saws and hammers.

The Russian men wore overall-type clothes, loose and lumpy. The women all looked squat, broad and shapeless in their unbecoming blanket shawls, heavy material skirts, probably for warmth, and ankle boots or clogs. Sex appeal for us was non-existent.

A diversion came as we passed two large flat-decked boats the shape of broad barges. Each boat was packed to the rails with men in grey uniform. They waved to us, not knowing who we were of course, and we all waved back, keen to establish an early friendship with our new Soviet allies. Our pilot hastened to inform us, however, that these were German prisoners of war being transported to concentration camps. We had seen such a camp earlier, a barbed wire enclosure with lookout towers and sentries shouldering rifles.

We were not feeling too warm towards the Germans, but when the pilot told us this we waved even more, shouting cheery, if rude messages. The Russian pilot could not understand our attitude towards our enemies. He simply spat.

On the afternoon of 1 September 1941, our convoy arrived at Archangel.

The information the Wing Commander had at this time on the *Llanstephan Castle* was that the object of our mission was to deliver the first batch of forty Hurricane IIs to the Russians, and come home. We would leave all our equipment with them, and possibly one or two engineering, wireless and armaments technicians. In the meantime more convoys would be delivering a further 200 Hurricanes to build the Russians' fighter force.

We reckoned we would probably be on our way home by the end of October. Or so we hoped. How sadly wrong we were.

After Liverpool's large floating landing stage, Archangel's wooden wharf, built entirely of poles and planks, was a primitive affair. If we had expected some sort of welcome after three weeks at sea, we were to be disappointed. A gang of peasants working on the quay, and a couple of sentries in sloppy khaki uniforms leaning casually on their rifles, watched the berthing of our ships with idle curiosity. Obviously they did not know who or what we were, and cared less.

When we had tied up, nobody came aboard. Nobody left our ship to go ashore. The Wing Commander said: 'We've come this bloody far. Now it's their move.' After an hour, however, the Russian Admiral's launch was seen speeding across from the other side of the river. It swung alongside the *Llanstephan Castle*. We lowered a ladder and the Admiral came aboard with Air Vice-Marshal Collier and Group Captain Bird who, we learned, had been at Moscow arranging details of our trip with the Russians.

Their conference with our Wing Commander provided the first really reliable information since we left Leconfield. We were all bound for Murmansk, but in three parties travelling separately by land, sea and air. There were no roads strong enough for our heavy lorries. The advance party would fly there immediately in Russian bombers, together with ground crews for those Hurricanes flying from the aircraft carrier *Argus*. The main party would travel by train, taking an estimated six days for the 600 miles round the south shore of the White Sea. This made allowance for the German bombing of the single line railway track linking Kandalaksha with Murmansk, which had to be mended before our party and equipment could proceed.

The Wing Commander and his party were to go by Russian destroyer taking them back through the White Sea (good luck to them!) and round the north coast into the Murmansk River. The destroyer would remain in the river at Murmansk as a flak-ship guarding our aerodrome.

It was decided that an engineering party should move on to Keg-Ost-Rof, an island aerodrome in the mouth of the River Dvina a few miles from Archangel, to assemble the Hurricanes that had arrived crated in our convoy. Flight Lieutenant Rook, Pilot Officer Woolaston and Pilot Officer Holmes would test-fly each aircraft as it was assembled, and sufficient pilots would wait at Archangel to ferry the Hurricanes to Murmansk when they were all completed.

The Air Vice-Marshal confirmed that one of our jobs at Murmansk would be to teach the Russian pilots to fly the Hurricanes.

He also gave us the cheering news that because of severe winters and shortage of daylight at these latitudes, operations would soon become impossible, and we would therefore have only a brief stay at Murmansk. My letter home, carried by one of the officers of the

Llanstephan Castle for posting when he arrived in England, bore these glad tidings, but it never arrived. The *Llanstephan Castle* was torpedoed on her way back. I never learned what happened to Icke and Vyle.

Plans went ahead speedily to get the advance party away, and they flew off the following day in three Russian airliners. The train party's plan came to grief right from the start. The Russians did not have the necessary equipment to unload our cargo from the ships on to the train. To save delay for the whole of the main party, therefore, one of our ships followed the Wing Commander's destroyer across the White Sea, with most of the main party in it. They would join a train at Kandalaksha and finish their journey by rail.

This party was placed under the command of Pilot Officer Martin Pratt, the cypher officer with whom I had shared a cabin from Liverpool in the *Llanstephan Castle*, and whose best man I subsequently became at his marriage to Edith in Marlow, when we finally arrived back in England. To those of us left behind while the Hurricanes were being assembled, money was the big problem. We all, naturally wanted to go ashore and buy souvenirs. Eventually the big moment came, and we were advanced 100 roubles each — worth £2!

Then we were informed that nobody was allowed ashore. Security. After much delay, passes arrived. Next came the problem of crossing the river to Archangel, nearly a mile. The OGPU (Russian security police) provided a river police launch for RAF officers only, forbidding the airmen at first to enter Archangel.

'We heard on the Wireless today (2 September) that a peace treaty between the Russians and the Finns was rumoured. This would be of particular significance to us at Murmansk, because the German lines in occupied Finland were only fifteen miles away. Before we had finally decided how such a treaty would affect us we heard that an official Finnish denial had been broadcast that any such pact was ever contemplated.'

I quote from a diary I kept at that time. It continues: 'It appears that I shall be on the *Llanstephan Castle* for another ten days or so while the Hurricanes are assembled. The engineering party will camp on the island aerodrome of Keg-Ost-Rof but I am luckier here with good English food, a first class cabin to myself now that Martin Pratt has gone, a luxury lounge to sit and read or write home, and a bath every day.

Flight Lieutenant Hodson, our interpreter.

Timber buildings at Archangel, with wooden footwalks.

'The mosquitoes are a pest. They breed in the bogs and infest the entire boat. Every time you swat one your find your own blood on the wall. It was no joke after all when they issued us with mosquito nets at Leconfield.

'The weather here is still warm and mild. The mosquitoes are thriving in this humidity. It is dark now by 8 pm and growing very cold at night.

'The local inhabitants are mainly of the peasant type, poorly clad and fed. They look dour and disinterested. They seem to carry on their work mechanically, without enthusiasm or ambition. They rarely smile — which, I suppose, is understandable. Finally, and unforgivably, they smell!

'Their cigarettes, which are one-third a hollow cardboard mouthpiece so that no tobacco is thrown away, are responsible to a great extent for the smell. Russian tobacco has a flat musty odour, lacking the sweet fragrance we enjoy from a Virginian leaf. It has the tang of a smouldering wet mattress. This, combined with body odour, vodka breath and clothing stops you dead on a still day or in a warm room.

'Their soldiers are quite different. Their uniforms may be drab (good camouflage?) but they are well fitting, and the men are fast moving, fast talking, and always ready to burst out into torrents of loud laughter. Their faces are flat and square, with boxers' noses and dark-set eyes. Mostly their hair is thin, cut short, and brushed down flat with no extravagant styles.

'Their strangest feature is their teeth. It is unusual to find a Russian soldier without his teeth encased, upper and lower, in a continuous coating of silver to the gums. They have no fillings. They protect against dental decay as we underguard a car.

'When the very cold weather arrived, about a month later, we learned that the peasants then sewed themselves into their quilted suits, and stayed in them for the winter. They were very obedient and a small group of officers handling a large work force of labourers, could achieve prodigious results.

'When we crossed the river into the town of Archangel we found almost all the men, except the very old, were in uniform. Women performed men's normal peace-time jobs. They sawed the wood, piloted the ferry boats, rowed the smaller boats, cleaned the streets, and drove the tramcars and lorries. We even found women on day and night sentry duty at the docks, armed with rifles and apparently quite happy to use their fixed bayonets given half a chance.

'Archangel was depressing. The river front, its most attractive section, with its white wooden buildings, was shoddy and in need of paint, with many dirty, broken windows.'

Always the windows were double-glazed. This was new to us then, and we always found it strange when opening a window to find a second set of windows on the other side of the sill. The roadways, to our amazement were not tarmac, but wooden planks. If a road needed mending, more planks were laid on top, leaving the old planks to rot underneath.

Footwalks were also made of wooden planks. These were on stilts about three feet high, with hand rails, to keep them clear of drifting winter snow. They were swept periodically, to prevent the frozen snow becoming a hazard. They were in a poor state of repair and a leg could easily be broken if a foot went through.

At every street corner raucous loudspeakers blared out. Excited announcers shouted messages in Russian. Whether they were instructions to workers, or news bulletins or promises of prosperity once the hated enemy was vanquished, we never knew. The reproduction was so crackling and distorted it must have been unintelligible even to the locals. No-one seemed to listen to them. Between the talking, tired gramophone records churned out scratched patriotic cavalry marches.

We found later that the people were allowed only to hear censored radio programmes over the public address system. Possession of a private wireless set was punishable.

It was impossible to recognise a shop from outside. Being state-owned, and thus having no competition, shop window displays were unnecessary. There was no advertising. A customer simply bought the article which happened to be on sale.

My diary continues: 'As the Russians have coupons for necessities, and are forbidden to buy luxuries without permission, stocks are trashy and uninteresting. The only cinema in Archangel has wooden seats and no ventilation. Upholstered seats would very quickly become "alive".

'We have been forbidden to drink Russian water unless it is boiled. We are advised to add sterilising tablets with which everyone is issued. The local drinking water is from the river and being near a town can scarcely be termed fresh!

'The Russians, now they know who we are, regard us as curiosities rather than allies in war. Some stare in sheer wonder that we have appeared from a country the other side of the world. Others cast shifty, suspicious glances at us when they think we are not looking. They obviously mistrust us.

'While passing a little wooden shed of a house, an old man sitting cross-legged and apparently dozing at his front door suddenly started shouting at me as I approached. I could not tell whether he was a fiery Bolshevik cursing me to damnation, and ready to throw a bomb at me, or was spouting a stream of anti-Hun propaganda for my benefit. I grinned at him in as friendly and encouraging a manner as possible to reassure him that we were both on the one side against the common enemy.

'Just then he rose to his feet, surprisingly nimbly, advancing with hand outstretched for mine. I seized it gladly, and shook it warmly. Suddenly, to my surprise and somewhat to my concern, he started dragging me into his house. This was enough. Whether he wanted to show me to his wife, or offer me vodka, or to slit my throat once he had me prisoner, I shall never know because I did not go in to find out.

'I dug my heels in and broke free of his strong grasp, freeing my right hand ready for my revolver. To my friendliest smile he replied with an ugly leer, so I went on my way. Back at the boat I asked Flight Lieutenant Hodson, who spent much of his childhood in Russia, what this was all about. He said: "Politics? Robbery? Genuine hospitality? Who knows? But it's fifty-fifty we'd not have seen you again if you had gone in." '

Our movements were watched and reported the whole time, wherever we went. Photography was of course absolutely forbidden, but that did not prevent me bringing back four 36 exposure cassettes taken when I was there.

We were offered permits to use cameras, but Hodson — knowing the working of their minds — warned us that this was probably a trick to obtain a list of all those with cameras, then confiscate them before their owners left the country.

Our first visit to Archangel was in darkness on the night of 2 September. We went down a rope ladder from the *Llanstephan Castle* into the naval launch, and sped across the river towards the swinging paraffin lantern guiding us to the quay. Fortunately Hodson had advised us to bring pocket torches to negotiate the raised footwalks. Our Russian guide was a charming olive-skinned girl in her early twenties. She had learned English at university in Kiev yet never before spoken to English people. Her speech was fluent and easy, her vocabulary extensive, with no trace of an accent. She would have made an ideal BBC announcer. She tried to discuss Shakespeare's plays as she knew many of them by heart, and was disappointed at our only passing acquaintance with the bard.

My diary goes on to record: 'A dozen of us went with her in the launch. We saw nothing of what was in the streets, as she led us straight to a Russian restaurant. This was to be our "night out" in return for bringing them forty Hurricanes. It was our first initiation to Russian food.

'On the table was a caraffe of yellow liquid which we took for white wine but which proved to be drinking water. She said it was safe to drink and that the colour came from the peat in the ground. On each side plate with a wooden-handled knife was a slice of black bread.

'Menus had been printed in anticipation of our visit in the two languages. It was slightly different from my birthday menu a couple of weeks earlier on the *Llanstephan Castle* in Iceland.'

The waitress recommended the salmon soup, so we ordered it. Hodson warned us about the vodka. Drunk neat — about one inch in a tumbler and tossed straight down — it has no immediate effect. But after a couple more a little man with a hammer inside your head starts hitting you behind the eyes, and you wake up with a splitting headache lasting 48 hours. He told us the vodka was in strengths of 45 per cent and 95 per cent. It was made from fermented grain. Both strengths burned with a pale blue flame if held near a naked light.

The salmon soup was skin, backbone, tail and fins of the fish floating in a tureen of boiling water, from which it was served. It tasted like uncooked fish smells. We had one vodka each, left the soup, and ordered an ice. With all the ice in Russia you would wonder how they could take an hour serving you with one. But the male interpreters who had now joined us made the most of that hour quizzing us about our lives in England, the war in Europe, and especially about our job here.

Neither the vodka (thanks to Hodson's warning) nor the persuasion of the interpreters worked, so we did not get our headaches and they did not get their information. Our ices, and the news that our boat called back for us, arrived together. We handed over our roubles to cover the bill and left.

Hodson told us a few days later he had learned that the restaurant to which we were taken had been in the OGPU headquarters. Our conversations had been bugged and our behaviour observed through two-way mirrors.

Next day, the party bound for Moscow left by plane. We never saw them again. I go on to record: 'We have now seen a few of the Russian fighter aircraft flying overhead. Although the propaganda posters illustrate the Russian air force in action in Stormovick low-wing monoplanes, not unlike Spitfires, their fighters are in fact all old biplanes. They have retractable undercarriages and seem pretty speedy, but are poorly armed and not fast enough to keep up with their own bombers, which are copies of the German twin-engined Messerschmitt 110.

'September 3. Today, none of our Hurricanes being assembled are yet ready to test-fly, so I made my first daylight visit to Archangel. Icke and Vyle went with me and we travelled there on a decrepit, evil-smelling ferry boat with paddles. We were again the subject of much curious scrutiny. Some stared openly as though we were animals at a zoo.'

Trying to pay our fare in Russian money, using the Russian language, made us a few friends. Most money transactions ended with our hands extended and our currency fanned across the palms, suggesting: 'Here, help yourself'. This they did with a laugh. Strangely, when the chance to rip us off was so easy, they never did. Perhaps their punishment if caught would be too severe. Perhaps they were just honest.

Women collected fares on the boat. We crossed the river several times the first week, and the fare-paying ritual became such a joke with one women conductor of sixty, in peasant clothing, shawl and stiff felt knee-boots, that in the end she would wave us away with a laugh and a flash of silver teeth, and we travelled free.

In prominent positions in all the streets and hallways of public buildings were large statues of Stalin or Lenin, and occasionally Molotov. The figures were never duplicated in Archangel although we later saw replicas in other towns. They were all fine craftmanship. The roads were badly potholed. But as all transport was military, and these vehicles were robust, no harm was done except to make the holes deeper. Footwalks were precarious with their broken planks.

'Very old, single-decked tramcars rattled along sunken and uneven lines. It is impossible to ride on them standing without holding the wooden overhead rail. They are usually full of soldiers.

'Dogs are rare. When you see one, it is lean like a wolf, scavenging for food. There are no cats. Perhaps the dogs have eaten them.

'The civilians have communal eating centres, paying for their meals with coupons. We never saw anything served other than stew and black bread. I saw a group of men and women stampeding to an English merchant ship one day when news leaked out that they could get hot water to drink with the bread. No wonder their faces are colourless, and their minds dull. The soldiers have better rations and carry them in string nets slung from their belts.

'The only shops of note we have seen so far are a furrier's and a chemist's. Fur slippers and gloves made by the Lapps were crude but quite acceptable. The fur is outside, with skin lining. But coats and hats were both of coarse fur like horse or reindeer, were badly cured, and smelt.'

The chemist stocked mainly medicines and candy. This looked and tasted (and probably was) very old. We bought some once out of curiosity, but not a second time. There were no manufacturers' labels on any containers or wrappers, probably because everything was state-made.

Strangely, the only people with whom we could converse were the children. They must be taught English at school. They loved to talk to us, and the women conductors let them ride free on the ferry just to try out their English. The world over, children all want to be friends. It is only when they grow older . . . We gave the kids some English coins, and this delighted them.

Still my diary:

'September 4 (fourth day here). Pilot Officer Pratt (Martin, my cabin mate) and Flying Officer Blackwell set off today with their party. They are bound for Murmansk, via the White Sea and Kandalaksha. Martin was quite sure they'd never make it, and would be shot by the Germans, eaten by polar bears or frozen into snowdrifts. He gave me his gold signet ring to take back to Edith. Why he thought I had a better chance of getting back than him, I could never quite fathom. Anyway I took his ring, returning it to him a couple of weeks later when we met up again at Murmansk.

'Actually there were some grounds for his fears. The reliability of the trains was in grave doubt and there was a distinct chance the Germans would have bombed the railway line again. From Kandalaksha they would be travelling 100 miles north, parallel and at times very near to the German lines. Wandering patrols could easily ambush their train. When we wished them farewell, we wondered if it was not goodbye, but they got through without much trouble in three days.

'The Wingco's party left on the Russian destroyer today, too.'

Flight Lieutenant Fred Gittins, the Wing engineering officer, was now hard at work with his troops at Keg-Ost-Rof aerodrome. The crated Hurricanes had all been transhipped there from the convoy, and unpacked. They were short of a kit for fixing on the heavy three-bladed propellers. The Russians, who are wonderful copyists, quickly made a kit from drawings.

'While I am waiting for my first aeroplane to test, I am visiting local villages in a jeep MT lent me. They are drab and disappointing. I expected colourful, traditional costume and primitive native life. But even here are endless piles of timber, rotting wooden streets and crude wooden huts. There are no drains. Cabbages grow on the roadside, where the earth is drier, the roads being built on dwarf embankments to keep them clear of the swamp.

'The locals are still wary of us. Strange, the women are less suspicious than the men and some of the older ones are starting to flirt outrageously.'

I drove round for three days. Then on 7 September, news came from the island that three Hurricanes would be ready for test tomorrow.

'On the wireless today we heard that the Germans were claiming they had shot down some English aircraft over Leningrad. This is a laugh. We are the only RAF contingent in Russia. The broadcast indicates that they have rumours we are here but are not sure where, and this is a probe in the hope that we will broadcast a denial and perhaps give a clue where we are. They are so naïve.

'Today Vyle and I walked eight miles along the railway track to another village. We wanted some exercise. We wondered if the smell would be the same there, or whether it was some special chemical or fertiliser or gas being produced at Archangel. Exactly the same. And obviously from the same cause. Nothing else was different either. Wood, wood, wood. Heavens, and we're short of it in England. It is stacked high for twenty miles and a mile deep along each side of the river. The river is awash with logs floating down from the forests. Tugs harness them into great log rafts a hundred yards square and haul them to the saw mills.

'We hear that the *Llanstephan Castle* is taking back to England some of the 300,000 Poles the Russians had taken prisoner. We had read about this in the newspapers before we left home. Word came through today that the carrier party will be flying off the *Argus* tomorrow for Murmansk. This means that the ground crews that left on the Russian destroyer with the Wingco on 4 September have arrived safely and are ready to receive our pilots.

'September 8. Today, Mickey Rook, Pilot Officer Dick Woolaston and I set off in a tiny motor-launch for Keg-Ost-Rof. Group Captain Bird, who joined us from Moscow, and Flight Lieutenant Hodson, our interpreter, were with us. A cabin just sat three if we crouched. The other two squatted on the floor on our parachutes. A disinterested middle-aged Russian took the wheel.

'The island is in the mouth of the River Dvina, just where it empties into the sea. Here we quite suddenly met rough water which buffetted our little boat cruelly. Head on into the waves, our bow was climbing crazily skywards then plunging over and down. Each time we dived the screw leapt our of the water and our engine revved madly. It was difficult to decide whether this fellow standing so stolidly behind the wheel really knew his job, or whether he was simply following orders to get us to the island, in fear of punishment if he failed. When Flight Lieutenant Hodson suggested we turned back he simply stared ahead, grimly tugging at the wheel which threatened to spin from his grasp each time we pitched down a wave. We sat back, resigned.

'Suddenly a wall of water as high as a house swept right over us, completely submerging our bows. It tore away our windscreen and stopped our engine. Now we are for it! Immediately the boat lost way, and wallowed out of control across the waves. We waited for the moment when we would take aboard a great torrent of water and be buffeted under.

'Feverishly we tore off the engine housing. Protecting the cylinder block from the spray as much as possible with our bodies, we scrubbed at the sparking plug insulators and high tension leads with hankies, to dry them out. We just hoped the magneto had not taken a soaking. We signalled to the Russian to crank. He tugged at the handle, and mercifully the engine fired first pull.

'Our pilot needed no second warning. He gave it full throttle and swung back round to get into the shelter of the river, while we fixed the engine cover. Riding with waves, wind and current, we made good time back to the *Llanstephan Castle*. It broke the monotony, anyway.

'September 9. Today they took the three of us out to Keg-Ost-Rof again, this time in a tug. The Russian commanding officer of the aerodrome personally flew us round one at a time in a two-seater Chaika to point out the bad patches on the landing field. The job was finding the good ones. With their light biplanes they could land to dodge the mud, but the heavy Hurricanes landing at twice the speed needed a long landing run particularly as brakes are useless in mud.

'That morning five Hurricanes were ready for us to test. There was tremendous excitement both among our boys and their Russian counterparts. Russian Admirals, Generals, Colonels, their Air Ministry representatives, technical experts, engineers — all were there to get their first glimpse of a Hurricane going through its paces.

'Micky gave me the first to test, making me the first pilot to fly a British war plane in Russia.

'Group Captain Bird briefed us that the Russian delegation were expecting to see something exceptional from the Hurricanes. They had heard about their successes against the Messerschmitts, Dorniers and Heinkels, in the Battle of Britain. Now they wanted to see just what they could do. This was carte blanche to give the Hurricanes all they'd got! If we'd flown like this at a British airfield we'd have been Court Martialled. The cloud was below a thousand feet, so the three of us were able to circle the aerodrome in cloud then spiral out of it at full throttle, sweeping at ground level across the grass straight at the delegation, and climbing up over their heads a hundred yards short of them.

'Flight Lieutenant Gittins never stopped talking that night about how well his aeroplanes performed and about the muddy uniforms of the Admirals and Generals through flinging themselves headlong on the ground as the Hurricanes roared over. We tore out from behind hangars at them, vertically banked above their heads, until red Very lights from the control tower indicated they'd seen enough. We did a couple of rolls and went into tight formation to land in a vic of three.

'We climbed out of our cockpits not knowing whether we were bound for Siberia or our own beds that night. But the Admirals and Generals were enthusiastic, and took us indoors and toasted us lavishly in vodka. We did not test the other two that day.

'On subsequent days, at the Group Captain's invitation we finished a test by beating up the *Llanstephan Castle*. This delighted the officers and crew, who had never up till now seen anything near their ship but hostile aircraft, dropping bombs or torpedoes, and strafing their decks with cannon fire. Now we came in at sea level, broadside on and well below her decks. I could look up through my windscreen as I approached at 300 mph and see the excited men at the rails waving furiously down at me. Then most of them would dive flat on the deck as my Hurricane went into a vertical climb to skim over the funnels and mast-tops and disappear into cloud. One day a Russian sentry on the quayside dropped his rifle and dived under a pile of timber.

'The local people of Archangel were very happy about the performance of the aeroplanes we were sending them. But they were convinced the pilots flying them were drunk, drugged, mad, or all three. We were gratified at this reaction. It meant the success of our mission, if the Russians had favourable first impressions of our fighters, for it was well-known that Stalin had asked Churchill for Spitfires.

'This week a Fleet Air Arm pilot named Lieutenant Lee turned up on the *Llanstephan Castle*. He had been picked up by a fishing smack after being shot down in flames by a Me 109 during a dive bombing attack from his carrier on Petsamo. His naval kit was destroyed by the fire and the salt water, so the Russians loaned him a Russian Commissar's uniform and hat. Soldiers now saluted him on all sides. He was useful to take on a shopping expedition because his uniform could get us anywhere. He was uninjured, and waiting to jump the next convoy home, and rejoin his ship.

'12 September. Today Micky Rook and Dick Woolaston with seven Sergeant Pilots took the first nine Hurricanes to Murmansk. This left six for me to test on my own, we having done three each of the first nine. I was to follow on with five more reserve pilots when these aircraft were ready. This led to the laugh of the whole trip.

'Now Micky Rook has gone, I have automatically become "OC Troops" on the *Llanstephan Castle*. Although we have on board both a Russian and a British Admiral, two English naval Captains, the Commodore of the convoy and an RAF Group Captain, I, although the lowliest form of Service life as a Pilot Officer, take precedence because in an RAF unit, the officer commanding is always the highest ranking qualified pilot, regardless of higher rank of others.

'13 September. I tested the last six Hurricanes today. They were all OK. It is a tribute to Gittins and his boys that apart from some minor adjustments to an occasional trimming tab, the aircraft were all assembled perfectly. The propeller kit the Russians made was first rate.

'As a final gesture of farewell, I beat up the *Llanstephan Castle* again on the last test. They enjoyed it, and the naval chief in Russia, Captain Brown, who was the following month made up to Admiral, invited me to visit him at his naval base when I arrived up at Murmansk. (They gave us a trip on a submarine there.)

'We heard today that our boys at Murmansk have been in action, and have shot down two Me 109s.

'14 September. As a token of thanks now that the Hurricanes are finished the Russians tonight invited the Engineering party, with Flight Lieutenant Hodson, our interpreter, and myself to a circus at Archangel. The main feature was a display by Caucasian dancers, of national dances of the Caucasus, in Southern Russia. They covered the styles of nearly twenty different tribes, being mostly mountain ritual dances wielding and throwing knives and axes, to the accompaniment of whoops and screams. Primitive string instruments, dating back to the 7th century which could have started their lives as anything from a coconut shell to a dried stomach, provided the music.

'The brilliant footwork in the dances outshone anything we had ever seen. Trained from childhood, these male dancers clench the toes and soles of their feet as one would a fist. Then they dance on the knuckles of their toes, wearing tight fitting boots with a paper-thin sole and an upper as soft and as pliable as a kid glove. They run, leap, and perform all manner of gymnastics on their toes to the rhythmic beat of the string instruments and drums.

'The RAF party was shown to a front row of seats, stretching nearly halfway round the circus ring. We were given a standing ovation from the audience as we took our seats, and again when we left. In contrast to this splendid affair, we witnessed a peasant funeral on the way to the circus. The hearse was a farm dray with a heavy black cart-horse in the shafts. The corpse lay flat on his back with hands folded across his chest. He was in a white shroud but bare-headed. He had a neatly trimmed white beard. Anyone who wished could pay their last respects as the cortège passed. The mourners all walked behind, heads bowed, and dressed in black. There were several weeping children. He was somebody's Dad. It was a sad sight.

'17 September. Today I led my flight of six Hurricanes to Murmansk. We went in two hops. We had been briefed when we took off from Keg-Ost-Rof to form two vics of three and circle until we were joined by a Russian P2 bomber. He was an exact replica of the German twin-engined, twin-tailed Messerschmitt 110 we knew so well from the time 36 of them made that daylight raid at Filton. I wondered what sort of diplomatic incident would have ensued if one of our chaps had shot down the P2 mistaking him for an Me 110. I took good care no one did.

'The P2 pilot set course at once for the White Sea, and we tagged behind. This stretch of water is quite narrow, but very long, and sharpens to a point at each end. We flew up the middle, from south-east to north-west, a distance of 298 miles. Then the P2 circled Afrikanda Aerodrome, north of Kandalaksha where we had been briefed to land and refuel. As soon as we had all landed he set course back to his own base.

'I was surprised and pleased to find some RAF fitters and riggers here waiting for us, Martin Pratt having dropped them off from his party.

'We had lunch here. The local commissars made every effort to get us tight. As leader of our Flight I was seated next to their top man on the main table. It was obvious he was in for a party, and equally obvious that if he could finish the day by shovelling the RAF pilots into bed with a few Russian girls in a cloud of vodka instead of completing their journey today, it would be a personal triumph for him. So I passed the word round: "One vodka each, and only then if you want it, and nobody — but nobody! has a second".

'This was the top strength vodka, swallowed neat and in one. It was with some relief that we found two of our engines refused to start after lunch. We all had a welcome walk in the fresh air and some more black coffee while the plugs were checked.

'By late afternoon we were airborne again. This time there was no P2 to lead us, and we had to do our own map reading, probably because our course due north was the whole way along the enemy lines.

'After a hundred miles of vigilance, with the sun sinking on our left and the Hun expected to come at us from that quarter at any moment, we suddenly saw a P2 shooting red flares as it headed towards us. It looked like a cry for help, as though he was either being attacked by German fighters or having to go down with engine trouble. But down below we saw our destination, a desolate space, between low hills, and devoid of buildings or runways.

'A careful search from five thousand feet and we were able to spot a few Hurricanes tucked in between trees on the airfield boundary. In line astern we went round and landed.

'There was hardly time to taxy in and switch off before the reunions started. These were the pals we last saw in Leconfield, Yorkshire, and now we were meeting up again in the Arctic Circle. It seemed unbelievable. Yes, Bushy, and Wag, and Tony and the rest and all seemed just the same. The party went on well into the night. Even Bernard Conybeare, our much loved and sworn tee-totaller bachelor adjutant, was rumoured to have had a small port and lemon to commemorate the occasion.

'Next day, despite slight headaches, we went down to flights and became operational.

'The Wingco said the Russians were losing bombers on raids over Finland because their own escorting biplane fighters were too slow. He had agreed we would do bomber escort and fighter interception, but had refused emphatically the Russian CO's request to make dive attacks on the German lines strafing troops and aircraft with our twelve machine-guns. He said the results of strafing would be spectacular, but he hated to think what would happen to any of our pilots who happened to be shot down.

'At this time we were expecting to be homeward bound by the beginning of October. But today, 18 September, the rumoured date slid back three weeks. Nobody could ever trace the origin of these dates. Mysteriously they leaked from the orderly room.

'19 September. All of a sudden, today a hush settled over our world. It was so quiet, you could actually hear nothing. Normally rattling lorries bounced along full of soldiers going to and from their duties. Open bins of stew for the troops clattered against each other in backs of trucks and vans. Now all was quiet. Overnight there had been a six inch snowfall. Roads and footwalks merged into one. Trees sagged under their load.

Russian sentry on sniper practice. Skis were now the main mode of transport.

Bushy and self outside 151 Wing Officers' Mess at Murmansk.

Vic Berg's prang. Two airmen died when they were flung off the tail on take-off.

Noon at our aerodrome.

'The Russians were not taken by surprise as we were. They see it happen every year. As a matter of smooth routine, horsedrawn sledges had already taken over as transport. The smallest children were on their way to school on skis. This was their normal life. To us it was something novel and exciting. We were all schoolboys again. Snowmen, and snowball fights before breakfast, then down to dispersal on three sledges all tied in a line behind a four-wheel drive jeep. We appreciated now the double windows throughout the Officers' Mess, for keeping the bitter cold at bay, while central heating boilers kept the rooms pleasantly warm.'

The Russians are masters of camouflage. From the air when we arrived at Vayanga it was difficult to pick out any aeroplanes or buildings on the ground. This was because huts were cleverly concealed among trees around the perimeter of the landing ground, and each aeroplane had its own blister hangar. These had an opening at the front just high enough for the aircraft to be pushed in backwards. They tapered away to the ground at the back and the sides, eliminating the shadows that reveal so much on a reconnaissance photograph. When the snow covered these blisters, it was quite impossible to pick them out as aircraft shelters.

Our crew rooms at the dispersals were similarly hidden. They had been dug out, then roofed at ground level, with ventilation shafts and a staircase added. Inside we had cast-iron wood-burning stoves with a chimney pipe through the roof, and twin tier bunks round the walls for reading or resting when not flying. Usually we spent our time on the ground toasting Russian bread on the stoves. They provided unlimited butter.

Slithering down to dispersal on our sledges, we wondered how we would manage taxying, taking off and landing in the snow. We need not have worried. Already, teams of tractors were pulling giant concrete rollers the height of a man, in clusters of as many as six, up and down the airfield pounding the snow flat.

We found as the weeks went by that a snowfall was something sudden. A clear blue sky would turn a heavy grey, then enormous snowflakes would cut visibility down to a few yards. But it was brief. As soon as it stopped snowing the sun shone through, the rollers were brought out, and the latest fall was flattened. This continued until our landing ground was covered with a foot or more of impacted solid ice.

Walking was very difficult. Progress could only be achieved by throwing your weight forward, walking stiff-legged and flat-footed. This was hard work on the muscles of the stomach and the groin. It was always a great relief to be back in the Mess at the end of the day, just for the joy of striding out on firm ground.

On 20 September we made our first offensive patrol over the German lines. This was a new experience, because although we had already flown many hours over enemy-occupied Europe, we had never yet flown over trenches full of soldiers. We could imagine the Germans taking pot shots at us with their rifles.

The soldiers on both sides were having a very rough time. There were only two main roads, one running north and south to make the boundary between Russia and Finland, and the other running east and west which takes traffic from one country into the other in peacetime. The terrain alongside these roads was bog and lakes in summer and frozen snow in winter, and this was the ground across which the soldiers had to fight. I was glad not to be in the poor bloody infantry. . . .

We could see the German armour moving up the road from the west, but they could not use it. They could not take it off the road on either side until they reached the crossroads, and the Russians held those at present. So their tanks, guns, and armoured vehicles were piling up, with nowhere to go, and were becoming a prime target for the Russian bombers. The same situation, of course, prevailed on our side with the Russian armour. The key to the whole of this part of the campaign was who held the crossroads.

Our first patrol was really to familiarise ourselves with the area. It was an easy sector to learn. You flew west into Finland, and east back home. On taking off from Murmansk you immediately crossed the river which empties into the Barents Sea only a few miles north, at the top of the Kola peninsula. Here the coastline went almost due east to west. If you were ever lost in the bad weather the immediate action was to fly north to the coast, then east to the estuary of the Murmansk river, and across the river to Vayanga aerodrome.

A disturbing feature of our recce was the heavy curtains of extremely accurate anti-aircraft fire that met us as we crossed the lines on our way back home. We assumed it came from the Germans, but were assured by the Russians that it was their own gunners who had not yet learned to distinguish Hurricanes from Messerschmitts.

'But do not worry, they will learn quickly,' we were assured.

They did learn, but not very quickly. We always had to be ready to take evasive action because if one or two stray shots came at us this always seemed to encourage others to join in. This, also, was the Russian system of air raid warning.

The first warning that a German raid was on its way came the moment their bombers took off and started grouping over their own airfield. Russian observer spies would radio the number and type of aircraft, their position and course to their anti-aircraft posts. The gunners would be ready to blast off the moment the raiders came in sight. The burst of gunfire in the sky would alert the Russian fighter pilots, sitting in their cockpits, strapped in and ready to go. They would start up and take off, and climb towards the shell bursts in the sky.

It was about now that the blizzards started. The brilliantly sunlit mountains would disappear and the clear sky would blacken. A bitter wind would spring up, and snow would drive almost horizontally across the airfield, swirling round the aircraft bays and the birch trees. All the footprints and tyre tracks filled up as you watched, but in a quarter of an hour the clouds had swept away and the sun was shining on a fresh new fairyland.

These blizzards were frequent, and at first frightening. To see your airfield disappear just as you were about to land on it was disconcerting, for there is no more lonely experience than to be in a solitary aeroplane over strange territory with nil visibility and probably not a lot of petrol, and the feeling that you will never see mother earth again until you hit her hard. But we soon learned that the blizzards were so local it was only necessary to fly a few miles upwind of them to a clear spot, and wait till the storm went through.

In these storms the temperature often dropped as low as 27°F below freezing, and it was a regular thing to have your breath frozen on your eyebrows and eyelashes. Aircraft had to be lavishly treated with anti-freeze to prevent cockpit hoods and panels being frozen into place.

It took time to grow accustomed to the daily routine of the Soviet aircrews warming up their machine-guns. Long bursts from their guns would be heard on the other side of the aerodrome, followed by the scream of bullets passing over our heads to finish in the hills behind our dispersal. After a while we learned to expect this, and to have faith in their gunners aiming high. We also learned not to take morning strolls in the hills until the Russian machine-guns were all warmed up.

Our own Brownings were all electrically heated. We never had a single stoppage throughout the Wing's tour at Murmansk.

There were no leaders, and there was no discipline amongst the Russian fighter pilots. They won a reward of a thousand roubles for each German they shot down, and the first one there had the best chance of getting the thousand roubles. When we were met by Russian ack-ack we had to be ready to avoid any trigger-happy Russian fighter pilots taking a shot at us too.

On 24 September the BBC mentioned for the first time that an RAF wing was operating in Russia. It did not say where.

On 81's first operational trip escorting Russian bombers, we were jumped by a squadron of '109s. The Germans were obviously surprised to see Hurricanes, and before they realised what was happening, Bushy, Wag Haw and Sergeant Waud had pinched one each. On the way home Scottie Edmiston spotted a Henschel 126 high-wing reconnaissance monoplane, rather like an RAF Lysander, and shot it down too.

Next day, we were jumped again. This time they sent a better team, for we got none and sadly we lost Sergeant Pilot Norman Smith. He was only eighteen. His body was brought in by the Russian observer corps and given a ceremonial funeral, on high ground overlooking Murmansk Sound in the 'Cemetery of Soviet Heroes'. Our Wing and the Russians both sent firing parties to his funeral, and the coffin was carried through the streets of the town with the Soviet Fleet Air Arm flag and Union Jack. Flight Lieutenant Fisher read the funeral service. It was a quiet and impressive ceremony for our first and also our last pilot to be killed there.

On 26 September I got an Me 109F. This was the first time we had met the rounded-wing Messerschmitts and we were glad to see that our improved Hurricane II could cope with them at the heights at which we were operating — which, because of the extreme temperatures, were never much more than 10,000 feet.

We were escorting a dozen Stormoviks to Petsamo at the time. Micky Rook had 'A' Flight in three sections of two, flying close escort to the right of the bombers. We in 'B' Flight were also in three pairs but a thousand feet higher, and a mile to the left to cope with the Hun from the sun.

The Messerschmitts came from behind, and at least five thousand feet above. They were streaking steeply down when I first saw them, sending out vapour trails from their wingtips in the freezing air. I bellowed a warning to Red leader, but Micky did not seem to get my call, and 'A' Flight cruised serenely on. There was no choice but to hope he would see them. Still transmitting a warning I swung round in a tight left-hand circle to attack head on.

Bushy was sticking to my tail. There were six Messerschmitts only three or four miles back now, diving at about thirty degrees and at terrific speed. When I had made half my turn and was heading towards the leader at ninety degrees he and his companion opened fire on the bombers. He had seen me and wanted to get in a quick burst before I intercepted. But he was well out of range and the tracer from his twin 20 mm cannons made a glowing chain of fire as the shells chased each other across the fading evening sky. The bombers and their escort sped on unharmed.

My quarter attack placed me in an ideal position but their leader was diving far too fast for accurate shooting. I needed at least four ringsights of deflection, reducing to two as the angle-off diminished, but to keep my bead so far ahead of my target on a vertical turn took him out of sight under my own nose. I suddenly saw also that drawing my sights so far forward put my bead right on to Micky Rook's Hurricane.

To Hell! Micky was safe enough at this deflection. I pressed the firing button and kept it pressed. The twelve guns blasted out blue flame in front of my wings. The airframe lurched momentarily with their recoil, as though an invisible hand had applied a brake and I was going to fall out of the sky.

I had no tracer. I was firing alternate armour piercing and deWilde explosive bullets, so I could not see where they were going. With such a snap shot I was far from hopeful. But it was a deterrent, for the other Messerschmitts broke away to the right without firing, and to my surprise did not return for a second attack.

Meanwhile the leader pulled out of his dive and was flying at tremendous speed over the top of the steadily plodding bombers. Possibly even now they did not know they had been attacked. Then the '109 rolled on to his back and from the inverted position his nose fell into a vertical dive.

The manoeuvre looked part triumphant, like a victory roll, and part evasive. But he kept going vertically down, spiralling slightly and at increasing speed. I had to take my eyes off him to look for other Huns who might be jumping me. But I knew if he pulled out of that dive before he hit the ground, he would do well.

We took the bombers to their target, stood off while they dropped their bombs and brought them home without further incident. At debriefing two Russian air gunners said they saw my Messerschmitt go in, so I must have hit him. My kill was not confirmed, however, until the following day when word came from German-occupied Finland by underground radio that what was left of the Messerschmitt had been found, with no survivor.

I was sad he never managed to bale out. That German pilot, whoever he was, was a resolute fellow. But I was glad to get an Me 109F — and the Russian bomber boys were over the moon. It boosted their morale no end, for they had been having heavy losses with their own fighters escorting, and this was the first German they had seen shot down.

The Wing adjutant wrote in his diary: 'Sept 26. 81 Squadron escorted Soviet bombers in a raid on Petsamo. Magnificent sight at take-off. First 'A' Flight 81; then Soviet fast dive bombers; then 'B' Flight; then a flight of Soviet heavy bombers. The sky above the aerodrome becomes full of aircraft taking station.

'They are all back in just over an hour, after a brilliant action on the part of 'B' Flight — perhaps the best thing the Wing has done yet. 'B' Flight was jumped by six Me 109s from cloud. When this happens, the Flight that has been jumped is usually pretty lucky if it gets away without loss to itself or its charges.

'B' Flight did better than this, however; they turned into the Messerschmitts, more or less each for each, getting in bursts as the opportunity offered after the first evasion of the "jump". They shot down three of them — all confirmed — and got back to base without a single bullet hole in any of their machines.

'The Soviet bombers carried out their mission unmolested and the Russian General telephoned a message of thanks.'

Back to my diary.

'Now that the RAF is getting a few successes in the air, the Russians are using us as propaganda. Swarms of reporters, photographers and newsreel cameramen have invaded us. We have been photographed standing on wings, climbing out of cockpits, taking off in formation, watching belts of ammunition being loaded into our wings for the machine-guns, shaking hands with Soviet pilots, with our arms round their girl interpreters, and always ending up with that internationally accepted sign of good spirit and optimism, the thumbs-up.

'At first this was all fun, but soon it grew boring trying to think of something new to say in the interviews, and different to do for the cameras. Often the photos were taken outside the RAF Officers' Mess. The Russians had built this specially for us. There was a large square white board on each side of the entrance. One read English Headquarters, 151 Wing, RAF and the other bore the Russian equivalent: Angleeski Shtap, 151 Krila KBC.'

This building housed all our administrative offices, our sick quarters, and upstairs the officers' ante-room and sleeping quarters. Two or three shared a bedroom, which was centrally heated and furnished with a table, a cupboard each, and iron beds. No water was piped into the building. Washing water was brought in, and heated by our batmen.

We ate at another building a quarter of a mile away. This is not far, but was a fair trek through deep snow in a temperature 30°F below freezing with a cutting wind. Food won few marks for variety, although it was plentiful. Soup was always mixed vegetable, mainly cabbage, the meat either horse or reindeer. The pancakes were excellent, served with jam or sugar. Sugar, green plum jam and butter were always in good supply. The bread was white, soggy when fresh and hard when stale, with no in-between. Always best toasted.

At first sparkling red and white wine and chocolate caramels were always on the menu, but when the railway line between Murmansk and the south was cut by German advances these items faded off the menu. Our Russian waitresses gabbled incessantly at us in their own language, shouting to make us understand. Their names were Mirosa, Norah, Ryeesa, Anya, Ira, and Lucie. They taught us the Russian names of our table dishes. They refused to attempt any English.

Our favourite food was thick, square slices of cold ham. One day ham disappeared from the menu, and we learned that the Germans had captured the crossroads, and with them went all the Russian food supplies. However, the Russians with a spirited counter-offensive, won back the crossroads a few days later, so our ham re-appeared supplemented by some even better Latvian ham pinched off the Germans. From now on, the ham was our war barometer. If there was ham for breakfast we were winning. This was amusing, but a more sobering side to the situation was that if the Germans held those crossroads and broke through the Russian line they would cut off the Kola peninsula and capture the entire RAF Wing.

To make up for the complete absence of fresh fruit and greens we were issued with vitamin tablets to take daily.

Our landing ground had obviously been bulldozed out of a valley between two lines of low hills. The surface was sandy, and in places sufficiently soft to tip a taxying aircraft on its nose. This broke a few airscrews, but after the blizzards, with the snow rolled hard and firm the trouble was removed.

One problem resulting from the extreme cold, was the snapping of the shaft drive to the generators on our Merlin engines. These shafts, or rods as long and as thick as a pencil, had an egg-cup shaped end, with teeth around the inside rim of the cup. The steel was skimmed specially thin near one end, to ensure breaking there under abnormal load, and avoid shearing more costly parts in the generator. The extreme temperature changes were snapping these shafts, and we had exhausted our supply of spares which were only available from Rolls-Royce in England. Once more the Russian engineers came to our rescue. Within 24 hours they had jigged up machines to make them complete with egg cup at one end with internal teeth. In two days all our aircraft were flying again. An engine modification cut out sudden temperature changes to the drive shafts and cured the trouble.

Recreations when not flying were at first nil. We returned daily at dusk on our sledges from dispersal to the Kremlin, as we called our Mess, to read a book, or write home. Quite often we would go to the steam baths. These are large rooms, each about the size of a squash court, with four or five giant steps leading from the floor at the front almost to the ceiling at the back. The higher up the steps, the hotter the steam. After ten to fifteen minutes you retire to the wash room, where a team of middle-aged women attendants, who seem faintly amused at the sight of naked men, throw baths of freezing water over your practically boiling body. As you curl up with the paralysing shock they smack your behind, laughing loudly. Impurities and inhibitions are washed away simultaneously at the Russian steam baths.

The convoy that arrived after ours brought 'comforts for the troops' — which included a wind-up HMV gramophone and one record of Vera Lynn singing 'We'll meet again'. Even letter-writing was difficult, for our life was centred around our operations, and these were all top secret. Any reference was forbidden in mail. One evening our hosts staged a cinema show for us, at the local hall. The film was entirely in Russian, but it was interesting trying to figure out the story from the behaviour of the characters. Some of our suggested versions of the plot would have quickly earned the film a double-X rating in England.

Occasional evening outings were arranged to Murmansk. But slithering over fifteen miles of icebound, narrow, winding roads, and round precipitous passes with only dim hooded headlights, was nobody's idea of a relaxing evening.

It was about this time that Vic Berg had his prang. When he was well enough to visit in hospital at Murmansk we went in and spent a few moments with him. Vic crashed through his keenness to get airborne when a German reconnaissance Ju 88 arrived to take photos of our airfield. The fitter and rigger ran back and lay over the tail of the Hurricane while Vic taxied out, to prevent it from tipping on its nose on the bumpy snow. But Vic, who wanted to get off without losing a second, opened up his engine the moment his chocks were away and roared out on to the airfield not realising his ground crew were now pinned over the tail by the force of the slipstream.

When the Hurricane reached flying speed and became airborne the weight of the two men dragged the tail down, the nose climbed vertically, then stalled, and the aircraft spun in and cartwheeled as the propeller hit the ground. The unfortunate fitter and rigger were flung high into the air to land 150 yards from the wrecked plane. They were both killed instantly. The plane did not catch fire and Vic was pulled out of the cockpit, the only part of the airframe that remained intact. The wings, engine and rear part of the fuselage were strewn in all directions.

Vic escaped with a broken right thigh and bad head injuries. He had no recollection when he recovered consciousness of how the crash happened. X-rays showed that his thigh had been set badly. It was broken and re-set after he arrived back in England on a cruiser many weeks later. All this, and poor Vic never once fired his guns in anger in Russia.

After Vic's accident there was practically continuous snow during the first week of October. Flying was impossible, so we did not know whether the Ju 88 pilot got his photos or not. On 6 October, the first clear day, we soon found that he had. About mid-morning all hell was let loose as the Russian guns opened fire a mile away along the river bank. For some reason we had received no earlier observer corps warning of the raid. As the barrage went up the Wingco came through on the ops phone and ordered both squadrons to scramble. 'Don't worry about who's with who,' he bellowed. 'Just get the bloody kites off the ground.'

Fourteen Ju 88s were bearing down on our airfield as 24 Hurricanes, taking off from all angles, tore into the air. It was a miracle there were no collisions. Then the bombs came. It was random bombing because the '88s, already split up by the anti-aircraft fire, were now obviously disturbed to see the Hurricanes climbing up to attack.

Bushy and I had been left on standby to keep two spare aircraft at readiness when the others came back to refuel. But the Wingco came through again to cancel this order, and told us to get our two aircraft airborne too, before they were bombed, and to fly a local protective patrol of the aerodrome.

The Ju 88s were still bombing at random as we and our ground crews legged it across the open space to our aircraft. There was no time to fasten parachutes or Sutton harness, and we left our helmets dangling on the reflector sights. My fitter already had my engine going and as he scrambled out of the cockpit I dropped into the seat. The rigger had dived under the airscrew and yanked both chocks away from the wheels. I waved my crew away, but they would have none of it and insisted on guiding me round the bomb craters on to the airfield. So I opened the throttle to full boost and left my loyal fellows standing with bombs dropping all around them giving me a good luck wave and a thumbs-up before they turned and dived for the shelters. Out of the corner of my eye I saw Bushy's plane tearing along fifty yards to the left.

My tail was off the ground and I was gaining speed fast when there came an almightly crump behind me. The blast of a bomb that missed me by feet lifted my tail as if it was a toy plane and I thought I would stand on my nose and then somersault. But the engine kept dragging the nose forward, and I hauled the stick hard back and somehow the tail came down and I had control again. I climbed up and started circling. By now the bombers had left so I stayed on aerodrome patrol. Bushy chased one but it climbed into cloud and soon he returned and tucked his wing behind mine. We pulled faces and made signs to indicate what a near miss it had been. Then we put on our helmets, and plugged in our R/T. Bushy had looked strange flying with his smoothly Brylcreemed dark hair. In due course we managed to fasten our straps but not our parachute harness.

The raid over, and no second wave following, Ops told us to land. The Wingco was already on the phone when I walked into dispersal. 'Thought you'd had it Holmes. You just disappeared in a cloud of earth and snow. I never saw you get airborne.' My ground crew came running in. 'Have you seen your airscrew, sir?' they grinned. I went out with them. The tip of one blade was missing and there were two jagged holes further down. The other two blades were either holed or chipped by bomb fragments. Bushy had a chip out of his bullet proof windscreen from the same bomb, and shrapnel through his fuselage.

Our boys shot down two of the Ju 88s for certain and damaged five others. Our only 'casualty' was Scottie Edmiston. He was taking off during the first flap and the blast of a bomb which landed in front of him stopped his engine. Fuming, he jumped out and stood on the wing yelling to his crew to bring a starter battery across to him. At that instant another bomb exploded and blew him clean off the wing into a deep snowdrift. Fortunately he was quite unhurt, but there was nothing left for him to do now but crawl out of the snow and run like hell for a shelter.

This raid had an interesting sequel. The German crew on one of the shot down Ju 88s were captured actually on our airfield, and questioned by our German-speaking intelligence officer. They spoke frankly, preferring to talk to the English rather than be handed over to the Russians for more 'rigorous' questioning. They said they had known for a month that we were at Murmansk. Their squadron had been brought from Norway specially to bomb us and our Hurricanes. They never came back a second time.

This was the classic occasion on which Mickey Rook was separated from the rest of 81 Squadron while chasing two Ju 88s. Returning to base, he was glad to spot what he thought were six of 134 Squadron. When he called up their leader to say he was joining up with them, the only response he received was for the leader to go into a steep turn towards him, his cannons blazing.

They were not 134 Squadron but six Me 109s.

There followed a colossal shambles, in which Messerschmitts all got in each other's way trying to take a shot at Mickey. He bagged one — confirmed later by the Russian observer corps — before he gained cloud cover and returned home with several bullet holes in 'Z' to bear out his story.

As a happy finale my ground crew were Mentioned in Despatches for their devotion to duty (and to me) by leading my aircraft out on to the aerodrome during the bombing raid.

On 16 September, when the Wing was doing far better than anyone ever hoped, with the score at 7-1 in our favour, signals had been exchanged between the Chief of the British Air Staff and the Head of the Soviet Navy, under whose command the Wing came while in Russia. Their messages were published simultaneously in newspapers in Britain and Russia, revealing for the first time that the RAF had not only arrived but was actually operating at Murmansk.

The signal from Air Chief Marshal Sir Charles Portal, Chief of the British Air Staff, to Admiral Kuznetsov, Head of the Soviet Navy and Naval Air Service, read:

'First operations by No 151 Wing, Royal Air Force, Murmansk. British Air Squadrons have arrived in the USSR and are now operating from Soviet territory against the common enemy.

'On this first and memorable occasion of our two Air Forces fighting side by side on Russian soil, I send you the warmest congratulations of all ranks of the Royal Air Force on the skilful and heroic resistance maintained by the Soviet Air Force against the German invaders.

'Permit me to express the confident hope that this may prove the beginning of ever wider and closer collaboration between our two Air Forces, each of which is already straining to the utmost to hasten the final defeat and collapse of the Nazi aggressors!'

Admiral Kuznetsov's reply read:

'Dear Air Chief Marshal,

'I am happy to confirm receipt of your telegram on the occasion of the first RAF operations at Murmansk.

'These operations are the very real expression of the inflexible will of the two great freedom-loving nations who have mobilised their armed and economic might for a decisive and merciless fight against the German invaders.

'I am sincerely happy at the fact that the lucky chance of beginning operations against the common enemy side by side with the RAF on an important part of the Front has fallen to the Air Force of the Soviet Navy.

'I take this opportunity of expressing to you, Air Chief Marshal of the Royal Air Force, my sincere regards and respects, N. Kuznetsov, Admiral, People's Commissar for the Navy, September 16, 1941.

The text of these two signals was transmitted from London to Vayanga aerodrome, where they were displayed on the Wing's notice board. I made copies for my diary and this is why I can produce them today. We felt pleased, and a little proud, that the head boys of the two outfits felt this way. Suddenly all that sea, and all this snow, and being thousands of miles from home, seemed worth it.

As the month of September passed, we became more accustomed to our new mode of life. Daylight hours were shortening rapidly. Dusk was now descending in mid-afternoon and we could watch the Northern Lights like searchlight beams criss-crossing in the sky over the North Pole.

The weather was now two extremes. It was either beautiful or foul. On a good day diamonds glistened everywhere as the dazzling sun reflected from crisp, hard snow. On such days in October only a quarter of a blood-red sun, rising at 11 am, would peep over the horizon at noon. By one o'clock it had gone again and evening had arrived.

Our flying operations were now drastically reduced with no night aids at Vayanga for homing after dark. But anyone caught up at dusk after a long patrol had little difficulty finding his way back to base because it lay in a bend of the river which stood out black against the white countryside.

When the weather clamped, heavy snow clouds rolled across the landscape and emptied themselves. Visibility came down to a few feet, and in a couple of hours another three or four inch blanket covered the ground and piled a layer of snow on to already overloaded silver birch trees.

In one such blizzard Wing Commander Isherwood invited me to climb with him to the top of the hill above the Wing operations room. We shared the rugger man's yearning for exercise. We set off, heads down against the driving snow. It was impossible to see the summit so we just kept climbing. At times we sank up to our armpits

INSTRUCTIONS

(1) Learn by heart the Russian phrase "Ya Anglicháhnin" (means "I am English" and is pronounced as spelt).

(2) Carry this folder and contents in left breast pocket.

(3) If you have time before contact with Russian troops, take out the folder and attach it (flag side outwards) to front of pocket.

(4) When spotted by Russian troops put up your hands holding the flag in one of them and call out the phrase "Ya Anglicháhnin."

(5) If you are spotted before taking action as at para 3 do NOT attempt to extract folder or flag. Put up your hands and call out phrase "Ya Anglicháhnin". The folder will be found when you are searched.

(6) You must understand that these recognition aids CANNOT be accepted by Soviet troops as proof of bona fides as they may be copied by the enemy. They should however protect you until you are cross questioned by competent officers.

Я англичанин

"Ya Anglicháhnin" (Pronounced as spelt)

Пожалуйста сообщите сведения обо мне в Британскую Военную Миссию в Москве

Please communicate my particulars to British Military Mission Moscow.

The silk identity Union Jack all RAF pilots carried for recognition by Soviet troops — to distinguish us from Germans if shot down.

Careless talk costs lives.

in snowdrifts, and though our breath turned our eyebrows to icicles, the exertion in the dry cold kept us pleasantly warm.

Near the top the cloud suddenly cleared and the snow stopped. As our goal stood out stark against the sky we began to race. Neither would yield, and it became an honourable dead-heat as we set foot simultaneously on the pinnacle. Then we flopped down on the dry snow, panting.

The spectacle from here was breathtaking. Hills rolled in all directions. The flat airfield far below could have been a frozen lake. To the west flowed the River Tulmola, ice free thanks to the Gulf Stream. To the north, black as doom, lay the cheerless and cruelly cold Arctic Ocean.

We had an extra round of toast each and a steaming glass of lemon tea when we arrived back at dispersal and the comfort of the wood-burning stove. Its chimney inside the hut was kept glowing a dull red from an endless supply of pine and birch logs.

About now we started combining our operational sorties with training sessions for the Russian pilots. We each had our own pupil, who would in due course take over our aircraft. Mine was Kapitan Markavitch. He would turn up with his interpreter, ask for me, salute smartly, and greet me through his interpreter. We then went through the usual formality of shaking hands, and got down to work.

He was an extremely experienced pilot, keen to learn. We read the Hurricane handling notes, of which he had his own translation, and discussed the controls, the instruments, and the handling characteristics of the aircraft. He got in and started up, taxied, braked, switched off.

On his fourth day he had a last check on the cockpit drill for take-off, the climbing, approach and stalling speeds, and the engine boosts. Then he plugged in his R/T jack, called Control for permission to take off, and was away. I was proud to see this handsome Russian flying my Hurricane. He circled the aerodrome twice, made a superb landing, and taxied over to me to give a delighted thumbs-up before turning and making for the Russian hangar. There the RAF roundel would be obliterated and a Russian star painted in.

Suddenly, I was a pilot without an aeroplane.

Later all our aircraft were returned to us after their stars had been painted on the fuselage. We were to continue escorting the Stormovik bombers on their raids until their own fighter pilots were trained to operational standard.

Just about now we had another spell of bad weather. The Russian Met men were very reliable with their forecasts because of the weather station at Spitzbergen, halfway to the North Pole. They knew the sky would be laden with snow for some days so the Russian pilots invited our two squadrons to a party at their Mess. Flight Lieutenant Hodson, our advisor on all things Russian, gave us a fatherly talk on the vagaries of vodka. But to no avail. The Russians have their own way of drinking a toast. They put one inch of neat vodka in a tumbler, click their heels, raise the glass to you with the greeting 'Zastarovia', swallow the vodka in one, and replenish the glass. If you sip your vodka, or even only half-drink it you are a cissie and they are offended, and walk away.

This is all right the first time or two. But when the beginning and the end of each conversation with any Russian pilot is 'Messer-schmitts!' — followed by drawing the forefinger across the throat with a slitting action, and spitting on the floor — it is hard to avoid spending a sociable evening drinking toasts in vodka.

Despite the stern warnings of our well-meaning and well-informed Hodson, casualties became very heavy indeed, the delayed action of real Russian vodka being almost lethal. Those who managed to slip away early crawled back through the snow to our own Mess with nothing worse than a blinding headache, and a hobnailed liver. But many were carried back bodily by the gleeful, and none too gentle Russians. One of our admin officers in a paralytic coma swallowed his tongue, and would have died had our MO, Squadron Leader Jackson, not fortunately been at hand to save him from choking by fishing it out with forceps.

This was not the end of the social scene, although we readily conceded that at this point it was without doubt one-nil to the Russians. The weather, we were assured, would stay bad, so we invited them next to our Mess. The visitors arrived in full regalia in a motorcoach which had an entrance each side at the front. It soon became apparent they had been warned that our Scotch whisky would be quite safe to drink provided they diluted it with plenty of water.

At their request, water jugs were placed on all our ante-room tables. With each double whisky they were handed, they slurped the glass half full of water. It looked like being a rather dull evening until some joker had the bright idea of refilling all the water jugs with gin. When the Russians started topping up their whisky with gin, the party immediately livened up. By the end of the evening, when they were leaving we had a great game pushing them into their bus at one side, and catching them as they fell right through, and out the other. Then we carried them round the front of the bus and pushed them in again. This game went on for quite some time, the funniest part being that our guests seemed to be enjoying it every bit as much as we were.

We decided this levelled the score.

There was a night bomber raid on Vayanga 48 hours later. Most of the 1,000 lb bombs they dropped failed to explode. The Russians informed us these had been made for the Germans by Polish prisoners who had sabotaged the detonators. At an RAF aerodrome an unexploded bomb is treated with great respect in case it decides to go off. The crater is cordoned off, and traffic diverted for fear vibration may trigger the mechanism. Then the bomb disposal experts arrive with stethoscopes and sensitive instruments and dismantle the monster.

At Vayanga half a dozen soldiers with shovels arrived in the back of a lorry, jumped off, and started digging. When they reached a bomb, they fastened a chain round it and winched it on to their lorry. They drove it to a lake about a mile away winched it off again and lowered it down to the ice. Then they retired to the other side of the lake and from behind sandbags exploded the bomb by machine-gun fire.

We asked the Russian officer in charge of the bomb disposal party whether he was not afraid his men might be killed. We would never be allowed to risk a man's life like this in England, we told him. 'Not at all,' he laughed. 'If they were in the front line fighting, they may be killed at any minute. They are lucky only to take the one small risk of the bomb going off and killing them.'

These soldiers dug up eight unexploded bombs on and around our airfield. At intervals we heard the stutter of a machine-gun, then the crump as each bomb exploded by the lake. Not one soldier was injured. We decided that if this was the Russian way of fighting a war against the Germans, they were going to win it.

One by one the Russian pilots soloed on Hurricanes. They had posted some of their most experienced fliers to Murmansk to form the nucleus of the first Soviet Hurricane squadrons, and these boys were not slow to tell us how good they were. They had been flying their Ilyushin I-16 a sturdy, stubby-winged monoplane, which they assured us was very difficult to fly. A pilot who could fly one of these, they claimed, could fly anything.

We assured them that the Hurricanes had no vice, and that any fool could fly them. After they had bent one or two Hurricanes, by heavy landings, and we had reminded them that 'only the best pilots can fly the I-16,' our message went home, and they started to take more notice of what we told them.

As this was something of an historic occasion the Russian Air-Officer-Commanding, Major General Kuznetsov, a pilot with thousands of flying hours in his logbook, flew the first Hurricane. The next was Kapitan Safonov, who was already credited with twelve victories and held the Russian equivalent of our VC, 'Hero of the Soviet Union'.

Our Hurricanes together with more already arriving in later convoys became a Wing of three Soviet Squadrons, Safonov, promoted to Lieutenant Colonel, being their Wing Commander.

One of their pilots, Kapitan Raputsokov, was made an honorary member of 134 RAF Squadron with the permission of Major General Kuznetsov. It was hoped that he would fly with the squadron on an operational mission. But before he could do so he was killed bringing home a Russian bomber hit by German ack-ack. He and his crew all died when they crashed near Vayanga aerodrome.

One of their pilots who commanded a Russian Hurricane Squadron was killed before we left. Kapitan Yakobenko took off one night with another squadron commander, Kapitan Kuharienko, in two Hurricanes to do a low-level shoot-up of Petsamo. But only Kuharienko returned, reporting that his companion had been shot down by ack-ack.

Day by day we handed over more of our equipment to the Russians. The agreement was that we were to leave them everything and take nothing home but our personal belongings. Lorries, petrol tankers, vans disappeared. Flying helmets, goggles, headphones and Mae Wests went too. We were allowed to keep our wool-lined flying boots for warmth, indicating that we were not German spies. We also kept as identification a folded Union Jack in a plastic holder which we always carried when flying to whip out and wave if we were shot down and had to make our way back through the Russian lines. The flag also had printed on it in bold letters, 'Ja Anglichani' — 'I am English'.

One of the items the Russians did not get was our whisky. Because beer is too bulky and heavy, spirits had been brought on the convoy for the troops. We had so many cases of whisky that a heavy wire netting cage was specially built to store it. An RAF Corporal and two of his cronies picked the locks one night, cleared out all the whisky, and hid it in the hills. The Russians caught them, and slung them into a local gaol. Our Wing Commander demanded their return to our unit, to be disciplined by the RAF, but this was one of the few favours the Russians refused. They maintained the men had committed a crime against the USSR by stealing Russian whisky. The last we heard was that they had gone to the salt mines in Siberia.

As our equipment became more depleted, and our presence less necessary, one query only was on everyone's lips. 'When are we going home?' Our job was done. Why were we still here?

On 10 October the great news came through that we must be prepared to leave for home on 25 October. Two days later, at a party celebrating Micky Rook's birthday, the Wing Commander breezed in and read out a cable he had just received from Air Ministry. It said '151 Wing to prepare to move south through Russia to the Middle East'.

Never did a birthday party become such a flop. Several guests retired to bed that night, very, very drunk. Here was the end of everything. We had endured the cold, the snow, the discomfort, the food — for what! To be sent somewhere at the back of beyond and probably to stay there for the duration of the war. Sickening thought.

Despair hung in a black cloud over the Wing after the promises we had been given of an early return to England.

It was the Russians who came to our rescue. They reckoned it would take the Wing four months to travel the 3,000 miles south through Russia and across the Caspian Sea. They said they could not provide us with the forty tons of rations required to feed 550 men for four months. Most important of all they did not want us travelling across all their lines of communication to the battle front.

I quote my diary written at that time: '20 October — There seems to be a remote chance now that we may not after all be going to the Middle East. There is still no sign though, that we will instead return home.

'26 October — This awful uncertainty persists. No aircraft now. Nothing to do but debate our fate. Maybe they'll send us to Moscow to operate there. Maybe the convoy route back across the Arctic has become too dangerous and they don't want to lose us! Maybe after all the publicity about the Wing in Murmansk they are afraid our return home would look like an evacuation, and the Hun will be saying he's kicked us out.

'There are whispers that the Wingco is sending rude messages back to Air Ministry, becoming ruder each day. We now go long walks in the snow to pass the time. We were enjoying the skiing, but that is finished because we have broken all the skis. Today we started a five rouble sweep on the date for leaving Murmansk for — anywhere!

'8 November. Still killing time. The boredom is killing us. Now seems possible we will stay here for the winter, and start operating here again next spring. Some suggest we may even go through Vladivostok to the *Far* East.

'Tonight the first mail since we left home has arrived. Twelve bags of it! First for three months. I had 24 letters. They took a day to read, and three days to answer. My replies went by submarine, for posting in England.'

One of the reasons the Russians fought in the air as individuals rather than as a team was that their pilots were awarded 1,000 roubles (about £20) for each enemy aircraft they shot down. Word came through from the Soviet authorities that this award was being extended to British pilots. The Wing Commander refused to allow us to accept the money individually and ruled that as the Wing had shot down fifteen, the 15,000 roubles — £300 — should go to the RAF Benevolent Fund.

About this time morale was sagging at the prospect of never seeing England again. Probably the weather was mainly responsible, but our return home date had been put back so often we felt like the donkey must have felt chasing his carrot. To cheer people up, the Sergeant Pilots decided to stage a variety show in their Mess. They constructed a stage, with curtains, and scenery. They scripted it themselves — uncensored, of course! It was a revelation to find the musical talent that emerged from ordinary day-to-day RAF blokes.

Wag was the Star. He could sit at a piano and charm anything from boogie-woogie to the classics from the keys with never a sheet of music. If anyone produced a lyric, Wag turned out the tune. The songs, or course, included rude references to all the personalities of the Wing, from the Wingco downwards. The rudest were to Air Ministry and their reluctance to let us go home. No-one escaped, and the sharper the barb the more enthusiastic the applause.

The favourite ran to over a dozen verses. It was sung by Sergeants Vic Reid, 'Avro' Anson and IBN Waud, accompanied by piano, trumpet and drums (all provided by the Russians). Entitled 'Hardships', it was really an ode to our more fortunate brethren still in the UK.

'9 November. The Russian General has presented the Wingco with a three-month old reindeer. Routine Orders posted today ask for any volunteer with experience of rearing reindeer — Father Christmas need not apply.

'12 November — Five more bags of mail arrived. They went to Moscow from Archangel instead of Murmansk.

'The Wingco has just come in and asked Bushy and myself if we want to go home! It is 9.45 am. We are to have our kit packed by 11 am and be ready to leave with a party of airmen. We are all packed and standing there waiting by 10 am. Two days later we are still waiting. Then told to forget it.

'16 November — Party of seven officers and sixty men as advance party today boarded HM minesweepers *Speedy, Gossamer* and *Hussar* at Rossta, the port near Vayanga. We lay at anchor that night and next day in the bay off Murmansk. I was on *Speedy,* with Bushy and eighteen men. We were told that we would sail round the peninsula and join a convoy preparing to leave from Archangel. The rest of the Wing were going home in two destroyers and a cruiser from Murmansk.

'Half way to Archangel our trio of minesweepers received orders to turn north to meet an incoming convoy and escort them back through the Russian minefields into Archangel. We met the convoy at latitude 76 on 22 November, in an Arctic gale.'

To be in a minesweeper in such seas is nobody's idea of comfort. Your chair slithered across the saloon deck while you sat in it. The plates would not stay on the table unless they were secured in box-like compartments. It was impossible to play a gramophone record. Drawers flew open, emptied their contents on the floor then, when the ship rolled the other way, slammed shut again. The revving of the screw when the stern came clear of the water threatened to shake the entire craft to pieces. And the smack as the keel flopped down on the waves again must, you fear, snap the vessel in two.

That four days gale seemed like four years.

Twenty miles from the mouth of the River Dvina heading into Archangel we met the ice. The river itself was frozen solid, but around the estuary it was mush ice, which was like frozen snow floating around in chunks, not solid enough to stop a ship. At the start of the icefield we dropped anchor. At 3.30 am we climbed down a ladder, walked across the ice from our minesweeper and boarded a Russian icebreaker which was to crush its way twenty miles to the convoy.

The procedure was for the icebreaker, which was named *Lenin*, to reverse a couple of hundred yards, then drive forward under full power at the six-foot-thick layer of ice. The bows were wide and flat like a toboggan so that the front of the *Lenin* rode high up on to the ice. There it would remain poised until under the sheer weight of the vessel, the ice would crack with an ominous rumbling. Then it would break and the *Lenin* would plunge with a sickening lurch through the ice crust into the water.

And back we'd go for another run. This went on for two days and nights, before we reached the convoy.

The icebreaker had no accommodation for us. We slept on the bare floors, taking turns to sit on the dining chairs, and sleep sprawled across the table, head on arms. The heat on this ship was unbearable for the Russians certainly know how to fight the cold. Consequently the panels in the walls had warped with the dry air and cockroaches crawled in and out of the cracks. These loathsome insects left us with bumps and bleeding. The food was cabbage soup, black bread and tea without milk.

A brass plate screwed high on the saloon bulkhead read: 'Built by Cammell Laird and Co Ltd., Birkenhead, England'. That shipyard was scarcely a stone's throw from my home, and before the war I attended all their launches as representative of *Lloyds List* newspaper — including that of the *Lenin*.

I was tempted to scratch on the wood beneath the plate: 'Reunited'.

'The river, a mile wide where our convoy is moored, presents a remarkable spectacle. It has now become a regular highway for traffic from one side to the other. Troops march across. Horses, probably with spiked hooves, pull sledges as big as lorries, laden with provisions, equipment and people. At night powerful searchlights are switched on to the wail of high-powered generators, and the activity continues. Parties of engineers are laying twenty miles of railway line up the frozen river for cargo to be unloaded direct from the ships on to trains to save the time of icebreakers smashing a route for them up to the landing stage.

'Our berths are already allocated for us when we reach the convoy. The organisation has been immaculate.'

12

Homeward Bound

'The airmen all went on a troopship and the officers were spread over a number of cargo ships. Bushy and myself were allocated to the Harrison Liner *Harpalion*, and the first mate had kindly vacated his cabin on the bridge for us. We were next door to the master, Captain Thomas, who was a rugged, gentle, genial Welsh giant. We felt that under his command no ship dare sink.

'Our quarters were most comfortable. Twin bunks with blankets and sheets against one wall, and a separate bathroom and shower. We and a Naval Lieutenant Commander who has a cabin further along the bridge, share the Captain's saloon.

'Captain Thomas tells us our ship has taken on a cargo of manganese ore at Archangel. This he assures us will have us swinging like a pendulum if we strike heavy seas. He was right.

'25 November — This is the first day after my first night on an English merchantman. I feel for the first time in three and a half months that I am really going home. The ship has an atmosphere of England about it. Being a cargo ship it is enormous, yet with no passenger accommodation. Our quarters are quite luxurious. The Captain's saloon has oak-panelled walls, plush couches, and tasteful furnishings. Indoors we are warm and comfortable. Outside our ship's hull is locked solid in six feet of ice. Our decks are deep in snow. Icicles festoon our rigging. Every water supply on the ship is frozen solid.

'Yet even in these truly Arctic conditions we get hints of home. Captain Thomas talks about Cardiff, and the nearby village where he lives. He knows Fairwood Common aerodrome well. A clock on his saloon mantelpiece has the maker's name Kelvin and Baird Ltd, Glasgow, on its face. Beside it a large glass ashtray proclaims the excellence of 'Lockside Ales' — probably won in a Glasgow pub, when our skipper called as a young midshipman.

'Beneath the mantelpiece is the most homely thing of all, a brightly flickering genuine coal fire, in a wrought iron grate, with coffee coloured tile surround and an oaken overmantel that would have graced any English dining room.

'This, then was our last billet before England. Not bad, provided we could break free of the grip of this ice, stay afloat for three weeks defying the rigours of mid-winter Arctic gales, and dodge bombs from above and torpedoes from below.

'26 November. Early this morning the *Lenin* gnawed her way through the ice and came alongside *Harpalion* to break us loose from our captive cradle. She worked around us until slabs of ice the size of tennis courts floated free, threatening to stave in the side of our ship when they drifted back against our hull.

'At ten minutes past noon our engines without warning throbbed into life. *Harpalion* trembled, sharing our excitement.

' "We're bloody well off," shouted Bushy, thumping one fur-gloved fist on the bridge rail and wiping an icicle off the end of his nose with his other. We weren't, of course, but it was a start. *Lenin* was making a channel linking all the boats in the convoy. As they were freed, their skippers started manoeuvring their ships up and down the channel before it froze solid again.

'At last they were all released from the grip of the ice. With *Lenin* in the lead charging up on to the ice, waiting while it crashed through, then backing for another onslaught, the line of merchant-men started their twenty-mile crawl to the open sea.

'We were fascinated to find that our convoy's departure did not in any way deter the Russians from crossing the river in pursuance of their duties. So quickly did the broken ice freeze again after a ship had passed that it would easily bear a man's weight before the next, a hundred yards behind, arrived.

'One poor chap, a bit too keen to cross, slipped on some slabs of ice which had not properly joined up, and he toppled into the water. Our crew threw ropes down, and soldiers on the ice fished him out and tied the ropes round him, but when he was hoisted on to our deck his body came up as stiff and as straight as a log, frozen solid.

They lowered the corpse back down again without even attempting to revive him.

'Other merchantmen from our convoy, moored further up river, had been broken free by two other icebreakers, which had also been using depth charges to blast a path in mid-river. These ships joined our channel and quite soon we were all heading slowly in single file towards the estuary. Twenty-four hours later, averaging a mile per hour, we were with our naval escort. Our icebreakers took back a newly arrived convoy.

'The Russians, even working at a temperature 46°F below freezing, were, we acknowledged, hot-stuff organisers.

'As the merchant ships manoeuvred to take station with their naval escort, a most impressive spectacle met our eyes. From over the Kola peninsula, silently climbing into the sky, came a squadron of Hurricanes. They were in beautiful battle formation, and heading for our convoy. Our Russian counterparts, as a goodwill gesture and a farewell tribute, were giving us a protective convoy patrol away from their country.

'Bushy and I could imagine Safonov's broad grin of silver-coated teeth as he led his fighter pilots towards us in their new Angleeski Hurricanes.

'All twelve waggled their wings in salute as they crossed the convoy, before breaking up into two flights of six to make separate patrols, one encircling the convoy and the other flying up and down the coast ready to intercept any raiders approaching from the battle zone. They stayed with us until we were well out of sight of land and their fuel was running low. Then Safonov must have called up the other flight to rejoin him for they came speeding in from the coast and the twelve re-formed as a squadron. Immediately they went into 504's "Hendon formaggers" — the formation we used in the Battle of Britain when we flew as a box in six pairs, and which we had taught the Russians.

'Through the powerful binoculars Captain Thomas passed to me I could plainly pick out my aeroplane "B", leading the second flight, and visualised Kapitan Markavitch sitting proudly at the controls. They made a long, low, sweeping salute over the middle of the convoy, climbed steeply and broke into feathers, re-formed as two flights and set course back for their base.

'Nobody ever said "Goodbye, and thank you", quite so courteously or so touchingly. We waved from the bridge: "Dos vudanye".

'*Harpalion* was the slowest ship, wallowing under the weight of its manganese ore cargo, and the others had to hold back to our speed. After 24 hours we have averaged 7½ knots. Captain Thomas told us our escort was being increased, and Bushy and I were quite amazed shortly afterwards to see plumes of smoke over the horizon ahead gradually materialise into two destroyers and a cruiser. Captain Thomas brought us a signal he had just received from the Commodore of the convoy saying 400 officers and men of 151 Wing were in the cruiser, and seventy more in each destroyer.

'The skipper says if we maintain 7½ knots throughout the voyage, we'll reach Kirkwall, at Scapa Flow in fourteen days. Better than we had hoped.

'29 November. *Harpalion* is proving not quite the luxury hotel we had expected. There is absolutely nowhere to exercise. Being a cargo ship she has no decks, and apart from one portion set aside for crew's accommodation the entire hull is devoted to cargo holds. The hatches, or lids, of the holds are surrounded by winches and wire hawsers so, although the vessel is very long, there are no flat surfaces suitable for walking.

'All that is left is the bridge, ten paces from port to starboard. I have to cross the bridge 176 times to walk a mile. With time spent turning at each end this takes nearly an hour. I make sure I do a military marching about-turn with knees well up to get the best benefit from the exercise. It is very boring because the view never changes — just our little huddle of ships plodding manfully through mile upon mile of black heaving ocean under a leaden sky.

'Now we are so far north that being mid-winter, it is continual night. We try to pass the time studying the stars which we are going to have with us incessantly for the next ten days and nights. The North Star no longer points to the North Pole, for we are almost there already, and the only way to follow it would be vertically upwards. I fished out my pocket compass to see how it sought magnetic north in these latitudes, but the ship's degaussing cable wound round our ship to neutralise magnetic mines screened my compass completely, and the needle just spun aimlessly.

'Our old friend the Plough, is still with us, and Orion's belt and his sword are just peeping over the southern horizon.

'Although the skies are now clear we are meeting very heavy weather indeed. *Harpalion* is plodding manfully along in the teeth of a fierce nor-easter gale. Despite her bulk, and her heavy cargo, she is bucking like a broncho. Waves wash over her bows and eddy between her hatch covers, frothing and swirling around the winches and derricks. Just as the little minesweepers did, her stern lifts clear of the water for her enormous twin screws to race, fit to fly off their shafts. The ship shudders violently each time the engines race, and groans as they slow to normal revs again.

'Our forward speed has dropped to 3½ knots in the gale. We covered only 81 miles in the last 24 hours. At this rate we'll be lucky to be home by Christmas — if at all!

'Today the cruiser flashed this signal across to us: "All personnel are to be warned that the Air Ministry consider it essential not, repeat not, to disclose in the UK that 151 Wing or its component squadrons are being withdrawn from Russia".

'This is obviously to prevent Lord Haw Haw from gloating over the radio that the Huns have kicked us out.

'Today the naval Lieutenant Commander who has been saying this weather is not bad and has been boasting about the really bad weather he has experienced while serving on trawlers has remained in his cabin, refusing all offers of food from the stewards. I don't think we'll get any more talk like that from him.

'The weather is actually getting worse. Twice while writing this in my diary I was thrown over the back of my chair. Each time I slithered on my back with the chair across the saloon floor and out through the open door, finishing in a heap at the foot of the stairs. All doors, including cabins, have to be hooked open at all times in case a torpedo hits the ship, warps the hull and wedges the door fast shut, making escape impossible. Playing cards won't stay on the table. Food won't stay on the plate. Sleep is impossible with the noise of the crashing waves, the howling wind, and the creaking hull.

'Suitcases, and loose items like shoes chase each other with the rugs around the floor. Coats swing to almost ninety degrees from the walls, and fly off the hooks and join in the shambles. Books topple over the ledges specially designed to hold them on the shelves. Drawers shoot out of the dressing table. We leave everything on the floor until the sea gets calmer.

'Our sitting room fire had to be doused in case the hot coals fell out on to the floor. The downdraught in the chimney three times showered the room with soot. A sooty saloon, with no fire and a temperature well below freezing, is a cheerless place. For the next two days Bushy and I stayed in our cabin where at least we had a radiator.

★   ★   ★

'1 December. Today we reached our most northerly latitude — 75 degrees — and turned west. We will be on this line for eight or nine days, or longer if we are delayed. At noon there is a trace of light for an hour that just enables us to make out the shadowy outline of the nearest ships. How the helmsmen manage to keep station in these conditions I cannot imagine, because the ever-present danger of submarines rules out the use of navigation lights.

'One quickly becomes time disorientated in perpetual darkness. You feel like a prisoner in a sealed cell. It is strange having to consult your watch to remind you whether the next meal is lunch or tea, or if there will be another meal before bed.

'This evening we had our first submarine scare. If we are torpedoed it will be impossible to launch boats in these seas. We have been in dangerous waters for some days now, since we have been sailing round the top of Norway, about 300 miles distant. Suddenly about 7 pm as I was writing this diary on my knee, there was a deafening roar. It felt as if our ship had been ripped open from stem to stern. I waited to see whether she would list to port or starboard, ready to climb up the side with the air bubble. Bushy came rushing in yelling "What the hell was that?".

'We ran out on to the bridge. The crew was collecting at action stations. The skipper told us there was a German sub around — which seemed pretty obvious — and that the explosion was a depth charge a destroyer had put down. At that moment there was another crump and a volcano of water erupted in the middle of the convoy. If the sub was there he must have been lying in wait for us right in our path.

'As we hurried indoors for our life jackets and warmest clothing a third depth charge exploded. We snatched up small personal items and stuffed them into our pockets, and ran out on to the bridge again. Four more explosions seemed to come from almost under our bows, but *Harpalion*'s Chief Officer assured us they were two or three miles away. That's not far when you're about a thousand miles from port.

'The convoy was now zig-zagging violently, each ship taking its own evasive action.

'We cursed the almost full moon which chose that moment to emerge from a bank of cloud into clear sky. The sea turned silver and the dark shadow of the ships stood out as sharp silhouettes. Ideal for subs. The sea looked angry, icy and uninviting.

'Five more depth charges exploded in rapid succession.

'The suspense, waiting for our ship to be suddenly split in two and blown up in a mountain of flame, was chilling. After half an hour, when nothing happened, and we were frozen to the marrow, we went into the mate's cabin. The three ship's officers there were all members of "The Raft Club" — for torpedoed sailors. We had no desire to join it. Of all topics, they chose to talk of sinkings at sea.

'They described how sudden it all was; what a small percentage of crew survived when a ship went down; how it was sheer luck if you were saved — like being sucked down a funnel and being blown out, or being caught in an air bubble inside an overturned lifeboat; how a torpedo in the right spot could down a ship our size in twenty seconds; how the first thing that happened was that the lights fused and pumps failed; then the ship rolled to such an angle that it was impossible to launch boats from either side. The steam radiators would burst and scald you; the open doors would slam shut with the blast and trap you like a rat in your cabin.

'After an hour of pretending we were not frightened, the chief steward brought us all cocoa and informed us that we were back on normal course again. Captain Thomas judged it almost certain the sub had been sunk. The depth charges had stopped when the soundings stopped. My thoughts turned to the brave men in the sub, German or not. If we had been scared in the comfort of our cabin, how must they have fared under fifty feet of water in a tin box that is suddenly split apart. But it was them or us. This was what war was all about.

'Bushy and I went back to our cabin, fished out the bottle of Gordon's Gin that Captain Thomas had sold us and drank the squadron toast "Here's to the next man to die". We began to feel better. Captain Thomas looked in last thing and dampened our spirits by advising us to sleep in our clothes, with our life jackets and a torch handy, and be sure the door was wedged hard open.

'I had one of my best nights yet. It was probably reaction after what did not happen, and resignation that there was nothing we could do if it did. We slept in our clothes for the next fortnight. There was unlimited hot water, so we took turns to read for an hour in the bath during the day with water up to our chin. Only trouble about this was that the swirling bath water tended to make you seasick.

'2 December. We knocked an hour off our clocks today. Did that make our journey an hour longer? Another strong headwind was knocking our speed down again. Do I wish I was back on firm ground in Murmansk or would I rather be here, half way home?

'9 pm. Just visited the chart room. We're making better progress than I expected. Did 140 miles today, despite the weather. We are near Bear Island, slightly south of it, and just under 1,000 miles from Kirkwall. We are slowing down to give two Russian ships who separated from us during the submarine panic the chance to rejoin us.

'3 December. More excitement. We are being shadowed either by German submarines, or a German raider, or both. At 10.30 am, still on course and in complete darkness, there was a distant wailing of foghorns. Long, shrill, moaning blasts. I was on the bridge at the time with Captain Thomas and the Chief Officer. As we watched, a green rocket went up from the Commodore's ship — signal for the convoy to alter course 45 degrees and start zigzagging.

'This obviously meant more submarines!

'I strolled to the other end of the bridge, and joined Bushy. "More of the dreaded torpedoes," he quipped, giving the recognised mouth twitch adopted by 504 in times of danger.

' "Keep your revolver handy," I told him. "You may be the first man to get a gong for shooting down a submarine."

'He grabbed my arm. He was in earnest now, and pointing. "Quick, the Commodore's signalling to *Harpalion*. What's he saying?" He fished in his pocket for a pencil and an envelope, and as I shouted out the letters being flashed across the water, he jotted them down.

' "All ships disperse, and proceed independently to destination", was the order that came across. The Captain had read it at the same time and he immediately gave full speed ahead on the telegraph. As the message was acknowledged from the engine room, revs started to build up. Soon the *Harpalion* was creaking and groaning, bursting her seams to push up her speed to 10½ knots. She shook so much I could hardly write. In the midday gloom the convoy was already breaking its tidy formation and spreading out. Ships were scurrying towards distant horizons. In a few minutes the dispersal was complete. Everyone had gone. We were on our own in the Arctic, ready to meet — what!

'Captain Thomas knew exactly what menaced us and explained what it was. A few days earlier the German battleship *Tirpitz* which had been skulking in a Norwegian fjord to hide from our Navy had weighed anchor and slipped out to sea. It was pretty certain she was up here in the Arctic because it was to this precise hunting ground that the other German raider, *Bismarck* came on her maiden wartime trip. The *Tirpitz*, with her deadly armament of 16-inch radar-controlled guns could sink *Harpalion* from twelve miles, without us even being able to see her smoke over the horizon.

'An hour or so after the convoy had dispersed we saw dimly silhouetted against bright cloud the next Murmansk-bound convoy approaching us. We passed within a mile and the only signal exchanged was that the cruiser and two destroyers which had been escorting us had turned to give added protection to the other convoy for the second half of their voyage. These were the naval vessels carrying the rest of 151 Wing. Our boys were on their way back to Russia again. We could imagine their comments having been half-way home.

'5 December — We've had three days and two nights alone in the Arctic since the *Tirpitz* panic. It's been a long time, but she's not found us. Wonder how the rest of the convoy fared? With our engines flat out we should have been making between 240 and 260 miles a day, but headwinds have kept our mileage down to between 140 and 150. I doubt this ship has a sound rivet left. Sleep at nights, with the throbbing engines, the howling wind and our luggage careering around our cabin, is quite impossible. The loneliness is oppressive and depressing. Nothing but water. Never offer me a cruise for my summer holiday.

'We are now 500 miles short of Iceland. It is another 500 miles from Iceland to Scapa. Even the last leg can be dangerous. We're still 1,000 miles short of the UK after nearly three weeks at sea.

'More excitement today. It helps to pass the time. We have edged down to latitude 72 degrees, and are enjoying a little daylight at midday. On the horizon smoke from a large ship has been spotted. Was this *Tirpitz* seeking us out? We waited for flashes of flame from her guns. Captain Thomas ordered smoke floats at the ready to cover our retreat. Not that smoke would fool her radar. But our raider was as worried about us as we were about him, and had already released his smoke floats as he turned away and dived like an arrow out of sight over the horizon.

'Later we saw her again, and identified her as *Hartlebury* who had been in our convoy before it dispersed. She was also bound for Iceland, and like us was feeling very, very lonely. Gradually the two ships edged in closer and we arrived at Iceland together.

'On the way into the fjord we missed by twenty yards a British mine which had broken away from its mooring in a nearby minefield.

'6 December. Having spent my birthday in Iceland on 20 August I am back to spend my Mother's birthday here on 6 December. The sight of any land after so long at sea under such conditions would have been sweet. But Seydisfjordur, with its narrow waterway between craggy precipitous cliffs rising sheer to 3,000 feet, and the rosy tint of the rising sun turning the snow-capped peaks mother of pearl, was a picture I will always remember.

'We dropped anchor at noon. Half an hour later the ship's cat celebrated the occasion by producing seven kittens under the saloon table while we were at lunch. Mother and kittens all doing well. All the ships leaving Murmansk with us are now at Iceland. We, being the slowest, arrived last. *Tirpitz* missed us all.

'Today — Pearl Harbor — that brings the US in. Good show!

'9 December — Left Iceland for Scapa Flow. Escort, two corvettes. Bit of a comedown after the cruisers, destroyers, minesweepers and aircraft carriers of last trip. Let's hope we don't need the heavy gang on this voyage, which should only take three or four days.

'11 December — Making good time, but 150 miles added to the route to avoid our own minefields. Can't grumble about that, I suppose. At midday a Hudson coastal reconnaissance plane turned up and gave us a convoy patrol. First glimpse of Scotland at Cape Wrath. A Liberator relieved the Hudson until after dark.

'12 December — 6 pm. Dropped anchor at Kirkwall. No one allowed ashore. Were able to send telegrams home saying we had arrived, but not where. To our surprise a Customs Officer came aboard to check for smugglers. From Murmansk, indeed! On top of my kitbag, which was packed to go ashore, was a small parcel containing four 36 exposure 35 mm films I had taken in Russia. It was addressed to my brother, a photographic chemist, for processing.

'The Customs Officer asked what the parcel contained and when I told him, he promptly confiscated the films. I stressed how important they were to the Air Ministry as a valuable record of an historic event. He still insisted upon taking them, but promised the films would be returned after censoring, providing they were not harmful to the war effort. I said goodbye to my photos.'

Three months later, after it was officially announced that the RAF Wing had now returned from Russia, I received by registered mail my four films, all fine-grain developed by Kodak, together with a complete set of prints. They were sent with the compliments of the Air Ministry accompanied by a flattering note praising the quality of the photographs, and mentioning that about twenty giant enlargements from my negatives were now included in a 'War in Russia' section at the Imperial War Museum in London.

I never bothered to take the matter up, because I was delighted to hear what had happened to my pictures, but I always thought (and still do) that this raised rather an interesting legal question about copyright.

Harpalion finally took us round to the Firth of Forth, and we disembarked at Leith. This could not have been more convenient as 81 Squadron was re-mustering at RAF Turnhouse, the airport of Edinburgh.

After we had said our farewells (and thanked Captain Thomas very much for having us) he gave us a beautifully coloured poster of a pink parrot, wearing a Nazi hat with a Swastika on the peak listening intently from his perch to a ship on the horizon in the background. Beneath the parrot it said 'Going ashore? Be careful to whom you talk, and what you say. You are in a position of trust. The safety of men's lives — perhaps your own — may depend on how well you can keep what you know to yourself.' In panels underneath, the warning was repeated in four foreign languages.

We arrived at RAF Turnhouse on 18 December, 1941, to marvel at Edinburgh's Forth Bridge spanning a misty skyline barely a stone's throw away.

Forces returning from overseas duty were entitled to extra leave, so for the second successive year by good fortune I enjoyed both Christmas and New Year at home. Early in January, on returning to

Turnhouse in the teeth of a bitter east wind, with even the grass grey, we found 81 Squadron was converting to Spitfires, and that we were posted to RAF Ouston. This, we found, was a modern aerodrome with two good intersecting runways, sited about six miles west along Hadrian's Wall from Newcastle upon Tyne.

We never had a chance to settle at Ouston. Rumours circulated from the start that those longest with the squadron were being rested from ops, and going to other jobs. Some were disappointed, some delighted at the thought of a different life, the rest just couldn't care less. The sum result, however, was unrest.

In the middle of all this, a secret signal came from Norway. The Germans were mounting an immediate low level daylight bombing raid on the Forth Bridge! This tip was taken so seriously that within an hour our twelve new Spitfires, with some very ham-handed pilots at the controls flying them for the first time, landed and refuelled at Turnhouse. We were ready for the raid.

Intelligence reported that Hitler was intending to destroy the bridge to break the rail link into Scotland and delay our army moving north when he revived last summer's plan for glider and parachute landings in Scotland, to march down into England through the back door. It was exciting to be back in the front line once more. Since we handed over our Hurricanes to the Russians at Murmansk, waited for ships to bring us home, spent three weeks in the Arctic getting here, then went on leave, we had quite lost touch with the air war. Now, in an hour, we were suddenly at readiness and raring to go.

The Germans did not make their raid that day. Nor the next. On the third day we had a message from Norway that the raid was temporarily called off through bad weather there. We were sent back to Ouston. The weather must have cleared suddenly in Norway, because a couple of hours after we landed at Ouston the Tannoy called us to action stations. 'Back to Turnhouse, quick!' we were told.

We went through the same performance again, though slightly better this time as we were now more at home flying the Spitfires. But again there was no raid and again, after two days we returned to Ouston. In the meantime a balloon barrage had gone up from ships anchored on the Forth near the Bridge.

When this happened a third time we began to wonder if some joker at the Air Ministry had us on a string. At all events, this time when we arrived back at Ouston our postings were through, and it was farewell to 81 Squadron and Fighter Command.

Most of the fellows were posted to operational training units. There they would lead pupil pilots at the last stage of their training around the sky teaching them formation flying and fighter tactics.

Bushy and self walking across the ice from our ship to board the Russian icebreaker.

Part Six
Instruction

13
Pupils from Canada

Bushy and I were lucky to be posted to No 2 Flying Instructors'
School, at Montrose on the east coast of Scotland, for a ten-week
flying instructor's course. Here the winter was bitterly cold, but the
air was crystal clear most of the time, and ideal for flying.

We were back at school with a vengeance. We soon discovered
that although we had been front-line fighter pilots for eighteen
months, with 400 flying hours on Hurricanes and Spitfires, we still
had plenty to learn about aviation.

To my surprise I found a few familiar faces at Montrose. This was
the first time I had ever arrived at a new station to find someone I
knew. Some of our 'F' Flight instructors from 5 FTS at Sealand, who
had now become very experienced, were on the staff here.

Barny Oldfield, a Flight Sergeant instructor from 'F' Flight, was
now commissioned and a Flying Officer. Pilot Officer Howie
Marcou, the handsome fair-haired Canadian with whom I made a
Pathé film of a fighter-pilot in training at Sealand, was a Flight
Lieutenant, and commanding a twin-engined Oxford flight.

The daily routine was similar to Sealand, with half a day flying
and the other half on lectures. Mainly our lives revolved around the
Flying Instructor's Bible, known as 1732 B, which lays down the
approved patter to accompany each demonstration a flying instructor teaches his pupils, thus ensuring that each pupil pilot works
through the same syllabus to a set pattern.

Learning the patter was hard. Demonstrating the exercise without
the patter took some mastering. But combining the two was the very

devil — you would find yourself sweeping over a boundary fence into a field while you were still talking about positioning yourself for the turn-in at 500 feet for your last final approach.

Most demonstrations started on the lines of: 'Now there are four points we must remember when stalling and spinning an aircraft . . . or doing a roll off the top of a loop . . .' Whether it was a precautionary landing, a forced landing, an engine failure on take-off or whatever, 1732 B always seemed to find four points to be observed if you were to do it properly. Probably it was good pelmanism, knowing you had four pegs on which to hang your hat, but remembering them all in the right order for the different exercises and synchronising them with your demonstration was not easy. This was how we spent ten weeks during March, April and May of 1942.

As we would be instructing on Miles Masters, we had to learn to fly them from the back seat. The rear cockpit hood hinged up to take a position similar to a motor cycle windscreen, and a lever raised the instructor's seat at least a foot to improve his forward visibility through this screen. Above 140 mph the hood would either buckle or blow on to your head, which was extremely painful even when wearing a stout leather helmet. So you lowered your seat, and sank into the depths of the fuselage for all exercises other than taking off and landing. You hoped you had a pupil who kept a good lookout for other aircraft.

It was very cold, very draughty, and very noisy perched up on the back seat. But with two twists of your muffler round your face, and leather gauntlet gloves with silk inner linings, you grew to like it. Soon you could handle the aircraft as well from there as from the front.

Night take-offs and landings from the rear seat were the worst because of the purple flames from the exhausts (never visible in daylight) licking past your face and spoiling your view. For one week we flew right through each night and slept in the day.

During the tenth and last week of the course we had the Chief Flying Instructor's tests. During every spare moment when we were not in the air, we would be reciting the patter and testing each other on the theory behind all the flying manoeuvres in preparation for these tests.

The CFI's test lasted an hour. Even the most experienced suffered from testitis. But somehow all but about three of our course of twenty qualified as day and night flying instructors on single-engined aircraft.

The end of the course was just one more excuse for a party. It was traditional that when each course ended, the course-pilots would invite the staff instructors to a thrash in the private lounge at the Park House Hotel. These invariably finished in the small hours with the shout of 'Bottoms up!' and some unfortunate was selected to have his bare bottom blacked with soot from the hearth after which willing hands hoisted him up face downwards for a cheeky impression to be stamped on the ceiling. Strangely, the hotel rather cherished these mementoes. Often a signatory was honoured with an invitation to ceremoniously append his signature to his very personal work of art.

Before we realised what had happened, our course had ended. On 28 April, 1942 Bushy and I were both posted as flying instructors to RAF Tern Hill, to which I had paid my pre-war visit after forced landing my Moth at Gnosall.

I said my goodbyes to my instructor, Flight Lieutenant Norman Smith, and to Howie Marcou and Barny Oldfield, and to Wing Commander Symondson who said he hoped to see me back on the staff at Montrose when I had had some instructing experience. Although I did not realise it, this had been the second chapter of what was to become a long and close friendship with Howie Marcou, even to the extent of being godfather a year or so later to his daughter Lesley. The friendship was to continue even after the war when he was back as a regular in the Royal Canadian Air Force in Quebec.

Tern Hill was not as I had remembered it.

My last visit there after my forced landing was as a civilian having his first sight of an RAF station. I was overawed then by the spacious landing ground, the giant hangars, and the tarmac roads criss-crossing the camp, linking the airfield with workshops, messes, sleeping quarters and the administrative block. But by now I was accustomed to aerodromes, having landed at 71 different ones, of all shapes and sizes, since I was last at Tern Hill.

It now slotted into place as a superb regular RAF peacetime station, an architect's dream of rosebeds fringing the messes, tidy lawns between the hangars, polished camouflaged cars sweeping back and forth, and no litter.

The extended training programme for pupil pilots arriving in droves from Canada, Rhodesia and the US stretched all the RAF training schools beyond their capacity. Several flights would be dispersed to work from satellite aerodromes a few miles away. Personnel would either live on these satellites, or travel by station transport each day, depending upon distance and the commitments of the MT Section.

Tern Hill's satellites were Calveley to the east, near Nantwich, and Chetwynd, south down the A41 Newport road. Each, with Tern Hill still its parent station, ran as a separate unit.

I was posted to 'D' Flight at Calveley. As the Mess accommodation there was full, I was billeted at Wettenhall Farm, where Joey Dutton and his charming wife Hilda had a pedigree Ayrshire herd. Their farmhouse, about a hundred years old with walls patterned by bricks of different colours, and built to last a thousand years, was on the south-east corner of the airfield, a quarter of a mile from the runway east to west. It was three minutes on a pushbike back into camp to eat and three minutes down the Nantwich-Tarporley road to Flights.

Calveley aerodrome was still under construction. The first runway was finished, and the second was a mess of lorries and bulldozers. Plasterers were working in the flight huts, where our flying kit hung amongst painters' trestles and plasterers' boards. Fortunately it was June so we did not miss the window panes. We and the builders pressed on, each with his own task, and because we shared the same goal there was never any friction.

Bushy came to 'D' Flight too. We had five pupils each. Mine were Sergeants Ralph, Feldman, Daley and Manger, and Pilot Officer Emmett. None had flown Masters yet, having been trained in Canada on Harvards. They did not know this would be the first time I had ever flown with a pupil! From now on, I was responsible not only for their standard of flying, but also for their lives. Each would be modelling his flying for all time on the way I taught him, as I had modelled mine on Douglas Shields'.

So I must be accurate always, aggressive yet confident in handling the aircraft and using the power of the engine to its maximum yet always with smooth restraint. Most important I must get my demonstrations right first time. None of this pretending you'd made a bosh of an exercise on purpose just to show what would go wrong if you did.

The biggest problem for our pupils, we quickly found, was map-reading and navigation. In Canada they flew in clear visibility over wide areas of featureless land apart from a road or a railway line. Probably one, and possibly both, led to the airfield, so they were never lost. But flying over England was a different proposition. The patchwork of fields and the maze or roads, rivers and railways made navigation very difficult, especially when an almost perpetual haze added to their problems.

One of my pupils was determined not to get lost. He was in the front seat, and as soon as we were airborne and climbing he craned round to peer back over the top of my head. A moment later he did this again. The third time I asked him, 'What the hell are you doing, Sergeant Ralph?' He replied, still intent on what he saw behind me, 'I'm just keeping the Wrekin in sight, sir. I don't mean to get lost.' The Wrekin was a prominent hill jutting out of fairly level country-side a few miles south of the airfield, and a valuable landmark.

Back at Montrose, on our Instructors' Course, all our flying had been either with a staff instructor who was drilling you in your 1732 B exercises, or a fellow course-pilot practising the exercises with you. As all the course-pilots were fairly experienced to be selected as flying instructors, there was little danger of an accident through faulty flying. Suddenly to have a raw pupil in the front seat was a new experience. It was now essential to cultivate an accident aware-ness enabling you to go right to the brink of disaster to give him every chance to rectify an error, before taking over at the last moment if he did not.

High up, doing spins or aerobatics, there was no problem. If he got himself in a mess upside down, perhaps in a roll or a loop, and started an inverted dive instead of recovering, then you left him to it. Sooner or later he would sort himself out, and it was far better to leave him to it than let him feel you had saved him from a sticky end by taking over. If he really needed help in such a situation he was probably not good pilot material, and should be scrubbed from the course anyway.

Exercises near the ground were a different matter. In landings, a pupil undershooting was in danger of tripping his wheels on the boundary fence. Or, if overshooting, he may still try to squeeze in with insufficient runway left, and crash into the far fence. Or he may lose his approach speed, and come near to stalling, particularly on turns where the stalling speed is higher.

I was over at Tern Hill one morning collecting an aircraft from servicing when a swan came on the circuit. The sun was very low, shining straight down the runway after a deluge of rain, causing the sun to reflect so that the poor bird obviously mistook the shining black tarmac for a river or lake. We watched fascinated as she flattened out, held off, and stretched her feet forward for the anticipated splash into the water.

The landing was sickening to watch. In a Walt Disney cartoon it would have been funny. The first touch started her somersaulting twenty or thirty yards along the runway. When she came to rest she lay stunned, too shocked to offer any resistance to the two airmen who sped out to her in the breakdown jeep. They seemed to understand swans, for they lifted her into the back, and one climbed in with her.

They drove her ten miles to a large lake near Newport and set her down near the water. She quickly made herself at home, paddling off to an island in the middle. Possibly this was where she originally intended to land. It was news to us that a swan needed a long stretch of water both to take off and land.

At Calveley, still with Corkey in mind, I was determined to teach my pupils as much outside the syllabus as possible. Flapless landings with Sergeant Audley involved approaching at about 120 mph instead of the normal 90. Without the throttle necessary when flaps act as an airbrake, elevator and rudder control became floppy, through lack of slipstream. It was essential also to touch down at the very start of the runway because of the longer run at the higher speed. These were subtle niceties Audley had to learn.

He did very well, and came in highly delighted to tell his pals of his achievement. I chanced to walk into the crew room to sign the Form 700, just as he was saying, 'We've been doing flapless landings. Bloody accurate, old Holmes!' Then he saw me, and vanished into thin air in a cloud of confusion. Far from upsetting me it did a lot to boost the ego of a novice instructor, and brought it home to me that even if your instructor happened to be younger than you, you always regarded him as a much older man.

After a couple of weeks No 8 intake were ready for their night flying. Flying in the dark is not easy at the best of times. Unless a bit of moon gives some hint of horizon, practically the entire trip has to be completed on instruments, which is a severe test of concentration for a learner pilot. I had done precious little night flying from the back seat at Montrose, and of course none with a pupil pilot. My total night flying experience was 2 hours 25 minutes dual and 16 hours 10 minutes solo, the latter mostly on Hurricanes.

When we arrived at Flights the cloud base was low, and dropping. The Met forecast was for drizzle, with fog on hills. There was no moon. It was pitch black. Flight Lieutenant Collingridge, officer i/c night flying, suggested that as it was touch and go if conditions would be suitable I, as flight commander, should do a weather test.

I sent Pilot Officer Emmett out to start up Master *8657*. When I followed him out, an airman was beckoning to me with his torch to show me to my aircraft. I ducked under the red port wingtip light and found the fuselage. I climbed into the back seat, switched on the cockpit lights, strapped myself in and checked the intercom. The chocks were pulled from under the wheels and two circling torches in the distance guided me to the runway. The duty pilot gave me a green to go and I lined up with the six flares, ready for take-off.

I confess that at this moment I wished I was back in the crew room with a magazine and a mug of hot tea. Or at dispersal with 504 waiting for a call to scramble. Or even in the pitch black Arctic.

An impatient green light flashed at me by the aerodrome control pilot brought me back to reality. I pushed open the throttle and the engine roared into life. The line of flares moved past on my left, slowly at first then as the airscrew blades bit and the acceleration pushed at my back, much faster. Checking with coarse rudder for swing, and holding the nose down to gain flying speed, the wheel rumble gradually died away and we were climbing.

'Wheels up, Emmett,' I called to the front seat.

'Right sir,' he acknowledged. The dual-controlled lever on my left jerked up and the green undercarriage lights on the dashboard went out. He sounded quite happy. Soon there was a slight thud as the oleos locked up and the red lights came on.

'Right, you've got her. Make a climbing turn on to 090 and level out at 1,000 feet. Then turn back on to 180 for the downwind leg. We'll do a couple of circuits and take a look at the weather. Looks lousy,' I added.

'Yes, sir.' The happiness had left his voice. He was concentrating very hard. I divided my attention between my instruments to check Emmett's progress, and the runway lights, to note our position.

As I looked to my left the lights faded, brightened for a moment then disappeared. Good lord, surely the generator had not packed up! How the hell was I going to get down either here or anywhere else in this blackness. Let's hope they fire off an occasional Very light for me to get my bearings.

Emmett, of course, had not realised the flarepath had gone. All his attention was centred on his left hand climbing turn. There was just one chance. We could have gone into low cloud, although the altimeter read only 370 feet.

'I've got her, Emmett,' I called.

Did I detect relief in his voice as he handed over?

I throttled back slightly and eased the nose down. The altimeter started to unwind slowly. At 180 degrees I stopped turning but kept descending. Still no lights at 280 feet. The generator *must* have failed.

'Tell me if you see those bloody lights,' I called to Emmett, and at that moment, with our height just below 250 feet — which is the minimum height laid down even for low flying exercises — I saw the flarepath, almost level with our port wingtip instead of way down below it. I wondered by how much we were clearing the tall silos on Joey Dutton's farm.

'There it is, sir,' Emmett shouted excitedly. He seemed to be enjoying the adventure now that he had handed over control.

'Yes, I've seen it. Do you want to land her?'

'I'd rather you did, sir.'

We came across wind and turned into wind at 200 feet. We dragged our stomach over the airfield boundary and touched down at number one flare. We rolled to a halt.

'Right, taxi her in Emmett. The taxying post's over on our left.' I tried to sound casual but I could feel my heart thumping. Collingridge heard our engine and came out to meet us. He'd been listening to records in the hut. I switched off and climbed out. 'How was it?' he called cheerily.

'Bloody awful. The birds are walking.'

'Cancelled?'

'Sure is.'

That was my first experience of back-seat night flying with a pupil in a Master. Pilot Officer Emmett couldn't wait to get into the crew room, to give his version of our weather test.

When we came off operational flying Group said it was for a rest. I soon found I was doing far more flying as an instructor than I ever did as a fighter pilot.

When I arrived at Tern Hill in May my grand total of flying was 803 hours. From that time I was in the air an average of five hours a day so that by the end of July I had passed the coveted 1,000 hours mark. This was an excuse for a celebration in which the whole course, both pupils and instructors, joined.

As my experience of flying with pupils grew, it became second nature to read their minds and anticipate their errors. When one did something wrong you would know instinctively whether he had recognised his fault, if he was going to try to correct his error, and how he would do so. If he over-corrected, which in their anxiety pupils often did, you must be prepared for the ultimate big error resulting from a multiplicity of small ones. But as you learned to get into the mind of your pupil, appreciate his reaction speed, and assess his ability, you grew to know with certainty just how far you could safely let him go with his mistake before giving him a little help, or if necessary even taking over control.

The 1,000 flying hours barrier is recognised as being a dangerous one to break through, because of the over-confidence it can bring to a pilot. There was an illustration of this for me when the Flight Sergeant asked me to fly a Master over to Tern Hill for a forty hours inspection. 'Will you tell them,' he said 'that occasionally she's not getting full power and ask them to check the boost.'

I signed the 700 and went out to the aircraft. The engine sang into life, and the fitter pointed to the tail, querying whether to lie on it while I ran up the engine and tested the magnetoes. I shook my head and waved away the chocks. After all, it was only a ten-minute hop to Tern Hill.

This was almost my undoing.

On the runway I opened up to take-off. She responded well enough at first but half-way along the runway still showed no sign of becoming unstuck, which raised doubts about the engine's performance. A glance at the boost gauge showed that I was only getting plus half a pound when, through the gate she should be giving five and a quarter pounds.

I let her go another hundred yards to give her the chance to get airborne on reduced power, but the urge was not there and I slammed the throttle shut before the point of no return. I was doing 80 mph and had about 400 yards in which to stop. Fortunately the brakes were good, and with the exceptionally wide undercarriage on the Masters, I was able to swing first to the left and then to the right, to kill my speed. I finished up with a ground loop on the perimeter track. Beside the track, driven into the ground, was a wooden post carrying a poison gas indicator board. One blade of the airscrew caught the top of this post, and chipped off the tip.

My over-confidence might easily have brought much more damage and I remembered this from that day on.

My first five pupils finished their course on 7 June and Sergeants Seymour, McAllister, Williams, and Dench, and Pilot Officers Williams, Stuart-Duncan and Taylor then came under my wing. I also had a Major Moody from an Army Co-operation unit allocated to me to be taught low flying for troop location. This was specialised low flying, involving concealment by keeping below tree height or in dips in the ground, and never allowing your aircraft silhouette above the skyline. To preserve the element of surprise you must approach a target from downwind to prevent your engine noise carrying to the enemy.

On 17 June we moved our Flight to another airfield at Chetwynd, near Newport. Here they had one decrepit old Hurricane, a landing ground entirely of grass, and an approach over high tension wires quite near to the boundary fence. It was here that I had the Borland twins as pupils, with Sergeants Audley, Forbes, Rodgers and Slade. I was to convert them all on to the Hurricane. But the engineer officer had had trouble with its hydraulics. He hoped they were right now, but would I please test-fly it before sending off any pupils?

I was only too eager. The last Hurricane I flew was in Russia. I put it through its paces, thoroughly enjoying myself for fifteen minutes then called Control to say I was coming in to land. But when I came to lower my wheels I found the hydraulics had packed up again. Neither the undercarriage nor the flaps were operating.

There was an emergency method of unlocking the wheels and allowing them to drop by gravity, then swinging the nose vigorously from side to side to throw the legs outwards by centrifugal force until they locked. This worked all right, but the flaps would not respond to hand-pumping. So I had to waggle sluggishly over the high tension wires and make a 120 mph landing on rough grass, bouncing like a bucking broncho. Fortunately the brakes operated by air pressure and were not affected, and a ground loop kept me out of a ditch at the far side.

It was with one of the Borland twins that I was as near being cut off in my prime as at any time during the war. Borland had done four landings with me dual and was having a final check circuit before I sent him off on his first night solo. We were stationary at the taxying post waiting to be signalled on to the runway. Regulations laid down that only one aircraft at a time should be at the taxying post, but somehow the aerodrome control pilot had allowed a second Master to creep up behind us.

With our own engine running we never heard him. The first inkling we had of another aircraft in our vicinity was when he buried his airscrew in our fuselage. He practically cut our aircraft in half, two feet behind my head. Fortunately the impact stalled his engine, and halted his progress, or his propeller would have gnawed its way along our fuselage chewing us up en route.

The ground crews put glim-lights round the two aircraft, moved the taxying post, and night flying continued. Sergeant Borland asked if he could leave his solo until the following night, and returned to the Mess looking rather white. He did his solo with his twin brother the following night, and next day both also flew the Hurricane.

About this time sodium flying was introduced as a method of practising night flying in daylight. On the runway was a flarepath of bright orange sodium lamps. The pupil wore goggles with dark blue glass that gave him the impression in daylight of a dark moonlit night. The flares showed up well through the glasses. There was sodium lighting also in the cockpit, enabling him to read his instruments through the goggles. The sodium flares simulated a flarepath at night.

The instructor was thus able to fly as safety pilot, keeping a daylight lookout for other aircraft on the circuit and speeding up the number of simulated night landings his pupil could make. By the end of July, I had sent fifteen more pupils solo by day and night, and also on the Hurricane.

On 15 August I was posted to RAF Hawarden, to take an air firing course, with a view to starting up a gunnery flight at Tern Hill. This course was all flown on Spitfires and I was delighted to break the record for the Unit with 38.5 per cent of hits on an air to ground target, 280 bullets finding their mark out of 730 fired.

But immediately I arrived back at Tern Hill, glowing with my success and keen to set up the Air Gunnery Flight, the Station Commander sent for me.

Group Captain Lowe was one of Nature's gentlemen. He was a first class pilot, life and soul of a Mess party, a strict disciplinarian. These qualities made him the ideal CO for No 5 Advanced Flying Unit at Tern Hill. In a civilian boardroom he would have commanded the same respect. His was the tall, knotty physique of the fit man of forty that accompanies an active brain. The blue, clean-shaven jaw could jut or laugh, the pale eyes melt or freeze.

'Sit down Holmes, old fellow. No bull.' (He wanted something otherwise he'd have kept me standing.) He generously indicated the easy chair near the same French window through which he had hailed me moments earlier across his trimly mown lawn. I removed my cap and sank into the comfortable cushions, guessing at his next move. It came as a question.

'How long have you been running our night flying flight, Holmes.'

'Three months, sir, since the beginning of June.' (He knew perfectly well. Must be working round to a compliment.) Here it came.

'And a damn good job you've done, too.' His eyes crinkled kindly at the temples as he smiled. 'No prangs — that's really something for a night flying flight. In fact, no accidents at all if we forget the night you and Sergeant Borland nearly lost your heads!'

I laughed politely at this little quip.

'Not easy to forget that in a hurry, sir.'

'I'm sure.' He seemed to be sharpening his tapering chin as he stroked it and weighed me up.

'Wing Commander Scott has asked for you to be posted back to his staff at Montrose. He's taken over from Symondson as CFI. How do you fancy that?

I sat forward eagerly. 'Flattered, sir. It means a lot. I'd like to go — no reflection on Tern Hill, of course,' I added hastily.

'You're right, it does mean a lot. But not, mark you, in terms of promotion.'

'How's that sir?' I caught his drift, but wanted to hear him say it.

'Well, you know, Holmes, there are some very senior types on the staff of an FIS — some are pre-war flying instructors, now too old for ops. They've been piling up the flying hours in their logbooks, getting AFCs but no promotion because there simply is no establishment for them. This happens at an FIS. If you went there, you'd be way down the queue.' He studied me through beetled brows. I waited for him to go on. I knew there must be more.

'Now, by the strangest coincidence — here, look at this.' He circled something in red ink on a sheet of foolscap, and he slid the paper across his desk towards me. I could see it was today's Daily Routine Orders awaiting his signature before going on the notice board. He had marked the announcement that Flying Officer Holmes was promoted forthwith to Acting Flight Lieutenant. I grinned my thanks. It looked good in print.

'Acting ranks are not awarded lightly, you know,' he reminded me. 'You'd be waiting another year for your substantive rank. You've got your second ring very early, but of course you'll lose it if you go to Montrose. And a year's increase in pay too, remember. You realise that?'

I nodded ruefully.

'So?' The bait had been laid, the trap set. Would I nibble?.

'Thank you for the promotion sir. I really appreciate it,' I said. 'But I'd like to take the posting at Montrose. I've enjoyed life here and it's under an hour home on my motorbike, but a staff job at Central Flying School carries prestige — and I'd end up a better pilot too.'

He nodded and sighed. 'I knew you'd say that, Holmes. Sorry to lose you. Good luck.'

He was a good loser. He shook my hand and patted my shoulder as he let me out through the French windows. 'You'd better get a train tomorrow morning,' he called after me across the lawn.

I went straight to the camp tailor to have a second ring sewn on to each cuff. The double band felt good. I had a celebration beer in the Mess, explained my sudden promotion to a mystified station adjutant while he issued my train warrant to Montrose, hauled my BSA out of the corner of the hangar, strapped my panniers with all my kit to the back mudguard and rode home to spend one night there as a Flight Lieutenant.

Next morning, 17 September 1942, the ring removed, Flying Officer Holmes entrained at 10.02 from Liverpool Exchange for Scotland. So ended my tour at Tern Hill, and possibly the shortest spell of any Flight Lieutenant on record.

Sadly, my link with Bushy went. We had gone flying and drinking together throughout our days with 504 Squadron at Castletown,

Hendon, Filton, Exeter, Russia and Edinburgh; then in Training Command, on our instructors' Course together at Montrose and finally as flying instructors in the same flights at Tern Hill and Calveley.

At least we'd both stayed alive. So far, at any rate. But the war was only half over.

★   ★   ★

On the second anniversary of my parachute descent into Chelsea, 15 September 1942, I reported back to 2 FIS at Montrose. Four months earlier I had completed my course there to become a flying instructor. Now I was back on their staff, teaching others as I had been taught.

There was a warm welcome from Howie Marcou and Barny Oldfield, my old Sealand instructors, and from Norman Smith who had been my instructor on Number 2 Course at Montrose between March and May. Wing Commander Scott, AFC ('Scottie'), the new CFI, a pre-war civil pilot of great experience, had a friendly chat about the job, and about the DFM he thought I had, which was now beginning to bore me.

I was attached to 'F' Flight under Flight Lieutenant Teddy Ballam, who had an AFM for his many hours as a Sergeant Pilot flying instructor. On 19 September I began my job of training Pilot Officers Booth and Gaston and Sergeants Carson, Pearch, Bell, Broom and Stevens to be flying instructors on Masters. This was No 15 Course — the thirteenth since I was last here. We had about twenty course-pilots. Twenty more, also on 15 Course, were going through on twin-engined Airspeed Oxfords in C Flight.

To cope with the amount of flying from Montrose it was necessary to use three extra aerodromes at Stracathro, Edzell and Fordoun. We were based at Stracathro. Montrose was steeped in tradition, having been a First World War RFC flying training school. The landing ground was almost entirely sand, much of it reclaimed from the seashore, and grassed. High sandhills heaped up along the east side stopped sand drifting across the airfield in high winds.

Originally it was an ideal flying field for slow, light biplanes, being firm, smooth and well-drained. But when the throttles were opened on the more powerful Masters and Oxfords, the airscrews tore up great lumps of sandy turf, and soon the ground became potholed and bumpy. Patching, or filling the holes was unsatisfactory, and eventually two runways were made by pinning heavy wire-mesh sheets to the ground with long metal staples.

Lorry loads of specially constructed steel netting arrived and the two runways were quickly constructed. They served their purpose well except that the tyres screamed and rumbled on the netting when landing and occasionally one burst if a hook worked loose.

Stracathro was two or three hundred feet above sea level, a well-drained grass landing ground. Edzell and Fordoun were new aerodromes hacked out of a picturesque valley, and runways were quickly laid there by brand new machines which arrived for the work. They were practically a one-man-band melting the macadam, spreading it in twenty-foot wide strips, and rolling it down at a speed of about a mile an hour. They were probably the forerunners of machines that a couple of decades later built our motorways.

The first two weeks of a new course were always devoted to teaching patter and exercises for elementary flying training on the Miles Magister monoplane, the baby brother of the Miles Master. The Magister was a pleasant little aeroplane except that sometimes it refused to pull out of a dive. This vice killed several pilots, including test pilots seeking the cause. Eventually it was cured by the simple expedient of fixing a narrow strip of metal along the top of each side of the fuselage, taking the airflow over the elevators which were being blanked off.

I had three near-misses in a Maggie. The first was when an engine cut at about 100 feet on take-off, as we were climbing over the sandhills towards the sea. A quick change-over to the other fuel tank cured the trouble momentarily, the engine firing again, though roughly. Hoping to get back and land I took a tight right-hand turn along the sandhills, gaining a little height. Over a street of bungalows at the south end of the field there was another splutter, so I turned away from the aerodrome toward the municipal golf course.

I was making my approach to the 15th fairway when the engine came on again. I played for safety by circling above the links to gain height before venturing back over the bungalows again.

At 500 feet with the engine sounding healthier I headed back towards the aerodrome. Sergeant Banister, in the front seat, turned and flashed a hopeful glance to me. But his gloved hands were gripping the sides of the open cockpit as he peered anxiously down at the bungalows on the boundary of the aerodrome, obviously weighing up our chances of reaching the field.

We left the bungalows behind and were half-way along the aerodrome perimeter, near the control tower, when our little engine finally gave up the ghost. I went into a glide juggling with the throttle, switches, and petrol cocks in the hope of finding the fault, but to no avail.

Sergeant Banister's gaze was now riveted on the ground, where, in a matter of seconds one way or another, we would undoubtedly be. This was no more than the final approach of forced landings that I had been teaching for six months. Except that this was for real.

With the nose down for extra speed for the turn we banked steeply round the control tower. Startled faces peered out at us from the top windows. There was insufficient height to continue the turn on to the runway, so we flattened out and landed diagonally across the wire mesh, running off the other side on to the grass.

Fortunately the aerodrome control pilot had seen our plight, and avoided a bad collision by stopping an Oxford taking off. Our engine died as we rolled to a standstill. We climbed out and started walking. Banister looked rather pale, and walked back to the Flight Office with me in silence. I noticed, however, that he soon recovered his tongue in the pilots' crew room.

The second Maggie trouble was while practising the exercise of re-starting an airscrew in flight. This was the recovery action to be taken when a propeller actually stops, stalling the engine. When demonstrating, the hardest part was stopping the propeller. To achieve this, it was necessary with throttle shut to pull up the nose of the aircraft almost vertically and stall it in a tail-down and practically stationary attitude. At that instant both engine switches are cut. The propeller wobbles to a halt, always a sickening sight to see.

This exercise was always done above 4,000 feet and over an airfield, in case the engine failed to re-start. After stopping the propeller it was necessary to dive the aircraft almost vertically to about 140 mph, which is very fast for a Maggie, meantime rocking the nose up and down in the dive to alter the angle of attack of the wind on the propeller blades, and turn the engine over compression.

Sergeant Heppenstall was too timid with his rocking. Perhaps he was worried about breaking the aeroplane's back, because it always felt as though this might happen. He was down 1,500 feet, still diving fast, when I told him to pull out. He did so gladly, but one finger of our airscrew still pointed upwards.

'Climb her to get all the height you can with your excess speed,' I told him. 'You're going to need it for your forced landing.' He regained five hundred feet then trimmed her into a gentle glide. 'You've got her now, sir,' he said.

'No, Heppenstall, you've got her,' I corrected. 'Let's see a nice no-engine forced landing on Stracathro.' I heard his hissed intake of breath, that sounded like quick blasphemy. Then he set about his task.

He checked the windsock, went to the downwind end of the field and started making S-turns down to 500 feet. Then he turned towards the field, side-slipped off his surplus height, and touched down well into the field, coming to a halt about the middle.

I could see he was delighted, but dared not show it.

'If you'll take the controls, sir, I'll put my chute under one wheel and give her a yank,' he called.

He climbed out, unlocked his parachute harness and wrapped it carefully round the canopy. Then he chocked the port wheel to prevent the Maggie running forward and catching him with the propeller when the engine fired. He gave me thumbs-up and I flicked the switches up. She fired first time. He donned his parachute and climbed back in. When he fastened his safety harness he called, 'Can we have another bash at that, sir?'

'Sure,' I said. This time he really rocked it, and by 2,000 feet, the engine had re-started.

Later, as we walked in to sign exercise completed in the authorisation book, I mentioned, 'Oh, by the way Heppenstall, about that re-starting engine in flight.'

'Sir?'

'Good show, Heppenstall.'

'Thank you, sir. Oh, and sir.'

'Yes Heppenstall?'

'Good show for you, sir, for letting me land it.'

'Now you know if ever you're teaching a pupil and that happens, that you really can land it. No panic.'

'No, sir.'

The third incident was with Flying Officer Gawronski who was, you will not be surprised to learn, a Pole. He was not stocky, with the squarish features characteristic of his race, but was tall and lithe.

His deep-brown eyes warmed with his ready smile. At Warsaw University he had learned excellent English. He was delighted when I nicknamed him Fred. He was one of my favourite pupils, even though he almost blew me up in my sitting room one evening showing me how much better than vodka his national drink Kmimkowka — pronounced Koo-meem-koof-ka — was by throwing some into the fire. The flames licked up the ceiling, cracking a mirror above the mantelpiece.

Earlier that day we had been practising forced landings in a Maggie at a field up the Fordoun valley near Laurencekirk. He had them taped, so I showed him some variations. I glided down, purposely overshooting the field so that we were about to hit the far hedge. At the last moment I eased the control column forward to drop the nose, and bumped the wheels hard on the ground. The Maggie bounced into the air just as many a pupil has done hamhandedly in a bad landing. It leapfrogged the hedge. Then, because there was a ploughed field the other side of the hedge, rather than pasture on which we could have set down, I gave the engine full throttle and we climbed away.

Fred then tried, made a perfect approach and bounced over the hedge, but when he opened his throttle the engine coughed. We sank slowly towards the soft, freshly-turned earth. I grabbed the throttle, pumped it frantically, and took the stick. Mercifully the engine picked up but our wheels had brushed the sticky soil. It was as though a hand reached up and grabbed us. If we went down surely we must overturn. The game little engine fought hard to lift us free of the sticky clutches of the soil, taking the weight off our wheels but unable to get us airborne. After twenty yards of being a moth fluttering along a fly paper we breasted a slight rise and we were airborne.

That night Fred light-heartedly demonstrated the inflammable properties of his national drink.

The scarcity of the egg by 1943 was so acute that one often wondered whether hens had forgotten how to lay them. In fact, the government took practically all of them and turned them into powder from which a concoction laughingly called scrambled egg could be made which looked and tasted like wet cardboard. Eggs that were sold on production of ration books had been preserved in water-glass and could be used only for frying and baking, although the aroma when the shell was first broken was reminiscent of the school chemistry lab on a hot day.

A fresh boiled egg for tea was a luxury one rarely enjoyed.

One spring afternoon I had a pupil practising forced landings in the Fordoun valley near Laurencekirk, when the farmer in whose field we had landed came out of his house and beckoned me to the hedge. We taxied across to him and he called me over. I unstrapped, telling Sergeant Chaffe, a New Zealander, to keep the engine going, jumped out and walked across, wondering what was worrying the fellow because this was an authorised practice forced landing field. Perhaps our plane was frightening a pregnant cow.

He was smiling, which was a good sign.

'A dozen eggs any good to you?' he called. I couldn't believe my ears. He might just as well have been offering me a bag of gold.

'They certainly would be.' I wondered where the snag was. Did he want a flip round in the 'plane, I wondered.

'Come into the house, then, and the wife will box 'em up for you, safe so's you can carry 'em. Will he be all right for a while?' He jerked his head towards Sergeant Chaffe.

'Just a moment.' I went back to Chaffe.

'Go off and practise some dummy approaches,' I shouted up to him above the noise of the engine. 'Don't actually land until you see me come back into the field, then put down and pick me up. I'm just going into the farm for a few — a few minutes.'

He nodded, knowing not to ask questions, and waited while I secured my straps safely in the front cockpit. Then he set off towards the far corner of the field to get his longest run for take-off. I saw him climbing away as I went into the farmhouse. She was a real Scots farmer's wife. Bonny and beaming, her grey hair was tied neatly in a bun. She wiped pastry off her hands on her apron to shake my hand when her husband introduced us.

'He's come for some eggs, Mary,' he told her. 'Put a dozen in a box for him — they're wholesale price,' he added, turning to me. First things first in Scotland, I thought. The box of eggs arrived with a pot of tea and a plate of buttered scones. There was home-made strawberry jam in a dainty bowl on the tray.

'You'll take a cup with us, won't you?' she beamed. I put the money for the eggs beside a heavy black marble clock built like a colosseum which stood on an enormous mahogany sideboard. I unwound my scarf and sat at a table heavy enough to sink through the floor.

They had a son fighting with the 8th Army in North Africa, they were quick to tell me, and I knew then that I was filling his place in their home and their hearts for a few moments. I could hear the sudden roar of Chaffe's engine as he kept opening up and going round again after a dummy approach to their field.

When I judged he would be getting low in petrol I took my leave, clutching my egg box, but not before they had extracted a promise from me to be sure to drop in whenever I was short of eggs. I kept my promise and by the end of his course Sergeant Chaffe was so expert at forced landings that he could land an aeroplane on a pin.

★　　★　　★

I first joined the RAFVR simply to fly, and during three pre-war years and the first three years of the war that was practically our only duty. Suddenly, however, at Montrose I found I was on a station still observing peacetime traditions.

Flying personnel, for instance, were also expected to take on the role of Station Duty Officer. As soon as my substantive rank of Flight Lieutenant was posted in Daily Routine Orders one of my first chores became that of SDO. From 00:01 hours to 23:59 hours Holmes became acting Station Commander. Any administrative problems arising in the absence of the CO were passed on to the SDO for his action. He must be prepared to deal with anything from a fire to a famine. What he said went, but heaven help him if the CO returned and disapproved his decision.

He had to stand in his best blue, and salute the flag when it was hoisted to bugle call at Reveille at dawn, and when it was struck to Last Post at dusk.

Taking my first Ceremonial Parade as Station Duty Officer was far more an ordeal than my first night flying solo. First you had to learn all the orders for calling the various flights and squadrons to attention, and marching them past the CO on the saluting stand. Then you had to practise shouting them at the top of your voice. You had to decide whether to be slightly refined and shout 'At-ten-shun!', or be more military with a real Sergeant Major bellow of

'Ten-shun!' or, simply: 'Sh-u-u-n!'; or very top drawer with a dignified 'H-u-n!'

Shouting at the top of your voice is something one normally never does.

To stand in front of 200 airmen, poised to spring when you give the word by bellowing it at the top of your voice, is an experience well to be missed. The dreadful thought is that having yelled 'Parade . . .' you forget the next order and dry up. Even worse you may give them the wrong order and have two squadrons walking towards each other in danger of a head-on collision.

There's always the chance too, of bursting out laughing. A bugler may fluff a note, or one of the RAF Regiment drop a rifle, or a drumstick may go flying out of the bass drummer's hand and hurtle through the air. All such trivialities can become hilarious situations.

On one parade a Sergeant Pilot who had been given a yellow fever jab for his overseas posting was standing at attention in the middle of the front rank of his Flight when he fainted. He did not crumple as one would expect, but fell flat on his face, as rigid as a post. Apart from a grazed chin he was quite unhurt because he had been so completely relaxed. But to get him off the parade ground without making a shambles of the ceremony was not easy.

Church parade was, if you'll pardon the unhappy metaphor, a bit of a bugger. Here you had to march the troops, with the band in full blast, past the CO to take the salute, then along the main road — hoping traffic will do the sensible thing and not get snarled up between a couple of squadrons. Finally the parade is halted, and Flights fall out in turn to enter the church. Then after the service they have to be fallen in again outside the church, marched back to camp, and heaven be praised — dismissed!

Quite the worst parade of all is the funeral party.

Two of my best pupils on 27 Course, Sergeants Ambler and Meadowcroft, crashed when they were together in a Master in our low-flying area near Aberdeen and hit a tree. The accident was reported by my other two pupils, Sergeants Chaffe and Holland, on the same exercise, who landed to tell me they had seen an explosion and flames.

The CFI thought it a fitting mark of respect that I, as their instructor, should officiate at their funeral. This entailed meeting their train at Montrose railway siding, loading their coffins from the luggage van on to a gun carriage, marching through Montrose to the cemetery, slow marching from the cemetery gate to the church with eight fellow course-pilots as bearers, and after the service, firing a salute over their graves by the RAF Regiment.

Then I returned to the aerodrome, and wrote to their parents, Ambler's being in Australia, and Meadowcroft's in New Zealand. They were not easy letters.

At Montrose aerodrome there were four Oxford and four Master Flights, and competition between them was fierce. Flying started officially at 8 am and the object was to be airborne as near to 08:01 as possible.

In 'F' Flight when Polly Flinders, an ex-fighter pilot, was our flight commander he always arranged for his ground crews to give overnight daily inspections to the two aircraft Flight Lieutenant Foster and I were flying. By 07:55 those Masters were already warmed up and tested and our pupils were taxying them to the flight hut door. At 08:00 exactly Foster and I signed the form 700s, ran to our machines and strapped in while our pupil taxied to the runway for take-off. Day after day our numbers were noted by the aerodrome control pilot as two 'F' Flight machines being first and second off the ground.

But came the day when the other Master Flight and an Oxford Flight, smarting at this daily indignity, followed the same routine and all six aircraft met on the runway, jostling for first take-off position.

Polly Flinders had his own remedy for this. Next morning he, Foster and I, having all been with fighter squadrons and well accustomed to scrambling into the air, taxied in formation to the runway. The aircraft from the other two Flights made way for our superior numbers, as Polly turned on the centre of the runway, and I lined up on his right and Foster on his left.

Polly nodded his head forward, a sign he was opening his throttle, and we set off down the runway in tight vic. We were told later that the sound of three Masters close together at full throttle climbing over the rooftops of Montrose at breakfast time brought most of the residents out of their front doors and many out of their beds.

'Scottie' was very impressed, but also very stern. It was a damn good show, he told us when he had the three of us on his carpet. But if other Flights tried it there might be a terrible pile-up one day in the Market Square.

'No more formation take-offs,' he thundered, 'and that order goes to all Flights.' But Scottie was grinning hugely as he showed us out. He had enjoyed Polly's joke — and the formation take-off.

By June of 1943 I had over 1,500 hours in my logbook, all on single-engined aircraft. The transition from singles to twins was the difference between a motorbike and a motorbus.

I had climbed up the seniority ladder at Montrose and was ready to have my own Flight, so Scottie thought it would be amusing to give me command of a flight of twin-engined Oxfords when I had never even flown one.

I had a dozen instructors under me, all experienced Oxford pilots, and I was the novice. There was only one answer. I spent an hour studying the pilot's handling notes, then Bill Dunnett took me for a ride in one of those big, waffly aeroplanes.

The difference between the Oxford and the Master was staggering. Instead of climbing in and sitting down you could walk round. The second pilot sat beside you, and there was room at the back for three or four passengers and a couple of bicycles. There was one set of controls for the flaps undercarriage and both engines, mounted centrally for both pilots to share, but each had his own control column, rudder and brake.

I took *1089* up solo for a couple of hours, concentrating on landings. While flying on one engine — a strenuous exercise, requiring hard pressure with one leg on the rudder to keep straight — I saw a Maggie doing an approach to the forced landing field near Laurencekirk. As it touched down the Maggie nosed over and flipped onto its back.

There was no sign of anyone getting out, or of anybody on the ground running to assist. It was a bit soon to be making precautionary landings in a field on my first trip in an Oxford, but there was no alternative. I recalled the stalling speeds quoted in the handling notes and sank the Oxford over the hedge. She dropped squarely onto three wheels, and responded well to the brakes. By the time I had turned to taxy to the overturned Maggie, its two occupants had crawled out. They were a bit shocked, but not hurt, and the instructor was slanging his pupil.

I made sure the petrol was turned off, left the pupil to guard his aircraft with strict instructions not to smoke, and gave the instructor a lift back to Montrose. I never asked him how it happened. He was not in my Flight, so it was not my responsibility. But he brightened when I mentioned the boggy state of the ground where they over-turned. This must have given him an idea.

I had only had my Oxford Flight a month when Scottie sent for me and told me that Air Gunnery was now to be included in the instructor's course syllabus. He said I was the logical person to start the Air Firing Flight. He added that Empire Central Flying School at Hullavington in Wiltshire had drawn up the air firing syllabus to be taught, and I was to be attached there for a week to learn it, and indent for what equipment was needed for an Air Firing Flight at Montrose.

I arrived at Hullavington on 19 July. It was like a repeat of Professor Jones's Gunnery Research Unit at Exeter except that here they had a team of several back-room boys with one pilot, Flight Lieutenant Johnson, teaching the practical side. I found that Professor Jones's GRU Assessor was now in limited production, and that ECFS had the first. They were delighted that I was able to tell them a little of the theory I had learned first hand from its inventor.

They had split the air firing programme into four simple exercises. The first was devoted to judging the range of your target before opening fire; the second to recognise its course or 'line of flight' when it was turning; the third was to judge the 'angle off' when firing — or the angle made between lines drawn through your machine and the target aircraft; and the fourth was the distance ahead of the target to aim (known as the deflection) allowing for the distance he would fly in the time taken for your bullets to travel from your guns to him.

This was all based on the obvious fact that if you were fully astern of your target you would aim directly at him, whereas if he flew at 90 degrees across your path you must aim a long way ahead with decreasing distances as the angle varied.

For the first exercise, you set on your reflector sight the known wingspan of your target — 38 feet for a fighter or sixty feet for a bomber. Turning a knurled ring altered the gap between two horizontal illuminated red neon lines on your sight at a range of 200 yards. If his wings exactly filled this gap he was 200 yards ahead. If they only half filled it, his range was 400 yards, but if they were twice the size of the gap he was only at 100 yards — so look out, or you'll crash into his tail if you have a fast overtaking speed!

Line of flight was not easy to judge, but was vitally important as your target must not fly over or under your bullets.

Solid scale models of all German aircraft were used to practise judging angle-off. Constant viewing of these models helped recognition of their silhouettes. From the targets' angle-off the deflection was calculated, a perfect shot resulting only when aiming the correct distance ahead, along the line of flight and from a range of 200 yards.

All the theory of these four exercises was practised by two aircraft taking turns to be target. A cine camera in the attacking plane was harmonised exactly with the aircraft sight, so that an accurate film record was made of the pilot's shooting. Later the cine film would be projected on the GRU Assessor. This was so accurate it was possible to calculate — because a gun was firing twenty rounds a second and making a cone of fire of thirteen feet diameter at 250 yards — exactly how many bullets would have hit the target (if any!) and which part of the target.

While Flight Lieutenant Johnson was demonstrating exercise 4 to me at Hullavington, the engine of our Master failed. We were above cloud because of ground haze. Johnny was a gunnery expert, not a flying instructor, and he immediately shouted to me, 'Here, this is your pigeon, you've got her'.

We had no idea where we were, being above cloud, and I did not know Wiltshire anyway. We trimmed to glide at 90 mph. Johnny opened his rear hood and raised the seat, 'to have a grandstand view'. I hoped we'd see some fields when we broke cloud.

We entered cumulus cloud at 7,000 feet, circling to keep near our home base of Hullavington. It seemed very quiet without the engine. When we broke cloud at 3,500 feet, imagine our delight to see in the haze to our left, a large grass aerodrome with two hangars at the far end. Johnny said at once it was Castle Coombe. We glided across the centre, looking for bad ground markers and checking the wind-sock for wind speed and direction. There was a clear run from one corner past the end of the second hangar, so we lowered our wheels and flaps, shed our surplus height, turned in and landed. Half a dozen airmen ran out, hoisted our tail off the ground, and pulled us to the tarmac on two wheels. By the time we had had some tea an electrical fault was located and remedied and we flew back to Hullavington.

Back at Montrose, after the ECFS Course, Scottie gave me three weeks to get our Air Firing Flight off the ground. The Cine Camera

Guns and Mark 11 Reflector Sights for which I had indented before going to Hullavington, were already here. These were installed in four Masters. One at a time the aircraft were jacked off their wheels into the flying position, and the camera gun and the sight were both harmonised on a target 250 yards away.

Corporal Gibb, a pre-war professional photographer, already had a first-rate photographic section under his command and was delighted to be involved in something more technical than taking passport photos for identity cards. He entered into the new venture with enthusiasm. He installed tall developing tanks for processing, fixing and washing 50-foot lengths of 16 mm cine film, wound in loops. His drier could handle ten films at a time.

Scottie was taken aback when I told him I needed a lecture room, film projection room, extension to the photographic section, an office for myself and two flying instructors. But when he realised these were all essential for the course to operate efficiently, he detailed Flying Officers Chris Edens and Vernon Warwick to the new Flight and allocated two lecture rooms and an office, all practically alongside the photographic section, to house us.

While the aircraft cameras and sights were being harmonised by the engineering section, Chris and Vernon helped me to prepare our two rooms. On tables down one side of the lecture room we set up the GRU Assessor, which consisted of a cine screen at one end with a gun sight marked on it and a 16 mm projector at the other which could be hand-turned to examine a film, one frame at a time. It was fan-cooled to prevent the film burning.

Blackboards on the end wall were for showing by simple trigonometry how the angle from which an aircraft was being attacked varied with the deflection allowance. On the walls were exploded diagrams of the reflector sight, and a Browning machine-gun, with steps in assembling the gun (which every pilot had to be able to do), and there were silhouettes of enemy aircraft seen from different angles.

The projection room, of course, needed blackout over all the windows. There was a nine-foot-square silvered screen at one end and a projector stand at the other. An electrician installed a junction box to give the projectionist control of all the room lights in the room. Chart boards had to be fixed along one wall for details of each pilot's exercises.

The first two Masters being harmonised, Chris and Vernon where separately given dual, then went up together, taking turns to be target. Afterwards they viewed their films on the projector and analysed their results on the GRU Assessor. When these two instructors were trained, the Montrose Air Firing Flight was born.

We had completed the 13th two-week gunnery course in early November, when one of the course pilots, a Flying Officer Gregson, stood up in the body of the hall at the passing-out review before the three Chief Flying Instructors. He delivered a fluent and obviously carefully prepared speech saying how much their course had enjoyed the air firing syllabus. It was so well presented it looked as if I had laid it on.

Several years later, while enjoying a flying film at the cinema, I recognised the star of the film, John Gregson, as being my appreciative course pilot. I realised then why he had put his speech across with such conviction, polish, and obvious relish. He was a gifted speaker.

Once the Air Firing Flight was running smoothly, Scottie informed me he would like me to start a Bombing Flight. This was really hard, because my knowledge of bombing was nil.

Back to Hullavington again where I was given bombs to de-fuse, bombs to load on to aircraft, and taught about the blast effect of TNT. The bomb-sight, based on the triangle of velocities, was a subject on its own. Next came the trajectory of a falling bomb, the effect of wind resistance and gravity, and its terminal velocity.

Having no bombing range at Montrose, the use of practice bombs was out, so we used flash bulbs mounted under the wings. The man with the bomb-sight in the nose of the Oxford would co-ordinate his height, ground speed and drift, tell his pilot 'Left a little, left, left . . . steady . . .' and when he pressed his bomb release a flash bulb under one wing would explode. The people on the range would plot the position of the flash on their chart and calculate where a bomb would have landed. There were four flash bulbs under each wing.

I indented for bomb-sights and flash bulbs and all the ground equipment. Four Oxfords were fitted with sights, another lecture room was furnished and decorated with bombing diagrams, and we started all over again training instructors.

When this Flight had gone through its birth pangs and put its first few courses through, I was appointed OC Applied Flying with responsibility for both Air Firing and Bombing Flights.

About now ECFS announced they were sending a Testing Flight

to Montrose for re-categorising staff instructors. Scottie put me in for my A2, and passing this qualified me to test course-pilots on single-engined aircraft day or night and pass them out as B (day and night) or Q (day only) flying instructors.

I felt by now that I had had enough applied flying. I put in a request for more hours in Oxfords and was given command of 'C' Flight at Edzell. They were in the middle of their night flying when I joined them, and I was glad to get my first twin-engined night flying into my logbook.

Night flying training was just now encountering a fresh hazard. A lone Ju 88 would occasionally nip over from Norway, flying in low below our radar, and mix with some of our training aircraft doing circuits and bumps. Of course, our machines all showed normal navigation lights to avoid collisions, but the Ju 88 would lurk around without lights. At a convenient moment he would pounce, give a quick squirt, and head for home, sending an Oxford and its crew down in flames. Several training aircraft had been lost to these raiders along the east coast, though not from our unit, so a Red Alert warning procedure was devised.

When an enemy raider was reported in the vicinity, the Red Alert would go out over R/T. Immediately lights on all aircraft and the flarepath would be doused and each aircraft would fly to his pre-arranged spot and circle there, avoiding the chance of collision.

On the first night I flew with 'C' Flight there was a Red Alert. It was a clear bright night and as we headed for our orbit point, the Ju 88 passed us from the opposite direction, his silhouette flashing across the full moon. We were within feet of a head-on collision. This must have shaken him as much as it shook me, for Control told us the raider had headed out to sea and gone homewards at high speed.

I did a Beam Approach Training Course while I was with 'C' Flight. Flight Lieutenant Ernie Powrie, who was considered by all of us to be a very old man indeed because he was nigh on fifty, ran the BAT Flight. This was a system of taking off and climbing away from the aerodrome, flying around, then returning and landing, entirely on instruments. It was a week's course. In the middle of the week the weather packed up, and all flying was cancelled, with the exception of the BAT Flight, Ernie saying we did not need to see anything anyway. He had two aircraft operating supposedly in different parts of the heavy overcast. Suddenly, over the aerodrome, the droning of the engines of two Oxfords merged into a sickening bang, and through the clouds we saw flames descending. The two Oxfords were locked together, and Ernie and three course pilots perished.

An experience I shall never forget at Montrose was being struck by lightning in an Oxford. The storm was black and angry over the mountains and we edged towards the coast to keep clear of it. Without warning a black cloud near us split asunder with a blinding flash and our Oxford shuddered sickeningly. The safety harnesses held us in our seats as the aircraft lurched and almost turned over. I expected to see the wings break away and go fluttering down. But she responded to the controls and came back level, and we kept flying.

Our only casualty was the magnetic compass. Instead of staying north-seeking the needle was spinning aimlessly round and round, demagnetised by the enormous electrical charge that had flowed through our aircraft. All our lights had gone. We were told later that we were safe inside, because we were insulated by the fuselage. But an airframe check after we landed revealed charred marks on the tailplane where the high current had fused the bonding.

Another experience that stands out clearly in my mind is the day my air speed indicator went on the blink. This instrument is the one always taken for granted, always trusted as completely reliable, and consequently never doubted. Imagine my surprise, therefore, when taking off at Montrose in a Master and glancing down to reassure myself that my speed as I was becoming airborne was about 95, to find it reading 140.

This was either an incredibly powerful Master, or I had held the nose down far longer than normal. As I climbed my indicator remained steady at 140. I levelled out, then put my nose down and dived. Still 140. This was a surprising, almost alarming, experience, because I had never known a false reading on the asi.

Landing without it was no particular problem. It was just a question of keeping fast enough for good aileron response and thus above stalling. I taxied in, according to my asi at 140 mph, which is a pretty fast walking speed. The rigger was mystified when he saw it.

The explanation was a simple one. The speed is measured by a small tube (the pitot head) under the wing. The forward speed of the aircraft creates pressure in the tube, actuating the needle. There is nothing mechanical to fail. But a bee had crawled in. The air pressure had blown it along the tube, wedging it there like a cork and sealing in the pressure. A tyre pump soon blew him out. Silly little b . . .

On 11 November 1943, ECFS came to Montrose again and the CFI put me in for my A1. This, he explained, was the top category for a flying instructor, qualifying him to test other instructors on both single and multi-engined aircraft by day or night. As my A2 was on a Master, the A1 had to be on an Oxford, with a further hour on the Magister covering the elementary syllabus.

Wing Commander Brembridge was my examiner. When he was satisfied with the routine syllabus he went on to experimental test flying, which was not part of the A1. All the manoeuvres he asked me to do were prohibited in an Oxford on safety grounds. We spun and we barrel-rolled; then we tail-slid from a vertical climb with one engine dead. The poor old Oxford plummeted backwards for a thousand feet, then lurched sideways into a nosedive. When we pulled out we had lost 6,000 feet. These manoeuvres were all very stimulating, but I wondered just how much punishment this rather frail wood-constructed fuselage and the wings would take. He was obviously calling my bluff, and I was determined not to miss my A1 through chickening out.

He gave me a good report, with the accompanying 'Exceptional' assessment as an instructor on all types. Scottie was pleased to have another A1 instructor on his staff for this reflected credit on him. A natural sequel was to go on the next Testing Flight visit to Erroll, thirty miles down the coast near Dundee.

This was a Fleet Air Arm Station, and when we arrived in a couple of Oxfords we were met by a naval Commander and 'welcomed aboard'. If we dropped anything it fell on the deck, we climbed companionways instead of stairs, and on the bridge at lunchtime we drank pink gins.

I had five instructors to test in a torpedo-carrying Swordfish. This was a fixed undercarriage biplane with a cruising speed of about 85 mph and a maximum of not much more. It was not a good start when I could not find my way into it. But in due course we got organised and taxied out for the test. The other four followed in rapid succession and by the time I had finished the last I felt I knew the Swordfish well enough to go off and sink the *Tirpitz*.

I went on several testing flight visits during the next month. The most enjoyable was to Tern Hill and Calveley where some of my former colleagues came up for test. Of course they all passed with flying colours!

★　　　★　　　★

Next I was sent off for a month's course at Central Gunnery School, at Sutton Bridge, Lincolnshire. This was all carried out with live ammunition, which was a change from the camera guns. The exercises were the same as I had been teaching for a year at Montrose, so the course was rather dull, but it had its lighter moments.

There was, for instance, the American Air Force Captain, who I shall call Harry Foxman. While the RAF pilots who were posted there had to be content to fly the clapped-out old Spitfires provided by the unit at Sutton Bridge, Harry Foxman had brought his own, personal, twin-fuselage and twin-tailed USAF Lightning. He did his course on the Lightning, making our Spitfires look rather slow.

But Harry was a great character. He sensed how impressed I was with his machine when he showed me over it. It was a single-seater cockpit, and he insisted that I sat in it while he explained the controls and the instruments. When he had finished he said: 'Okay, buddy, off you go.'

'Oh sure, buddy,' I retorted.

'Gee Ray, I'm not kidding,' he insisted. 'We don't have 700s to sign and that sort of bullshit like you have. This is my aeroplane, and I'm responsible for it, and if I want to send you flying in it then that's between me and Uncle Sam. There's just one thing, though, don't bend the bastard or it will sure get complicated.'

I took him at his word. It was too good an opportunity to be missed. It was a joy to fly. And I did not bend it.

Not so enjoyable was a trip in one of Sutton Bridge's Spitfires. They were all old reject planes from squadrons and were forever giving trouble. I was doing a No 5 exercise which was a vertical camera gun attack upon a Wellington. You started about 5,000 feet above the Wellington, travelling on opposite courses. When he was immediately below you, you half-rolled on to your back then completed the second half of a loop, bringing your target into your sights as you came into the vertical position above him and completing the attack by skimming behind his tail.

At the start of my second No 5 attack, something fell past my face as I half-rolled. It dropped into my hood, and seemed quite big and heavy. I decided to investigate just in case my aeroplane was falling to pieces, which would not have surprised me. I stayed inverted while I reached down past my head to search the hood, and very quickly my hand came out clutching a large, oily bolt.

It was long enough and strong enough to hold together some very important parts of my aeroplane.

I gently rolled the Spitfire back to level flight and radioed to the Wimpey that my aircraft was u/s and I was breaking off the attack, and was returning to base. At least I hoped I was returning to base. The only bolt of that size I could think of was one that would be holding together the linkage for my control column to the ailerons and elevators. I could not understand why even now the controls had not lost all meaning and gone completely floppy. I slid back my hood, ready for a hasty exit.

Very, very gingerly I tried a little bank. Then a very gentle climb and dive. So far so good, but how long would it last! I called base and asked them to clear the runway and be sure nothing baulked me. When I arrived over the airfield the ambulance and crash tender were manoeuvring into place beside the tarmac. I did a very gentle circuit with no bumps or stresses, as I lowered the wheels and flaps. I coaxed her on a trickle of engine ever so carefully to the runway. Even up to the last few feet from the ground I expected the controls to go crazy and nose-dive me into the ground.

I heaved a sigh of relief as we touched down and coasted to a standstill. Back at Flights I handed the bolt to the Sergeant, who was plainly puzzled. 'They don't have bolts like that in a Spitfire,' he said with confidence.

'Then what the hell's it doing on the floor of my cockpit?' I demanded. 'If nothing else, it could have jammed my controls.' He agreed, and apologised, making me feel a heel because it looked as if I was blaming him.

I never found where that bolt came from. Obviously it was just a bolt from the blue.

Part Seven
Photographic Recce

14
Posted Killed

In November 1944, with my flying hours now topping the 2,000 mark, Scottie sent for me once more. Coastal Command were howling out, he said, for pilots with previous operational experience, for photographic reconnaissance. They must be experienced, he explained, because with the second front pushing the Germans back across Europe, the photographic sorties were now very long, requiring pilots to navigate solo in Spitfires to targets four or five hundred miles behind enemy lines.

Group Captain Frankie Coleman, our Station Commander with a First World War DSO won in the Royal Flying Corps, shook me by the hand with the parting words, 'Now's your chance for a few gongs'.

I thanked him.

At Dyce, Aberdeen's Civil Airport now used by the Queen when she visits Balmoral, the RAF had a hangar in one corner for PR training.

The Dyce course was absorbingly interesting. First we had to learn in detail the map of north-west Europe, and study the weather characteristics over that area. Then we were taught the operation of the 20-inch and 36-inch focal length cameras installed vertically in the fuselage of the Spitfire, and the method of taking and of interpreting stereoscopic photographs.

A stereo pair of photos is two pictures of the same subject taken from different places, as viewed by two eyes. To achieve this the camera is set to expose automatically at pre-selected intervals of between three and six seconds depending upon height and ground speed. With each picture overlapping the previous one by fifty per cent, every subject is on the second half of the first photo and the first half of the second. Then, when they are viewed through special glasses, the first photo with the left eye and the second with the right eye, the detail on the pictures merges into one and stands out in astonishing relief.

Having learned the theory of this, the eight pilots on our course spent a month putting it into practice. We made long trips photographing four or five 'targets' in the south of England, then flying non-stop 600 miles to the north tip of Scotland to photograph two more. We finished the course with a couple of operational sorties across the North Sea to Norway for the experience of single-engined flying over water and over enemy territory.

It was during one of these trips that, officially, I was killed.

At the start of the trip I discovered my flying helmet had disappeared from the locker I shared with Flying Officer Arthur Flynn. As he was already airborne and must have taken my helmet by mistake, I took his.

I flew down to Wiltshire and photographed two factories, then across to the North Wales coast to snap Llandudno pier. Next I set course for Caithness for a shot of our old 504 airfield at Castletown. But on the way, near the Scottish border the cloud thickened over the Lowlands, with heavy rain blotting out the hills. I tried to call base for a Met report but my radio was dead. I was in the position every pilot dreads, in cloud over high ground with no radio.

I could have gone back but the weather had deteriorated behind me, too. There was no choice but to press on, hoping for a break in the overcast further north. I flew on ETA until I judged I was over Dyce. The cloud here was thick, and Dyce is at the start of high mountains. I went on another hundred miles. By now I was over the highest of the Highlands. Still the cloud was solid and the radio dead.

My fuel state was now giving cause for concern. I was soon to make the choice between descending through cloud hoping to see ground before I hit a hill, or baling out. After another ten minutes, with the petrol gauge alarmingly low, my prayers were answered. I spotted a hole like a tube going down through the cloud, showing clearly that at the bottom was the sea. It made me dizzy to look down it, but if I could get down this hole, keeping the water in sight, I must miss the mountains.

I shut my throttle and started a tight spiral left-hand gliding turn, losing height round and round the funnel. It was very narrow and I kept running into cloud. Also, the hole seemed to be moving quickly to the north-east, which was strange because the met report had plotted the wind from the north. At 3,000 feet, the hole suddenly closed, and I lost sight of the water. My gauge showed only ten minutes' flying. There was no choice but to keep circling down, hoping I stayed over water.

At 500 feet I had still not broken cloud, but at 300 feet I breathed a long sigh of relief as I spied blue waves below, almost close enough to touch. At 200 feet the cloud was a dense ceiling of mist above me. I looked round for some land. Although the visibility was fair, there was no land in sight in any direction. This part of Scotland is only about fifty miles wide, and obviously a change of wind had taken me out to sea. But on which side of Scotland was I? Was I over the North Sea or the Atlantic? Should I head due east, or due west? The wrong way would drop me in the drink.

On the basis that the hole in the cloud was tending to move eastwards into the Moray Firth, I decided to go west. I had five minutes' fuel. If I was wrong and found no land, I would have to climb into cloud, to gain sufficient height to turn upside down and bale out, because a ditched Spitfire tips on its nose and dives straight to the bottom, giving the pilot no chance of escape. This happened to Pilot Officer Sanders only a couple of weeks earlier when he ditched with engine trouble, and they never found him.

After two minutes I saw cliffs a couple of miles ahead. Thirty seconds later I was skimming over the top of them, almost grazing the grass while my head was practically in the cloud, and ready to belly land on the first bit of flat ground I could find. To my amazement I spotted an aerodrome with cross-runways and blister hangars swirling in the mist right ahead. It was like a mirage. I dropped my wheels and flaps and sank gratefully on to the nearest runway, hoping no-one was landing the opposite way.

Somebody fired a red Very light to direct me to the control tower, but half-way there my engine coughed, so I taxied clear of the runway on to the grass where the fuel finally gave out. I switched off, climbed out, slid the hood shut behind me, and shouldered my parachute. As I set off across the grass for the control tower I realised to my amazement that I was at Wick, 150 miles north of Dyce, the aerodrome at which I flew my first Hurricane when I joined 504, before it had runways.

I was met at the door of the tower by the duty Sergeant. 'Welcome to Wick, Flying Officer Flynn,' he greeted me.

'Flynn? No, Holmes — Flight Lieutenant Holmes — from Dyce.'

'Yes, we know you're from Dyce, sir. The Observer Corps have been tracking your progress for the last couple of hours. But they thought you were Flying Officer Flynn.' An airman interrupted our conversation. 'Excuse me, sir, Dyce are on the phone for you.'

I went into the office. Squadron Leader Saint was on the line. 'Glad you're OK Flynn,' he said. 'What went wrong? We've been trying to call you.'

'Bloody radio packed up. Not a whisper. But the other thing that went wrong, Johnny, was that you got the names mixed up. I'm Holmes, not Flynn.'

'Oh God, sorry old boy, but you've been posted as killed. Mountain rescue found a bod on the hills near here with your name in his hat. He was trying to find his way through a stuffed cloud. Assumed it was you.'

'You know I'd never do anything so dangerous, Johnny. But I can explain the helmet. Arthur Flynn took mine from the locker by mistake so I have his. Nice memento.'

'Sorry about the mistake,' said Saint. 'Glad it wasn't you.'

'Me too' — almost adding that it nearly was. 'Before you go Johnny, what the hell am I doing up here at Wick? I'm 150 miles above Dyce.'

'We tried to call you to give you a new Met report. You ran into the edge of a depression, and the wind took a complete arse about face!'

'Thanks. By the way —'

'Yes?'

' — sorry about Flynn. And will you indent for a new helmet for me? I don't think, somehow, I'll be wanting mine back.'

I finished my course at Dyce on New Year's Eve, went on leave, and reported to RAF Benson, in Oxfordshire, the site of the King's Flight, on 9 January 1945. It was to be the start of my tour of ops on the sky-blue photographic Spitfire XIs and XIXs. This, though I could never have guessed it, was to be quite the toughest time of my war.

What had I started when I went up to Prestwick to learn to fly a Tiger Moth?

★ ★ ★

I reported to 309 Squadron at Benson, twelve miles south of Oxford. This was a training squadron for pilots before being posted to an operational squadron. Two Spitfire and two Mosquito squadrons drew replacements for their losses from 309.

With 309 I did three practice trips over southern England, to qualify me for operational flying. The ground training schedule included visits to the photographic section in the nearby village of Ewelme, famous for its watercress beds, and to our photo interpretation unit ten miles away at Medmenham, a soap magnate's private castle tucked into a loop of the Thames near Marlow. Both sites were off the aerodrome to miss any bombing. The loss of either of these sections would have been disastrous.

We took our aerial photos vertically with two cameras which occupied the full depth of a Spitfire fuselage. Each carried a magazine holding 500 whole-plate pictures measuring 8½ by 6½ inches. The camera lenses, the size of small saucers, had a focal length of 36 inches, which was a remarkable optical achievement by their makers.

Photographing over targets, the cameras would make an exposure about every three seconds depending on ground speed, and practically a full magazine would be used on successful sorties. Each plate, exposed from six miles up, would cover an area on the ground measuring about 1,000 yards x 800 yards. Filters over the lenses reduced haze, improving detail and contrast.

To process exposed films, magazines were clipped to a cabinet of developer the height of the ceiling and the length of the darkroom. Inside the cabinet, the film would be drawn many times up and down over stainless steel rollers, emerging at the other end as development was completed. From there it would be fed into similar cabinets of stop bath, fixer and wash. After five minutes' fan drying, in a dust-free cabinet, the film would be married to a roll of same-size printing paper, and contact exposures made. The contact paper went through its own developing, fixing, and washing processes and each print emerged dried, trimmed and serially numbered to identify it with the pilot's trace of his sortie on a large scale map.

When Bomber Command had a raid planned it was simple to turn up the latest photos of their target, and print large quantities for distribution to the squadrons making the raid.

After I was posted to ops we were encouraged to visit Medmenham and meet the staff there as often as possible. Interpreting vertical photos was a skilled art and it was helpful if the pilot knew the problems involved, to try to avoid them. The interpreters were all specialists in finding chinks in the enemy's armour, and a good clear photo was of untold value to them. Some would specialise in ships, some railways, some airfields and aircraft, and others on oil refineries. The military experts would trace troop movements, and the scientists sought new secret weapons like flying bombs and rockets. Often secret hideaways would be hidden in forests but footpaths in early morning dew would betray them.

It was fascinating to find what these men could learn by careful examination of the photographs through powerful stereo lenses. In one room at Medmenham I found a back-room boy in ecstasy over my photos of a synthetic oil refinery at Merseberg. It was a beautifully designed refinery, almost perfectly rectangular in shape, with all the various sections fitting together with the precision of the works of a wristwatch. He had identified every working part of that refinery as though naming the components of an engine. He knew exactly the use of each building and the output of each machine. By examining bomb-damaged parts he could estimate the drop in output.

The same interpreter took me to a board covering one complete wall. Every German oil refinery was on that board like a football league table, with details of maximum output, parts damaged, parts repaired, and present output. He told me Bomber Command never aimed to destroy a refinery completely. 'Much better,' he said, 'to damage it just sufficiently to give them hope of repairing it. PR photos tell how they're getting on with the repairs. Then, when they're about ready to go into production again, we biff 'em once more. But again only enough to keep 'em busy mending it.' With a grim smile he added, 'It breaks their little Hun hearts that way. We like to think of them crying themselves to sleep every night.'

The Merseberg oil refinery photos were taken in Spitfire *PL966* on 8 April 1945, together with pictures of the now famous Colditz prisoner-of-war camp. In March 1946, when the war had been over some months, I read the following paragraph in the *Daily Telegraph*, under the heading PETROL TO BAKING POWDER. 'Berlin, Tuesday — The great Merseberg Leuna synthetic oil plant at Halle, once one of the chief cogs in the Nazi war industry, and before Germany's surrender a prime target for Allied bombers, is now producing baking powder.'

On another visit to Medmenham, I was shown mosaics they had mounted of my pictures of Bremen and Kiel. Encircled in yellow pencil which showed up well on the black prints, were the nests of cigar-shaped submarines alongside wharves at Kiel, being refuelled for sea.

From collections of trains at marshalling yards they could tell which battlefront was being fed with supplies, men or munitions and where the Allied armies could expect the next counter-attack to be launched. Enormous conveyer trains seen up near the Baltic coast led to the discovery of the deadly V2 rocket bomb being made at Peenemünde, near Rostock, Hitler's most deadly secret weapon.

On 7 February 1945 the eighth anniversary of my first solo at Prestwick, I was posted to 541 PR Squadron for operational work. 541 took as its emblem the elusive wild sky-blue flower, the Bird's-eye Speedwell.

John Ludman was posted to 541 with me. We reported to Tim Fairhurst, the CO, who after a chat attached us to 'B' Flight where John Shelmerdine was our flight commander. He immediately briefed us to go on the 'Nursery Run', to the Channel Isles. This was every new pilot's first trip. It was a long way to Jersey from Oxford. We could have taken a direct line over the Isle of Wight, the Channel and the Cherbourg peninsula. But to miss the still occupied part of France we were told to head west from Benson to Portland Bill then fly due south. This took us parallel to the Brittany coast about twenty miles out to sea until we passed over Alderney, photographing it en route. South-west took us to Guernsey, then south-east to Sark with pictures of both islands, continuing on to Jersey where we had to photograph St Helier, Corbière lighthouse, and the hill on which the Germans had their anti-aircraft gunnery school.

Whenever a new boy went off on his first trip, the old sweats in the Flight made it sound as hairy as possible. They warned us of the swarms of Messerschmitts likely to come up like bees from the Brittany airfields, but most of all we must beware of the accuracy of the German gunnery instructors on Jersey who knew exactly the height to fuse their shells and were deadly on deflection.

John Shelmerdine was more down to earth. 'Just keep your eye open for the '109s — you'll probably not be troubled by them, but don't count on it,' he advised. 'As for the gunnery school, we know they're short of ammunition there, and are only allowed one shot at each Spitfire. But they make every round count.'

He was right about the Messerschmitts. I left an hour before Ludman and though I searched continuously saw no sign of any German air activity. It was a superb day. Clear winter sun in icy blue sky. Crossing out over Portland Bill soon I had a view of the north coast of France, stretching up to the narrow straits of Dover and our own white cliffs. Then, as I came level with Cherbourg after about ten minutes, I could look into all the holiday beaches down the north coast of Brittany.

Then I saw the Channel Isles ahead and turned to my maps to search for the right targets. Over Jersey, I left the gunnery school until the last, snapping St Helier and Corbière on a right-hand circle, and approaching the gunners from the south, hoping the sun behind me would make things harder for them. I increased my revs to 2,850 and watched my speed rise.

I felt the bump when the shell exploded behind my tail just as I started my cameras running. I looked back and I saw the white puff of cloud dead on my height, and immediately behind. My sudden burst of speed had made all the difference.

I had my photos, and I headed home, triumph in my heart at the completion of my first successful photographic mission. I passed Ludman on his way out just as I was making landfall over Portland Bill and we rocked our wings in greeting. Speech was forbidden over the air, but the wing wagging said everything. I met him at dispersal when he arrived back. He was already out of his cockpit discussing something with his ground crew near the tail.

'Bloody good shooting,' he said pointing to the fin as I joined them. 'Shelmerdine was dead right. Look at that with one poop.' He indicated a ragged hole through metal skin. 'All I can say is I'm glad they didn't have half a dozen to throw at me. I'd have come home like a ruddy colander.'

This was our first photographic venture over enemy territory, and our baptism of fire. It was the start.

I was well aware that at Benson a whole new life lay ahead of me. I was now to become a lone ranger. A scout. A spy in the sky. I was to be taken to a briefing room, shown top secret maps, given highly classified information about a target, and sent to photograph it. If I succeeded, then 'Good show, old chap' and a tiny coloured flag came out of the ops room on the wall map. And I would be given two ounces of boiled sweets, five fags and an egg. I would also be allowed to select 5 prints from my sortie as a memento. Call it bribery if you like, but this last reward was a wonderful incentive, and today I still value my album of photos recording all the trips I made across war-scarred Europe.

The day after my Channel Isles trip I was sent there again. I was keen for something more ambitious, but this was good tactics. It gave me a second sample of leaving the English coast behind and of flying over the Channel to hostile shores. It also gave me more confidence in my navigation.

I was calmer making my way down the French coast than on the previous day. Then, I was waiting for swarms of Messerschmitts to materialise. Now I felt I would see them first. While the adrenalin was, admittedly, surging freely, I was more on my toes and less on edge.

I used the same dodge again over the gunnery school at Jersey. This time I dived as well as increasing speed. I was pleased on looking back to see his shell had burst up at my original height, and a couple of hundred yards back. I wondered how the gunnery instructor would explain to his pupils that he had under-deflected twice on consecutive days.

There was an Air Ministry Order at this time that pilots must not do more than one high-altitude trip every three days. Our aircraft were not pressurised, and it was a strain to live on bottled oxygen at low atmospheric pressure for several hours on end. So it was three days later before my next op.

This was to the Ruhr. I was briefed that it was heavily defended by anti-aircraft guns, and to expect a hot reception. They were right. But these gunners could not hold a candle to the fellow at Jersey, who hit John Ludman with one round. Here it was random shooting, and I had no trouble getting to my targets.

The most interesting feature about my Ruhr photos was that, with the February sun being so low, bridges across the Rhine, and high masted ships berthed at the quays, threw long shadows across the water that made sharp silhouettes. This simplified identification of the ships from the photos.

My next trip, the following day — although I should have had two days off — was no nursery run with no random gunners. My targets were 200 miles south of the Ruhr at Mannheim and Ludwigshafen on the southern stretches of the Rhine where it bends due east into Germany. Without continuous searching for interceptors it could have been a pleasure flight. For many miles my route followed the picturesque river, twisting through valleys fringed by hills and forests. Every few minutes I passed a Snow White's castle that seemed to float in mid-air. Then the Rhine bent left and a branch of the river carried on south, and I knew I was there.

I did not linger long taking photos. They were easy to locate with the two rivers, two bridges and the railway. Strangely, I never saw a fighter either on the way out or returning back home. That did nothing to relieve the suspense of the searching and I enjoyed my 'operational egg' for supper, feeling I'd earned it.

The end of February and beginning of March saw a spell of bad weather across Europe. Photos were impossible. Then when the weather cleared, disaster met us, for we lost four pilots from 'B' Flight in four days. Gwynn Brookes was missing from Leipzig and Tony Scargill from Bielefeld, both on 5 March. George Platt ditched in the North Sea returning from Bremerhaven on the 7th and was never found. Garrett Godden, one of our two South African pilots was lost also on the Bielefeld trip on the 9th.

On those four days, consecutively, I went to Hamburg, Kiel, Hamburg again and Holland. No two-day rests between sorties now. The danger signs were showing in the Flight. Chaps were getting edgy. The trips were growing longer. Four or five hours was quite a spell to be up there alone, relying on a single engine and your own navigation while you play cat and mouse with a ruthless enemy.

The Holland trip on the last day I made twice. First time, just as the Dutch coast came within gliding distance after forty minutes over the North Sea, my engine faltered and began running rough. Black exhaust smoke ribboned past the cockpit. Burning oil — probably a broken piston-ring. Turning back was to be avoided when casualties were mounting. There was always the white feather implication. But it would be foolhardy to press on with a protesting engine which could at any moment give up the ghost.

Regretfully I turned back. Closing the throttle slightly reduced the backfiring. By gentle nursing I kept my height while sacrificing speed. My main object was to reach England. Ditching a Spitfire is fatal, and baling out into the North Sea in March about as healthy.

Crossing the coast I called base, told them I was in trouble, and was returning if I could get that far. Now that I was safely over land I started losing height about a thousand feet a minute and arrived over Benson still at 12,000 feet. The misfiring was worse. The airfield from that height looked the size of a pocket handkerchief. Control said the ambulance was in place beside the runway. I circled the field half a dozen times, shedding my height and trying to get my eyes in focus for the landing. I was still at about 500 feet and half a mile short of the airfield boundary, when the two fire tenders awaiting me reversed off the runway and set off hell for leather back across the turf to their stations. They had made their own assessment of the situation. Happily they were right. As I taxied back to dispersal another Spit started up. Its form 700 was thrust into my cockpit for signing as I switched off my engine. 'Flight Lieutenant Shelmerdine said to get off right away,' my rigger said. 'Weather's clamping over Holland.'

I was feeling a bit drained after nursing my aircraft back across the North Sea. 'Tell Shelmerdine to get stuffed,' I growled as I signed. I never meant him to, but apparently he did tell him, for the CO sent for me after I'd completed the second sortie.

'This is it,' I thought as I knocked on his door. 'Here we go again.' But he greeted me with a warm grin. 'You've been pressing on a bit lately, Holmes, have 48 hours' leave,' was all he said.

Shelmerdine was waiting outside 'Nice photos you got,' he said, 'I've just seen the rushes. Two more flags off the board. Good show. Enjoy your leave.'

Good sort, John!

15
Hamburg Sortie

The briefing officer was tall, pink-faced and cleanshaven. He could have been a young curate in RAF uniform. In fact, he was a university languages lecturer in peacetime, and now, in war, an expert on codes and cyphers, and a Flight Lieutenant.

He pressed a switch and my CO, Squadron Leader Tim Fairhurst, and I watched a roller blind which extended the entire length of one wall slide upwards to reveal a neon illuminated map of north-western Europe. The English Channel, the Thames and the rivers of France and Germany were pale blue. The land mass was green except where it turned to orange then brown with height. The Swiss Alps, lower right, were almost black. Black lines indicated railways.

A touch of other switches sent the map rolling sideways so that the North Sea, the Baltic ports and northern Germany where the Kiel Canal starts, came into view. Pins with mushroom tops of various colours pockmarked the map. The colours signified the priority of targets to be photographed. Some around The Hague pinpointed V2 launching sites, others, near Calais, flying bomb ramps. There were submarine bases, railway marshalling yards, synthetic oil refineries and airfields for fighters, bombers, experimental aircraft, or simply maintenance units. All had their degrees of importance for photographing, and for destruction by Bomber Command.

Hamburg, with its port of Harburg, was a top priority.

'We've not had pictures of this area for three months,' Tim Fairhurst complained. 'The weather this winter had been bloody lousy and not one pilot who went in good weather came back. The Hun is fighting like hell to keep our recce planes away.'

I did not need reminding that 541 had lost three pilots on the Hamburg run alone.

Fairhurst went on: 'Met have an unusual forecast. I say "unusual", because I can't see for the life of me how they can be so sure of themselves. But they are.' He approached the map, picking up a long pointer, and indicated Hamburg, about 500 miles due east of RAF Benson. 'From here to Hamburg it's ten-tenths cloud down to the deck without a break. Solid, and raining like Hell all the way.

'But here —' and the pointer continued south-east through Luneberg, until it reached the River Elbe thirty miles from Hamburg, '— it's clear and sunny.'

'Any targets there?'

'No, but Met say this clearance, which is roughly circular and about twenty miles in diameter, is a freak temperature inversion — something to do with a cold air stream blowing from the Alps.

'This pocket of clearance is moving north-west at 15 mph. Around midday Hamburg and the port at Harburg will bask in sunshine for at least half an hour.'

I glanced at my wristwatch. 'I'll need to get cracking.'

'It'll be a lousy trip to Hamburg,' sympathised Fairhurst. 'Even lousier arriving back at Benson with no visibility for landing.'

I told him, 'I'll see Met about winds and make out my flight plan. Would you mind phoning 'B' Flight and asking them to have an aircraft warming up in fifteen minutes, with camera heaters switched on, and a full ninety-gallon drop tank. Oh —' as an afterthought, thinking of Dyce, 'ask them to stick a Very pistol and a few cartridges in the cockpit locker — may come in useful if my R/T packs up when they're talking me down.'

I was airborne at 10:28 hours, giving myself an hour and a half to Hamburg. Before I could jot A/B and the time on my kneepad the Spitfire was in cloud at 150 feet. Wheels up, I called Control to tell them I was off the ground, and started a gentle climbing turn to make a circle back over the airfield. By the time I had completed the circuit I was at 5,000 feet and came out of the turn on 083 degrees magnetic. The Spitfire and I continued to climb at 180 mph plus 9 boost, 3,000 rpm and 4,000 feet per minute.

To go straight on to instruments in a Spitfire XIX immediately on take-off is a stimulating experience. This happens at night, of course, but then there is practically always some sort of horizon or hazy landmark to reassure the pilot that he is right way up.

The 2,100 hp Griffon engine, exactly twice the power of the Merlins powering all the earlier marks of Spitfire and Hurricane, drives a five-bladed propeller. So great is the torque at 3,000 revs in fine pitch that there is a tendency to twist the aircraft around its own propeller. On the runway this can burst the starboard tyre during take-off. As a consequence, until airborne the boost, which on override can go up to 20 lb for climb and maximum speed, has to be kept down to no more than 7 lb, or about half throttle.

I throttled back to climbing boost, reducing revs to 2,650 and trimmed the rudder tabs to keep the aircraft flying steadily on 083 degrees. The altimeter wound speedily up to 10,000 feet. This gave me a comfortable feeling of reassurance. At least I was well clear of all hills between here and Switzerland. And at a safe height to bale out in case of engine trouble — which would be the only choice in such weather conditions.

I concentrated hard for the next ten minutes, interpreting messages from the blind flying panel and engine instruments. I switched over from the gravity fuel supply to the ninety-gallon drop tank and, when I was sure the petrol flow was continuous, switched off the main tank. I settled down to fly an accurate course at a steady climbing speed.

At 28,500 feet the Spitfire levelled out, still in cloud, and I coarsened the airscrew to 2,250 revs while leaving the throttle fully open. The drop in pressure with height had progressively brought the supercharged boost down to plus one. In clear weather conditions the Spitfire would make a trail about 500 feet above this, and I had no wish to run into the clear weather at Hamburg and reveal my presence there with a sudden white plume of condensation. Settling down to a cruising ground speed of 410 mph, I checked the course and took a deep breath to relax myself and relieve the tension which had persisted practically from the moment Fairhurst first told me I was going to Hamburg.

It was always the same. You're in the Mess in foul weather playing whiskey-poker or darts, or reading a 'Saint' story or writing home, or listening to Vera Lynn, and you get a buzz to go to briefing. Then the knot ties itself in your guts, and the adrenalin starts coursing. A job. Where to? Something special or just a tin pan alley run? You never wondered if you'd come back or not. Or if you'd get shot down, have to forced-land or bale out.

These things would never happen to you.

Must be crossing over the coast near Harwich now. London would be back beneath my tail, mouth of the Thames way down to the right. At the time I gave no thought to the landing that lay ahead three hours hence with visibility QBI (remembered as 'Quite bloody impossible'). Plenty to think about before then.

Well over the North Sea now, the Dutch coast ahead. German radar would soon be picking me up. I switched on the R/T and listened. Almost immediately there came the familiar faint wail as the enemy's invisible radio beam swept past. It was repeated a second or two later, as the beam came back, then again, faster, as with each sweep the radar operator came nearer to fixing my position.

The wails merged and became louder as a second beam, then a third, locked into position, a plot on the German operations board. They could now follow my every move, noting any change of track, speed or height. From the course I was steering they would anticipate the target was Hamburg, reckon my time due over it, and have fighters sitting waiting. I wondered if Met were right that it would be clear there.

From now on it was a battle of wits. A game of chess.

Sod that noise. I switched off the radio.

There was still nothing to be seen outside but swirling wet cotton wool. It was hard to imagine that five miles below people lived in houses and drove motorcars, or tended their animals on farms. All wishing me dead.

I checked the course again, then my watch, and finally the map. I made a pencilled note on my kneepad that we should be over the Zuider Zee, the Dutch inland sea. Just half-way to the target. Still another 69 minutes to go. A life-time. Maybe my lifetime. I replaced the pencil, tied to a string in case I fumbled it, into a slot alongside the pad.

I marked my progress along the pencilled track across my map with a cross every five minutes. A quick glance at any moment showed the exact position. I scanned ahead along the pencil line to Hamburg, visualising the railways, canals and occasional lakes we would be crossing. I refreshed my memory yet again about the landmarks round Hamburg, so that I would know how to run up to the target without consulting the map at a time when there could be fighters about.

After ten minutes I decided to play a game with the Hun, and make it a bit harder for him. Very gradually I altered my course to starboard. After five minutes I was steering fifteen degrees south of the original course. The gradual alteration would not at first be noticed by the radar operators, and by the time they realised I had changed course we would be well south of the previous track, heading on a new bearing, probably Bremen. This would mean bringing up more fighters from airfields round Bremen, or diverting the Hamburg defenders. I hoped for the latter, because that would leave Hamburg unprotected.

Just to add to the confusion I swung the Spitfire hard to the right and flew for one minute due south, then continued east again. Then I decided I had laid enough red herrings for one day, and concentrated now upon getting straight to Hamburg, taking into consideration the deliberate alterations of course I had made.

First the drop tank had to go. There was no gauge for reading its contents but at a gallon a minute the consumption was easy to reckon. I still had about twenty gallons of 130 octane in the tank, but plenty to get me home with the two 66-gallon wing tanks replacing the eight machine-guns, and my 85-gallon main tank. (PR Spitfires were unarmed.) I would need full manoeuvrability should my Spitfire be intercepted over Hamburg, and the drop tank limited this considerably. Besides, twenty gallons of fuel could start a sizeable fire.

Bremen was as good a place as any to drop it. The tanks always burst, making a beautiful petrol bomb.

I shut the throttle and raised the nose until the speed dropped to 140 mph. The controls became sloppy and the Spitfire wallowed. At a higher speed the air pressure would have held the drop tank too hard against the aircraft's belly to be able to force it away. I switched the fuel supply on to the starboard wing tank, made sure there was no air lock in the supply, and unlocked the drop tank. My right heel found the plunger on the cockpit floor, and kicked down hard. The aircraft bucked violently with its change of trim. The tank, which had been up to that moment a long blister along the Spitfire's belly, fell away, tearing its umbilical from its parent and starting its ungainly tumble to earth.

I opened the throttle again, and swung the aircraft round as I always did to catch a glimpse of the tank spinning lazily downwards. It disappeared almost at once in the dense cloud. I calculated I was now south-west of Hamburg, giving the German radar the impression that we were heading still further east. Now I swung round to north-east.

The new course was to the port of Harburg, a few miles short of the city along the River Elbe. This was where the shipping lay while convoys formed to transport troops and supplies to other war zones. British Intelligence could identify these ships and by tracking their movements often shed light on any new action the enemy was planning. Important rail links were made at Hamburg with Berlin further east, Bremen to the south-west and Kiel and Lübeck and the Baltic coast to the north.

Now the cloud was quite suddenly thinner, becoming even wispy. It was lighter. The rain stopped beating the windscreen. It looked as though those Met wallahs might be right, after all. Sure enough, splashes of blue appeared above. Then all at once I was sitting on a shimmering white eiderdown, the sun blazing down, dazzling my eyes and warming up the cockpit. The quilt exploded, and there, through straggling cloud wisps, was the ground.

Not only the ground! By heaven, my navigation, despite the changes of course, had worked like a dream. There was the River Elbe, a shimmering, slimy snake dragging its lazy way over green fields and through dense woodland. Not three minutes' flying to the north the fields ended at the docks of Harburg.

Suddenly my heart gave a bound. Above the Spitfire was a con trail, a twin trail, probably an Me 262 jet. He was fast, and armed with four 30 mm cannons. The reception committee were in attendance. They were circling, waiting patiently for me. Will you come into my parlour . . . ? My ruse hadn't been so clever after all.

I weaved and looked back to be quite sure we were not making a trail, then headed straight for the target. The jet — I could see only one but he had to have a pal — was still circling and had not yet spotted me 5,000 feet below. Full bore, diving slightly for extra speed, I headed for the four fingers stretching out into the river that were the quaysides where the ships berthed. Even from five miles up I saw immediately that something was missing from the dock scene below.

It all appeared bare and white as if under a blanket of snow. Then, as I was starting my cameras, I realised what was lacking. The quays were a mass of dust and rubble. There were no buildings. The ground was pock-marked with bomb craters. This was Bomber

Command's revenge for the Luftwaffe's blitzes on Coventry, Liverpool, Birmingham and London. The bombs had flattened the warehouses, blown away the dock sheds and cranes. Fire had completed the devastation.

I banked vertically to sight my run along the east bank of the river, picked a cumulus cloud to aim at, and levelled out with the Spitfire's nose pointing towards the cloud. I switched on my two vertical cameras to take photographs at two and a half second intervals. A flashing green light confirmed when each exposure was made to produce pictures in stereo pairs.

The Messerschmitt pilot had now spotted me. He was diving angrily from the rear at a tremendous overtaking speed. With no guns to fight back, and no chance of outpacing the German jet, the Spitfire's only chance was evasion.

I slammed the throttle closed. The engine backfired as though it had already been shot. The speed dropped to 300, 250, 200 mph. Through the blister hood I could see the Hun now less than 2,000 yards away, and closing the gap. He would open fire at 1,000 yards. With my speed well under 200, I yanked the Spitfire into a vertical right-hand bank then hauled the control column back into my belly until my eyeballs seemed to be rolling down my cheeks.

I blacked out completely with the centrifugal pull and I kicked on hard right rudder. The aircraft went into a fit of convulsions at this ill-treatment. Streamers flew from its wingtips as it spun down vertically off a high speed stall. The Messerschmitt, at three times the speed of the Spitfire, was firing futilely because he could never turn tightly enough at his speed to get the deflection on the Spitfire. The whirling tracer from the four 30 mm cannons was passing behind me. Surprisingly, I even heard the throaty bark of the guns. Then the Me 262 flashed behind as I eased out of the spin.

The Hun would take ten miles to complete his turn at that speed and would probably even lose me. There was certainly time for another run over Harburg. The cameras were still running (bad show!). But there were 500 exposures in the magazines. A second run was made, this time along the west side of the river. Then I headed for the cloud bank, gaining its welcome cover as a second Messerschmitt, probably answering the call of its leader, was positioning himself for attack.

I sang most of the way home. Crazy songs, made-up words, mostly rubbish. I was jubilant. The sound of my own voice, which came back loud and clear through the radio headset, eased the tension. I did not care that I had to land at my base in the sort of weather that made the birds walk.

I started shedding height over the English coast, and was down to 2,000 feet by what I reckoned to be Oxford. Ops had kept the air clear of all other aircraft.

Control vectored me over Benson at this height. I set their barometric pressure on my altimeter so that it would read exactly zero on landing. With wheels and flaps down now they sent me out on a wide loop to bring me on to the runway bearing, three miles downwind of the airfield.

By losing height and flying the headings Control gave me, I heard the pips of the outer marker beacon 1,000 yards from the runway at 300 feet. I picked up the pips of the inner marker on the aerodrome boundary at 150 feet. At that instant I came out of cloud, saw the runway ahead with sodium flares along its edges. Muttering a prayer of thanks, I shut the throttle, held off and was down. The rumble of the wheels along the tarmac was a welcome sound.

I insisted on taking my own camera magazines up to the photographic section. I smoked a cigarette as I watched them being clamped on to the developing tank. Then I went up to debriefing. Twenty minutes later, debriefed, I was inspecting rush prints of my photographs of Harburg, all serial-numbered and dated for plotting.

Bomber Command was delighted at the pictures, because they showed their crews had done their job well, and did not need to go there again. There was nothing left to bomb. A set of prints went to Intelligence to identify the ships and assess the full effect of their damage on the German war effort.

I was given a set, too. And an egg for lunch.

The trip to Kiel, two days later on 9 March, was very similar. Again it was a target that had a top flag priority rating on the briefing board. It was suspected that the Germans, in a bid to destroy our Atlantic convoys, were turning out U-boats like hot cakes at Kiel, but either the winter had been too bad for photography or they'd

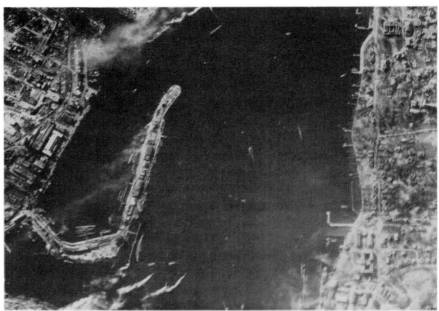

Submarines at Kiel.

An oblique photo of Bielefeld Viaduct shows seven arches smashed, and railway lines hanging in mid-air, with water-filled bomb craters.

shot down any pilots who managed to take pictures. We still had no coverage about their progress with the vessels.

I was going there on the first clear day for weeks. I was told they really wanted those pictures.

The Nazis were equally keen we should not get them.

The crossing of the North Sea, Amsterdam and Zuider Zee was without incident. Visibility was perfect. Along the north coast of Germany thirty miles to my left I could make out the emerald necklace of the Friesian Islands, merging into a hazy purple land mass that was Denmark, where the mainland turned abruptly north. On the far side of the Danish peninsula just inside Germany lay Kiel, my target.

I expected they would send up jets to intercept me again, so I headed well south of Kiel to lay a false trial, and spotted two Messerschmitt Me 163 rocket fighters taking off from an airfield near Bremerhaven. I let them climb below me for two minutes knowing they could not see my blue Spitfire at my height, then altered course 45 degrees to starboard, taking me even further off course for Kiel. When I saw them correcting for my change of track, I swung left to due north and went like a bat out of hell for my target. (The Me 163 only carried enough fuel for eight minutes' powered flight. When it was exhausted they became gliders.)

Half-way there, Lübeck on my right gave a good checkpoint, making Kiel easy to find because the port snuggled into the left-hand side of an enormous basin. This sheet of water was several miles wide and flowed north round the top of Denmark and through the Kattegat into the Atlantic Ocean. It was dotted with large ships.

From that height, at first glance, each ship appeared to have a large raft moored alongside it. But closer examination revealed that this 'raft' was in reality five or six U-boats moored side by side. They were fuelling from their mother tanker, preparing for sea. Along the coastline were more clusters of submarines tethered alongside quays and jetties, probably already fuelled and waiting for crews to take them to sea.

I switched on my cameras and made my first run, photographing the dockyards at Kiel which were building these killer craft in such quantities. I continued up the coast to the Kattegat, cameras running all the time. As I turned to fly back south along the opposite side of the basin I spotted two circular condensation trails ahead of me just south of Kiel. They had obviously been sent up to intercept me as I turned north near Bremen but were a couple of minutes late. Although they had missed me, they were still circling, and were between me and home. I felt cut off and trapped.

They solved my problem for me when their trails suddenly stopped while they were on a southerly heading. The endurance of a jet in those days was very limited and I sensed they had been recalled to their base somewhere near Hamburg, probably assuming I had escaped to the north across Denmark.

I completed my run down the Basin, then swung round and made a third run across to Kiel, following the Kiel Canal due west across country until it entered the Elbe near Cuxhaven. The backroom boys would be glad to know what shipping was using the Canal.

It was a dodgy run back . . . Jerry knew I had the pictures and was not letting me get them home without a fight. I needed to go north of the Friesians and Holland before I got clear, but was home for tea. The same night, before the U-boats could escape to sea, a thousand bombers blasted hell out of them. That must have broken Jerry's heart. It must also have saved a few of our merchant ships and their crews.

At 4 am on 23 March my batman gently shook my shoulder. In those days we slept on the brink of consciousness.

'What is it Sam? An air raid?'

'No, sir. Sorry it's so early, but ops want you in briefing at 05:00. They say you're to have a good breakfast first-orders.'

That meant only one thing, A long, early trip.

'Thanks, Sam.' I fumbled for my packet of Players to which I had now resorted. Sam was there with his lighter already aflame. He left a mug of tea on my bedside table, near my keys and cash. 'There's sugar in it. I know you don't like it, but you'll be needing the energy.'

I retched as I sipped it. But I downed the lot. Sam was loyal and devoted, and he knew best. I lit my second cigarette going into the dining room. A pretty little blonde WAAF, fresh as a daisy, obviously briefed by Sam, approached.

'Porridge, scrambled egg — from a real egg, out of a shell — toast, marmalade and coffee, sir?'

She was no more than eighteen. She should have been spanked and sent back to bed. But she was doing a grand job. I thanked her, sat alone at a table, and finished my cigarette while she brought my meal. She was ready to chat but somehow I wasn't.

At 04:55 I walked into briefing.

The Wingco was there, and the station commandant hovered in the background. This must really be something, to get the top brass out of their beds.

'This one is really something, Holmes,' the Wingco said, not knowing he echoed my thoughts as if breaking a dream. 'Top hush, you're to have no outside contact before you're airborne.'

He went on to paint the picture.

The Germans, he explained, had only one rail link of any note running between Berlin and north-west Europe. This crossed a wide river at Bremen by a high viaduct bridge many hundreds of yards long, rather like our own Forth Bridge. If we could bust this bridge, we could upset their communications for weeks, play havoc with their troop movements, and prevent supplies, tanks and munitions and, most of all, fuel, getting from the factories and oil refineries to their forces fighting at the front.

It could shorten the war dramatically.

He went on to tell how the high command intended to achieve this. A giant daylight raid of American Flying Fortresses was to be mounted on Hamburg docks, about a hundred miles north-east of Bremen. Accompanying the Forts would be a squadron of Lancasters each carrying a 'Ten ton Tess' — the 10,000 kg Grand Slam bomb designed by Barnes Wallis of Dambusting 'bouncing bomb' fame. This had just been used successfully a few days earlier, on 14 March, in an attack on a similar viaduct at Bielefeld, further south.

A few miles after Wilhemshaven, by which time all available enemy fighters would be busily engaging the Forts, the Lancs would break away to the south and attack the Bremen bridge. These bombs, the Wingco said, would cause such terrific explosions that the dust clouds would make photography impossible for some hours, possibly for days. I was to work out a flight plan to Bremen that would synchronise exactly my time of arrival with that of the bombers, and take my photos as the bombs were falling.

The Met Officer came in with the wind speed and direction along my route, and the ground speed the bombers expected to maintain. He forecast no cloud. 'B' Flight phoned through to say *PL952* was warmed up and ready whenever I wanted it. I drank two cups of coffee and smoked two more cigarettes. I never thought I could smoke four before 6 am.

At 06:50 word came through from Bomber Command that the bombers were taking off from aerodromes dotted over Essex, Kent and Norfolk. There were 800, and it would take them at least fifteen minutes to form up. At 07:20 we heard they had set course for Bremen, and I worked out their ETA there. As I would be flying at nearly twice their speed I delayed my take-off until 08:10. I climbed to 30,000 feet above Benson and set course for Bremen at 08:17.

It was a clear morning and the light was excellent for photographs. I expected no trouble from German fighters. They would be too busy with the bombers even to notice me at twice their height, and the radar would never pick me up with all the other plots. The sun was low, bright and dead ahead. At 29,300 feet where I made no trail, it was below my nose, and didn't trouble me. Twenty miles from Wilhemshaven I spotted the bomber force ahead and below at 17,000 feet. The sun glinted off the top of their wings like a shimmering sea stretching to the horizon on both sides.

The fighters were already attacking them diving on the bombers which had closed into tight formation to concentrate their defensive firepower. An Me 109 went down trailing smoke as I watched. I saw the Lancasters peel off to the right, heading for Bremen. The fighters did not seem to notice this and kept attacking the main force.

When the Lancasters were ten miles from Bremen four fighters detached themselves from the other battle and went after them. I watched this like moves on a chess board. The Lancs were now in line astern on the east side of the bridge, with their backs to the sun for better bomb aiming. I was now circling their target and my banked turn gave me a clear view of the battleground. Still no fighters came near me.

In single file a hundred yards apart the twelve Lancasters, tiny as toy models, crept across the landscape. They ignored the fighters. Their pilots and bomb aimers would be concentrating on their run up, their gunners hard at work pumping lead at the Messerschmitts. Near the bridge the fighters laid off and the flak took over. The gunfire was murderous. Jerry obviously valued his bridge and had prepared for such a raid. The bombers just kept going. From my height the bridge looked no wider than a length of wire stretched taut across the river. It was going to be a very difficult target. They had one bomb each, only one chance. There was no pattern bombing about this operation — everything depended on precision. If no-one breached the bridge the whole plan would be abortive.

I saw the explosion as the first bomb hit the river bank to one side of the railway line. The earth bloomed like a rose opening, I switched on my cameras, and concentrated now on flying backwards and forwards across the bridge, filming continuously. As I had to fly straight and level I could only see the bomb-bursts when I turned at the end of a run. The dust clouds were already rising. After the last Lanc had unloaded and headed for home I went into a steep turn above the bridge and examined the damage.

My heart sank. I had hoped to see gaping holes in the bridge arches, but it still seemed intact. There were three bomb craters in the earth at one end, and two at the other, but the best these could have done was to uproot the railway lines, which would speedily be repaired. To my amazement there were bomb craters visible through the water in the river bed itself. The explosions must have blown mud and water high into the air, leaving enormous holes still to be seen even after the water flowed back into them.

Then I found what I wanted. On the very edge of the west bank a bomb had dropped plumb on the railway line, blowing the river bank away and leaving the end of the bridge hanging into the water. Railway lines and bridge girders twisted into the air like a spider in its death throes. The bomber boys had done it again.

As I headed for home after them I counted only nine Lancasters. One of these, with heavy black smoke trailing from its port wing, was rapidly losing height and after a few minutes it crashed and exploded in flames in a wood near Groningen.

My stereo photos bore out my visual sighting. Within half an hour of landing back at Benson jubilant messages of congratulations were being signalled to all the bomber squadrons who took part.

I enjoyed my second breakfast.

16

The AOC Drops In

One of the highlights of our days in 541 was the evening — a few days after the Kiel trip — when Brian Fuge threw a party at The George in Wallingford. Brian, like John Ludman and myself, was a Flight Lieutenant who had just completed a tour as a flying instructor, John's being in Rhodesia.

This was a very special party. Brian's wife — I wish I could remember her name — was due to go into a nursing home for their first baby. Brian was off on leave after duty next day to motor home and be with her at the birth. His excitement at the impending event was infectious. There just had to be a party.

His car was already loaded with his kit, ready for the quick getaway and journey home, so we drove down to the 13th century George pub at Wallingford, a couple of miles along the Oxford road from camp, on two bicycles and my 1935 Austin Seven Ruby cabriolet. (Oh, that I still had it today!)

Our route took us round the airfield. Nobody warned us, of course, but a team of men from works and bricks were busy re-surfacing the perimeter track with molten tar. As we roared round a right-hand bend, singing songs appropriate to the occasion, we ran on to the tar quite suddenly. It only looked like water, as though someone had been washing down an aircraft. Suddenly all four car tyres completely lost adhesion. There was no longer any such thing as friction. The cyclists, following, managed to stop when they saw our fate.

An attempt to steer the car into the skid was met with a steering wheel spinning as freely as a top. The Austin pirouetted gracefully once, twice, three times. As we completed the last full circle both nearside wheels slid simultaneously broadside off the skid pan and came to a jarring, sickening stop on the grass. It seemed we must roll over. But at exactly 45 degrees we remained poised. Now what? We sat there long enough to wonder whether we would finish the roll or drop back on to four wheels. It seemed most likely that our wire-spoked wheels would collapse under the strain and drop us on to our brake drums.

Without anyone giving the order, the five of us in the little car flung our weight to starboard, and this won the day. We flopped back onto our two off-side wheels with a thump, bounced a bit on our leaf springs, and the car then sat there as if nothing had happened.

So we resumed our journey to The George.

I can see Brian now in that timbered lounge with its whitewashed walls a yard thick. He was leaning against a black oak and leaded-light partition, his pewter pint pot waving aloft, and starting to slur happily as we drank to the safe arrival of baby Fuge. The laughter in his eyes melted their normally blue icy as he wiped a tear from one cheek and beer froth from his short blonde moustache with a sweep of his hand.

'Here's to my daughter,' he kept toasting. 'It's going to be a daughter you know, fellers.'

So we spent our time finding names for her — some beautiful, and some bawdy. No one got drunk. We had to fly next day, and our trips now stretched to five hours across the full width of Europe almost to the Russian lines. Someone banged at the piano, the locals joined in, and soon a sing-song was in full swing.

Next day it was Berlin. The Mosquitoes had started bombing the German capital nightly, and the Lancs and Fortresses were blasting hell out of the enemy's oil refineries, their aerodromes and what few factories they had left. Photographic coverage was vital to check for total destruction or whether anything remained still to be wiped out.

Ron Smyth, our flight commander, begged Brian not to go. Tim Fairhurst, the CO, all but ordered him to push off after breakfast and get home. But our losses had been heavy and Brian was the last man to shirk his obligations.

John Ludman took the early run, Brian next, and I was last, at about two-hourly intervals. When I took off, John would be an hour from home and Brian nearing Berlin. We had different targets so we never expected to meet. I was doing the airfields to the north.

Over Hanover, one and a half hour's flying from Benson, I shut off my engine and pulled my nose up to drop speed to 140 and shed my ninety-gallon drop tank. As I looked down to watch it flutter away leaflike, I noticed the tiny cross runways of an aerodrome five miles below. Crawling along one white runway like flies on a table-cloth were two Me 163 rocket fighters. I watched them with idle curiosity, assuming they were on some local mission or even a practice flight, and noticed they turned sharply through 180 degrees on to my course, climbing steeply. I felt happy that they could not possibly trouble me. By the time they struggled up to my height I, at 410 mph, would be miles away.

Nevertheless, caution and mistrust that was now inbred kept me watching them. Each minute, after my routine round search for German fighters, I finished glancing down at them. Very soon I realised that not only were they now at practically half my height, but they were still holding station immediately below me.

The truth suddenly dawned why we had lost four pilots in as many days. These '163s which could reach nearly 600 mph, could climb at 410 while their radar controller kept their plot exactly on mine. They were ascending vertically under my belly, the blind spot. What a perfect way to attack! Just ascend, as though in a lift, then at the crucial moment drop back a hundred yards, and let fire.

I could see them clearly now, black spots against the ground, but much bigger. I hoped they could not yet see me. My blue Spitfire, up in dazzling blue space, was difficult to locate. They would probably still be flying the courses their controller gave them. I turned 45 degrees to port and put my nose down slightly to build up my speed to 470, an extra mile a minute. They continued on course for two minutes until my new position was detected on their board, then I saw them suddenly swing on to my course. This was proof I was their prey. So I bent back ninety degrees to starboard and flew at right-angles to them, maintaining my speed for five minutes.

Then I made corrections for my deviations, climbed back up to regain the 3,000 feet I had lost in gaining speed, and headed for my target. By now the '163s were no longer to be seen, and I knew even if they spotted me now that they had not the fuel to chase me. But I watched for jets coming up from other airfields and hoped Ludman and Fuge were doing the same. I made a mental note to tell all pilots when I landed of the Hun's latest interception tactics.

The sortie was otherwise uneventful, but John came to meet me when I landed. His ruddy features had lost some of their colour. 'Brian's not back yet,' he announced anxiously. 'Suppose you didn't see anything of him this time?'

I told him about the '163s. 'I got jumped by a couple of those bastards near Hanover,' he said. 'They must have been trying the same trick but they came up too far behind me, and I saw them first and buggered off. Looks as if they have done a better job with Brian.'

He was probably right. We could only guess what happened. They delayed posting him missing until after his baby was born. A telegram arrived at the Mess for him next morning. The CO opened it, then pinned it up on the Mess notice board. It read: 'F/Lt Brian Fuge, RAF Benson. Darling, you've got your daughter. Congratulations and love.'

As one Fuge left this world, another arrived. I often wondered if they met, fleetingly, half-way.

★ ★ ★

Vernon Warwick, who helped me to start the Air Firing Flight with Chris Edens at Montrose, was posted to PR before me, but to a Mosquito Squadron. I was glad to join forces with him again at Benson where we had two squadrons of Spitfires and two of Mosquitoes.

The Mosquitoes had a longer range than the Spitfires, and a bomb aimer's window enabled the navigator to lie on the floor and guide his pilot over long targets like railway lines, rivers, canals and lines of docks. The Spitfire, on the other hand was faster and more manoeuvrable for smaller and less accessible targets.

It was not long before Vernon had me flying his Mosquito. It handled rather like the twin-engined Oxfords at Montrose, much more powerful, of course, twice as fast, and cruised effortlessly at high speed. There was excellent visibility all round and it landed with a reassuring thud on the runway with no bounce and no tendency to swing like the short-fuselaged Oxfords.

Vernon gave me the sad news that Howie Marcou, who had finally achieved his dearest ambition by getting himself posted to a

Lancaster pathfinder squadron after four years of instructing, had been shot down. He was simply posted missing, with no further news. This was very sad, because my path had crossed Howie's so often, and he and Snooks had presented me with a lovely God-daughter, Lesley.

I was sadder still when Vernon was himself shot down two days later. He was doing a long haul to Peenemünde on the Baltic coast, about 200 miles due north of Berlin, where the Germans were making their V2 rockets. The V2 was giving a considerable headache to our High Command. While the V1 flying bombs, launched from ramps in northern France, proved easy for our Typhoons to shoot down before they reached London — although many did get through with tragic results — the V2 rocket bomb arrived silently with no warning. It was launched vertically by rocket, and at a height of seventy miles keeled over in an arc, cut its motor and dived without a whisper on to unsuspecting London.

First news of the arrival of a V2 was the explosion. The terror of the unknown was kept from the long-suffering population for some time by attributing these mysterious explosions to fractured gas mains.

We had only two answers to the V2. One was to bomb the factory making them at Peenemünde, and it was while photographing this and the trains bringing the bombs to Holland, that Vernon was shot down. The other answer was to destroy the launching sites.

On 21 March I had an experience which was unusual but of some significance. When crossing the Dutch coast about fifty miles north of Rotterdam, bound for Bremen and Hanover, a white corkscrew of smoke began to climb vertically from the ground just ahead and below. I ran my cameras and watched, fascinated. As it climbed it became apparent it was some type of anti-aircraft shell being aimed, far too accurately for comfort, at my aeroplane.

Scarcely five seconds later, another white corkscrew followed it from practically the same place. They spiralled up together so fast that there was no time to dodge them. As I held my course and watched, the first swept upwards less than a hundred yards ahead. My aircraft bucked and rocked as I flew through its trail. The second was slightly to my right, but still too close for comfort.

When I looked up they were both spiralling high into the stratosphere. Then, almost together, as though suffering the same defect, they suddenly keeled over and dived into the sea less than ten miles from the Dutch coast. My photos later showed that these were not anti-aircraft shells as I had at first assumed them to be, but V2s intended for London. Their launching site had been cunningly chosen, from the public square in the centre of The Hague. The Germans knew we would not attack this launching pad because the Dutch were our allies. We would never bomb their city.

Our Typhoons did, however, attack the sites with rockets. The Dutch were warned through the underground to keep clear and the Typhoons put the pad out of action long enough to give London some welcome respite from V2s. While they were there the Typhoons also attacked oil storage tanks at Rotterdam with rockets, and the deadly accuracy of their attack was shown in photos of burned-out empty tanks but with no surrounding damage.

If I thought I had stumbled across a secret weapon on that trip, I was even more convinced I had a few days later. It was my first sight of UFOs.

Near Hanover, always a hot spot, I saw many miles away to the left a black spot with a circle round it like a planet, moving at incredible speed. It made an arc, sweeping across the horizon ahead of my aeroplane then dipping slightly and passing out of sight under my starboard wing. I watched carefully, for I was sure it was manoeuvring for an astern attack. It re-appeared below the trailing edge of my wing, and as it swept along I became aware that it was followed by a line of similar aircraft. Were they aircraft or UFOs?

I looked to the left again, and saw that quite a swarm of these objects were now describing the same arc around me. Were these ships manned, or were they radio-controlled German secret weapons to home on to my aircraft and destroy me?

As I swung back again to look for more, the rubber tube connecting my oxygen bottle to my face mask caught on the seat lever and stopped me moving my head fully round. I reached down to free it, and found it was trapped. I raised the seat a trifle to free the tube and as I did so all the little space invaders suddenly faded from view.

I had been experiencing strange hallucinations through oxygen starvation. I turned my oxygen full on to saturate my blood again. The images on my retinas had been so clearly defined, and chased each other at such speed across the sky, that I have often wondered in later years whether this may explain some of the sightings of UFOs reported in different parts of the world. Could oxygen starvation be occurring for example, by deeply inhaling tobacco smoke, filling the lungs with carbon monoxide, and cutting off the oxygen supply to the brain? Or just having your collar too tight!

★   ★   ★

With our trips lengthening as the targets for bombing probed deeper into the heart of the enemy, so did our squadron losses mount. It was a good shot in the arm, therefore when the following letter appeared one day on our notice board at Flights.

From: Commanding Officer, 541 Squadron, Benson

March Operations, 1945

Total sorties	175
Operational hours	608.15
Killed or missing	6

Last month was at the same time extremely successful and disastrous.

The weather was unusually good, and the total of sorties was almost as good as last September. The targets were mainly Bomber Command oil and aerodromes. Some very good sorties were flown to Berlin, and the coverage of the large Berlin area was better than we dared hope for at this time of the year.

Our losses were unusually high. This appears to be due to combinations of bad luck all occurring at the one time. With the war situation in its present state, I do not think that we shall have as much trouble from now on.

All pilots are to be congratulated on their fine effort which must have imposed considerable strain.

The following messages of congratulations have been received:

'Congratulations to you and your pilots on the completion of a lengthy photographic programme on March 25th covering Bomber Command attacks during a long bad weather period. I appreciate the difficulty of obtaining photographs of attacks by my command which vary so greatly in type, and in distance from your base. The completion of these vital tasks is a good show. Success to your operations.'

From AOC in Chief, HQ Bomber Command.

'The Committee has noted, of recent months, with great admiration, the many most hazardous sorties which the aircraft of 541 Squadron have carried out. The Committee would be glad if you would convey the appreciation of the JPRC to the Commanding Officer and Officers concerned.'

From JPRC Benson.

'The working committee would like to express its appreciation of the excellent job performed by the photo reconnaissance groups last week. In the course of a few days, more than 40 German synthetic oil plants, oil refineries and benzol plants were covered by UK-based planes, an achievement which has contributed materially to the planning of current bomber operations against the German oil industry.

'The oil production Committee is fully cognizant of the difficult operational conditions under which photo reconnaissance of oil plants has been secured during the winter months, and recognises how those engaged in photo reconnaissance have taken every advantage of limited visual opportunities to obtain the needed cover. May we take this occasion to express once again our continued awareness of the co-operation and spirit of the groups concerned. Without their assistance the success which has been achieved in the bombing campaign against German Oil could not have been realised.'

From Combined Strategic Targets Committee.

These people must have meant what they wrote, for the letters were followed up at the end of March with a morale-boosting visit to Benson personally by Air Commodore Waghorn, the Air Officer commanding our Group.

A heart-to-heart chat with an Air Commodore is not something that comes your way every day, and it pepped us up immensely. He stayed for lunch in the Mess and met everyone afterwards in the ante-room. He was so popular that he was persuaded to stay on longer than he had intended. He sent his staff car back by road, with one of our pilots in it. He said he would borrow one of our Spitfires to fly himself back to his base, and our pilot could return the Spitfire to Benson.

It was also a way of impressing upon us that Air Commodores could fly Spitfires.

As he taxied away from our dispersal he gave us a cheery wave, and a V sign through the open hood. We waved back but without the V sign. Good type, we agreed.

At the runway there was no delay. The aerodrome duty pilot knew who was at the controls, and gave him priority over a Mosquito from 543 trying to get down after a railway marshalling yards sortie in the Ruhr. Open went the throttles of both the Spitfire and the Mosquito as one took off and the other went round again. The Mosquito brought his wheels and flaps up, and with the speed he already had, quickly overhauled the single-engined machine now with its tail up and just getting airborne.

Suddenly we found ourselves staring, aghast.

Instead of holding down his nose, and letting speed build up to about 140 for the climb, the AOC was treating the Spitfire like a

Tiger Moth. No sooner was he airborne then he hauled it into a steep left-hand climbing turn. He was still within the aerodrome boundary, and if he intended to make a spectacular departure he certainly achieved his object. The lower wing flicked under in a high-loading stall, the top wing rolled in the start of a spin, and before the machine had spun even half a turn it had dived inverted into the ground and burst into flames.

The burning wreckage was in a field less than 500 yards beyond the runway but was practically burned out when the fire tender crashed through the hedge to it. The AOC, flung out by the impact, lay a few feet from one smouldering wing. He was not burned, but was dead.

It was an honour I would have chosen to be spared, but on station duty orders a day or so later my name appeared as Officer in the air in charge of AOC's funeral. It was to be a splendid ceremonial affair, despite it being wartime. The coffin was to be taken by road from the mortuary at Benson through Oxford to a country church three miles north-west where the service and burial would take place.

As the AOC had in his group an American Wing of twin-engined twin-fuselaged Lightnings at Mount Farm, it was planned that twelve of these Lightnings, nine blue PR Spitfires and three South African low-level PR Mustangs would make a fly-past, dipping in salute as the funeral party made its way from the hearse at the lych gate through the churchyard and into the church.

The Lightnings were to take off from Mount Farm, and fly a few miles south to Benson. Here the Spitfires and the Mustangs already orbiting would join up with the Lightnings, making an impressive formation of 24 assorted aircraft.

Meanwhile I, as 'Officer in Charge funeral in the air', was to be up at Oxford locating the cortege in the city traffic and shadowing it along the road to the church. I was to call in Yankee Red Leader, who would be circling with his wing well out of sight and earshot of the church, at the exact moment to bring him over the coffin when they bore it at slow march up the church path. It was a splendid plan, spectacular and impressive. Unfortunately it did not take the weather into account.

On the day of the funeral, 5 April, there was steady drizzle. Cloudbase was 900 feet, forward visibility about three miles. But after all, it was the AOC, and the order was to go ahead as planned.

Three separate phone calls came through to Benson from the Oxford Police complaining that a blue Spitfire, obviously one of our photographic machines, appeared to be lost over their city. It kept circling between the university spires near a sports field. Perhaps, they suggested, it was looking for a forced landing ground.

This was, of course me, with flaps down, flying as slowly as possible in appalling conditions to locate my funeral procession crawling through rain-drenched streets. At last I found it, and shadowed it north to the Woodstock roundabout where I knew it would turn right and speed up a little for the last leg of its journey.

It had been arranged with Yankee Red Leader that over the R/T the code name for the church would be 'Target'. So at this point I called him up, told him the procession was now three miles from target, and asked him if he knew the position of target from where he was.

'Sure do, buddy,' came Red Leader's reassuring reply.

'Good show. I'll call you again in exactly four minutes, and give you your ETA over target,' I promised. I started my stop-watch.

'OK buddy, and Out.' His transmitter clicked off.

The road climbed slightly from here lowering my cloudbase. But the cortege was making steady progress and I was timing it, to give Yankee an accurate estimate of its arrival time. Suddenly, when we were still less than half-way to the church I spotted a wing of Lightnings, Spitfires and Mustangs heading directly at me out of the gloom. There was no escape other than up into the cloud, to let the formation scrape under me. When I came down again they'd gone, and I called up Yankee Red One.

With American and British relations well in mind I contrived to keep the edge of my voice as I told him: 'Make one more complete circuit, then come in on target, and you'll be spot-on for timing.'

'Thanks, pal.'

The funeral procession slowed down at a village, possibly for traffic lights but was maintaining a good average. I reckoned Yankee Red One would be dipping in salute right on the needle. It really was murky now. Where it was hilly I was not much above the tree-tops. As I circled ahead of the cars I was thankful at last to see the church below me.

I flew south following a lane that crossed the main road to leave a clear path for Yankee Leader and his boys who were due any second.

The cortege stopped at the lych gate. The cars emptied, and the occupants formed a procession. Bearers shouldered the coffin, manoeuvred through the gateway, and started their slow march up the path, followed by the mourners. The path was lined for fifty yards on one side with RAF officers in blue and on the other with American Air Force officers in khaki.

'Come on Yankee Red Leader,' I shouted into the R/T, 'If you don't come now, you'll be too bloody late.'

The AOC's coffin slowly completed its journey up the path. I was the only aircraft around so I politely dipped my solitary Spitfire in salute as the coffin was carried through the doorway.

The small procession disappeared after it into the church. The door was shut. It was probably slammed. I circled a moment or two longer, sick at heart that Yankee Red One had let us down so badly. There had been no further response after my last entreaty over the radio. Then suddenly through my headphones came a familiar voice.

'Hello, Ray, it's John here.'

John Ludman was leading the section of three Spitfires in the Spitfire and Mustang contingent from Benson.

'Come in John.'

'Yankee's lost his bloody self on the wrong side of Oxford,' he said, blatantly ignoring all R/T code procedure. 'But I've got the target pinpointed and we'll be there in two shakes. Watch out, we're coming in fast and low.'

Fast and low was right! Within a minute, three Spitfires like a streak of blue light hurtled into view at hedge height from the south-east. They aimed straight at the church, so low that I felt sure its tiny spire would be sliced off. In a flash they were gone, and were up at cloud base turning steeply and getting into position for another swoop.

'How was that Ray? Shall we have another bash?'

'That was just fine, John,' I answered. 'But I think we'll leave it at that. Hello Yankee Red Leader, what happened to you?, I called. Not surprisingly there was still no answer.

By the time I landed back at base stories were already circulating about the AOC's air salute. Our station Commander, who was at the church service, had radioed from his car immediately it was over. He was sorry, but not surprised he said, that the Lightnings got lost. 'Our own fault for letting them lead.'

Later, over drinks in the Mess, he told us: 'The congregation was on its knees in prayer when those three Spitfires came over. They made such a roar I thought the flaming roof had gone. Just the organ playing soft funeral music, then whoosh! Half the people dived under their seat. I'll swear the AOC jumped three inches off his trestles.

'Probably killing himself, laughing,' he added, sliding his tankard across the bar for a refill.

That was the last we heard of it.

★   ★   ★

The low cloud that made Air Commodore Waghorn's funeral fly-past such a fiasco spread over north-west Europe for several days, ruling out photos. But on 8 April I was briefed for oil targets around Dresden, Leipzig, Chemnitz and Halle with photos on my way back of the town of Nordhausen. Nordhausen I did not know. It was just a name on the map of some place about 200 miles south-west of Berlin. It had never justified a high priority flag on the ops room map. Suddenly it had become top priority.

I jerked a head towards the flag. 'What's suddenly brought Nordhausen into the news!' The briefing officer grinned. 'You may well ask. Have a look at this.'

He opened a file marked Top Secret, and turned up a signal. It explained that top-ranking Luftwaffe officers had moved to Nordhausen from Berlin because our non-stop bombing raids on the capital were upsetting communications and were a danger to their personal safety. They moved out to Nordhausen secretly, to conduct their air war from there. Unfortunately for them, the secret had leaked and the previous night our bomber force had gone out with express instruction 'to bomb the city centre with intent to kill top-ranking Luftwaffe personnel evacuated there from Berlin'.

The bomber boys had done their stuff. My photos showed the aerodrome one mile to the south was practically unmarked. Between the aerodrome buildings and the town in the railway marshalling yards, were a few scattered bomb craters. But a few hundred yards further north, where the main railway line encircled the southern suburbs, an area of devastation started which worsened nearer the city centre. Here, what had been the heart of Nordhausen was now only white dust and rubble. This was the first time I had ever seen a city bombed 'with intent to kill persons in it'.

It underlined the cruel horror of war, and the cold callousness with which both sides were fighting it.

With so many fellows going missing, it was hard to remember what good news was. About mid-March, however, when our armies were gaining ground across Germany, I received a telegram from Snooks Marcou in Scotland. She had stayed at Montrose when Howie was posted to Lancasters, because they had rented a bungalow there and she was prepared to stay for good after Howie was shot down and posted missing.

She sent me the joyous news that not only was Howie alive and safe, but the German hospital in which he was a prisoner had been freed by the Americans. He had broken a leg landing in a tree in his parachute. The Americans had flown him back to England and put him in hospital a few miles south of Oxford. Could I visit him there? She could not get away because of the two young children.

I immediately applied for, and was granted, permission to motor down to see him, and within an hour my little Austin Seven was bounding along at close on forty miles an hour, which was really pushing it. There was a wonderful reunion. He looked good — a bit older perhaps because his toothbrush moustache needed trimming. His leg was mending well, and he was now convalescing and would be well enough quite soon to rejoin Snooks back at Montrose.

Though I lost many good pals, here was the Canadian with whom fate had kindly kept me in close contact at regular intervals throughout five years of war, still alive.

17
Help from a Hun

Berlin was always a dicey trip.

First and foremost, it was the German capital, the life's blood and heart of Hunland. You had the feeling as you crossed the coast that scores of Luftwaffe pilots were waiting to win Iron Crosses sacrificing their lives to stop you reaching their beloved city. Then there was the sheer distance over featureless countryside. True, the odd river or railway, and an occasional lake or town, gave a map pinpoint but if you had a long spell above ten-tenths cloud it was the devil's own job finding yourself when you finally saw ground. Worst of all, your track crossed Hanover, base of their crack pilots and Me 262 twin-engined jets.

We had been having trouble jettisoning our drop tanks. These were the shape of a baby's pram, about as deep and as wide but much longer, and tapered at the back. They were shaped to nestle snugly under the Spitfire's belly so that one-third of a ton of petrol was supported against the fuselage by the airstream in flight.

Because the airstream was also an obstacle to jettisoning the tank, a simple modification had been designed to help to separate it from the fuselage. A rod was installed to pass through the cockpit floor near the pilot's seat. It had a flat plunger on the outside end. As the pilot kicked down with his heel driving the plunger down six inches, it forced the tank away. This broke the seal. The air would force its way into the gap, blowing away the tank.

Before I took off on this trip in *PL952*, the Flight Sergeant rigger beckoned me aside. He was very apologetic. 'I'm sorry, sir, you should have been flying *SR395* but she's sprung an oil leak. '*952* is in good nick but unfortunately she's the last for the drop tank mod.'

'You mean you've not had time to test it?'

'I mean she's not been done yet. She's the only one that's not. But,' he added hopefully, 'she's a grand kite and we've never had any complaints about not shedding her tank.'

'That's OK, Chiefy. Thanks for telling me. I'd have been hunting round the cockpit looking for the pedal — they're a helluva job to find.'

I'd never had a hung tank before this trip. I actually spun the machine over Hanover, trying to jettison it. I waggled it, and shook it. I locked and unlocked it several times in case the mechanism had jammed. What would I not have given for a kick-release! The clear order was to go back home if your drop tank stuck on. This was fair enough. The aircraft lost 45 mph, and manoeuvrability with its extra drag, tended to waddle, and used more petrol.

On the other hand, it had taken me an hour and a half to get to Hanover, and I was now more than half-way to Berlin. But, most important of all, with our recent losses it must not be thought I had found an excuse to cut short a dangerous sortie. So I locked the tank in position in case it blew off at speed and knocked my tail section off, and pressed on due east.

The photography was uneventful. I located my marshalling yards and Rechlin Larz and Perlberg, two of their secret test aerodromes, recorded them, and headed home. Back at Hanover at 29,000 feet I spotted a '262 twin-jet about three miles behind approaching like a bat out of hell. With my drop tank keeping my speed down to 360 mph he had an overtaking speed of at least 200 mph and was growing rapidly bigger as I watched, his twin engines like two evil eyes. I had no chance of outstripping him.

My only hope was to outmanoeuvre him by turning his extra speed to my advantage, then seek refuge in the cloud layer 15,000 feet below. I continued on a straight course for a few seconds more, letting him believe I was a sitting duck, and shut my throttle fully. The engine backfired and the automatic coarsening of the airscrew was a powerful brake. My airspeed needle wound back dramatically.

He would not open fire at above a thousand yards. If he did, he'd probably miss. Gambling on this I let him close in to that range. By now my speed was around 200. I swung into a tight vertical turn so fast I lost all vision. My cheeks felt on my chest. Half-way round, as I heard his cannons booming I turned the Spitfire over and dived inverted for the cloud cover. There was not much cloud, but sufficient for hide and seek. I knew he could not be following me because of his speed and must be taking a wide sweep. I kept diving vertically, spiralling slightly in case he had somehow got on to my tail. My drop tank was protesting loudly. It was probably buckling with the buffetting. As I neared the speed of sound my elevators began shaking. The control column was vibrating and would not respond to my tugging. Instead it was being forced forward taking my dive way past the vertical and starting an inverted loop.

It was the drop tank that saved me. Its drag stopped me going through the sound barrier and as the air became denser at lower altitude we dropped below supersonic speed and I gained control again. I was still hurtling down almost vertically as I hit cloud which was barely a couple of thousand feet thick and I came out through the bottom still diving steeply. I had to practically loop the loop to regain the cloud.

I was by no means safe yet. Lower down I became the prey of German fighters who would know I was in trouble. I must have been seen diving through the cloud. And even in cloud the '262s could find me, with their newly-developed night flying equipment enabling them to home blind on to an aircraft in complete blackness. Alert to this possibility, I made repeated changes of course, yet always trying to gain ground towards home.

Petrol was now becoming a worry. More fuel was being used for less speed at 14,000 feet. I must climb back to 29,000 for fuel economy at the risk of standing out for miles around as my silhouette emerged from the snow-white cloud cones. The climb would swallow even more fuel.

I stayed twenty minutes in the cloud until the '262 would be low on fuel and have to head homewards. Then I edged warily out of the cumulus. I made a careful search all round and started the climb. It was painful dragging that empty, useless, tank with me every-where I went. I would have given anything to be rid of it. I was over the Ruhr, with Brussels Melbroek my objective, when I first became sure I'd never make it. My needle was hovering depressingly near the empty mark on the gauge. I decided to send out a Mayday call in case there was some nearer airfield who could home me in.

To my profound relief I had an immediate response. My saviour was so loud and clear and reassuring as he asked, 'How can I help?' that I knew my lucky star was shining. I explained quickly that I had five minutes' fuel, was at 30,000 feet over the Ruhr, and wanted somewhere to land nearer than Brussels.

'We're practically below you,' he laughed. 'Your luck's in. Just turn on to 355 degrees, lose height to save your fuel and we'll home you in.'

I thanked him and turned a right-angle to starboard. Then I checked my map to see where he was taking me. With the battle lines altering daily, I was probably being brought down on to a French, or even a captured German aerodrome. My heart nearly missed a beat when I saw that his course was taking me to the southern part of Holland which the Nazis still held. The German bastard, with his beautiful Oxford accent, was probably killing himself laughing at the smooth way he had cut in and the thought of me running out of petrol behind German lines. They'd get me, and my aeroplane, and most of all my films.

I called him up and told him I'd rumbled him, and was heading back home again. 'Well, chum, it was worth trying,' he laughed. 'Better to have loved and lost than never to have loved at all.'

He came on again a couple of minutes later. 'Still airborne?' he inquired. 'Yes — sorry to disappoint you — Chum!' I was saying, when at that instant my engine cut.

I was now down to 22,000 feet, above cloud, over enemy territory with no petrol, and not much hope. I trimmed for a speed of about 140 mph to stretch my glide, and headed due west in the hope of crossing the lines. The chance of finding an airfield was remote, and it was going to be a wheels-up belly landing. It was impossible to say as I came through cloud and saw ground from 12,000 feet whether our armies or theirs were down below. At least I'd left the Ruhr, as I knew by the black pall of smoke in my wake.

At 6,000 feet I spotted the autobahn ahead and to the right. It was straight and two lanes wide. I'd have to touch down between any bridges that crossed it. I lowered my wheels, and their drag increased my rate of descent, but I still had sufficient height to glide across the roadway at 1,000 feet. I dropped the flaps and side-slipped to keep short of a bridge I saw at the last moment. The road was clear of vehicles and it was as good as landing on a runway.

At the end of my run I turned across the road, to have a view both ways. Who would get to me first, the English from the left or the Germans from the right? Almost at once a camouflaged lorry roared up and half a dozen Tommies jumped out and ran at me. 'If it's petrol you need,' a Corporal shouted up, 'we captured a dump of aviation fuel in five-gallon drums down the road. Would that be any good?'

'Just the job. How long to get some?'

'Ten minutes. We'll be right back, sir.'

He left a couple of fellows with rifles with me while he went off in the lorry. They only looked nineteen, but they'd probably killed a few Germans. I climbed out and had a yawn and a stretch, and offered them my Players. We all lit up.

'Where's the enemy?', I asked.

'They're dug in at the end of this road,' said one, a fair-haired boy, slipping his rifle sling off his shoulder to ease the load. 'Bet you're glad you don't have to lug one of these bloody things across Europe.'

We heard the lorry approaching as we were finishing our cigarettes. I made sure they'd stamped them out properly. By the time I'd climbed up on to the engine and removed the cap from the main tank they'd pulled up and were passing a drum and a funnel up on to the wing. I checked the labelling. Hundred octane. I wanted 130, but this would do if I kept my boost down. The drum was sealed and the Corporal stuck his bayonet through the soft metal before I could stop him.

'You'd have blown us to kingdom come if that had made a spark,' I told him. 'It didn't,' he grinned. The fair-haired lad came up on to the wing and together we hoisted up the heavy can and emptied it into my tank. We put two more in and I checked the cap was safely on, and climbed back into the cockpit. I was fortunate that this was one of the few Spitfires with a cartridge starter. Most need a trolley battery to turn the engine over, but on this, firing a cartridge blew the engine round over compression, and one of the 24 sparking plugs nearly always fired. There were six cartridges. I primed the engine which was still warm, and it started with a welcome throaty rumble at the second attempt.

I fastened my straps, waved my thanks to the Army and took off down the autobahn, clearing the bridge with comfort. As I looked back over the bridge they were still standing by their lorry, waving.

I waggled my wings. Almost immediately I spotted the railway line I had seen on my map that took me in a wide left-hand sweep to Melbroek airfield, twenty miles away. I landed there and re-fuelled. They signalled my safe arrival to Benson.

An hour later I was back at base. As I taxied to dispersal the Flight Sergeant walked out to meet me. I told him my drop tank was still locked on.

'Wouldn't the plunger kick it off for you?' I stared at him. 'What bloody plunger?'

'I'm sorry sir, it's my fault telling you the mod hadn't been done, I only found out after you'd gone that they'd worked overtime on her last night to finish it.'

'You mean I've had a plunger on her all the time?'

'Fraid so, sir. But you seem to have managed OK, would you mind unlocking the tank and giving the plunger a kick to test her. I'll catch her when she falls.' I climbed back in as an airman joined the Flight Sergeant under the nose, 'Right sir, kick her,' he shouted.

I found the plunger and pressed with my heel. I felt the aircraft rise slightly on its oleo legs as the heavy tank dropped away. They lifted it up and I locked it back on again. 'Seems fine, sir,' the Flight Sergeant called. 'Works a dream. No trouble.'

'No trouble. Jolly good. Thanks, Chiefy.' I hauled my chute out of the cockpit, tucked the magazines of film from the cameras under one arm and went off to de-briefing. What the hell!

★   ★   ★

My last operational sortie of the war was on 25 April, to Hitler's hide-out, the Eagle's Eyrie at Berchtesgaden, high up in the Bavarian Alps. It seemed a fitting finale. This was the Führer's love-nest retreat to which he decamped with Eva Braun whenever his military problems were driving him mad at Berlin. I was told it was both a romantic, centuries-old castle in which he had held fabulous parties, and an impregnable heavily guarded fortress. Its rooms were furnished with every luxury, its gardens exotic.

This was to be yet another secret mission for me, because Bomber Command were planning as a nice wind-up to the war to blast Berchtesgaden to hell. Why should Adolf not suffer the final humiliation of having his romantic retreat reduced to rubble like our cities, they reasoned.

I hoped Hitler would be there when I photographed the place. There was every likelihood he would have scampered to it like a frightened rat now that the Russians were storming Berlin. In fact, it transpired he had holed up with some of his generals in his Bunker in the Chancellery grounds at the German capital where, three days after my trip, on 28 April, he married Eva Braun. Two days later they both, with Goebbels and his wife Magda, committed suicide after Magda Goebbels had first poisoned her six young children with cyanide capsules in chocolates.

It was going to be my longest trip yet, about six hours, and the furthest behind enemy lines. I expected it to be dicey because even at this stage of the war the loyal and loving Luftwaffe pilots would be determined at all costs to protect to the last their beloved Führer's hide-out. I need not have worried. Not a single aircraft came up to intercept.

The most memorable part of the flight was the view approaching the Alps after passing two large lakes at Ammer and Wurn, fifty miles south of Munich. Although I was at 30,000 feet, these towering, snow-blanketed land masses could have been banks of pastel pink and blue cumulus cloud ahead. Though only half my height, they rose so steeply it seemed they must block my path. Even when I was above the white peaks and glaciers they were so high I felt, although I was 15,000 feet higher, that I was barely skimming over them. My cockpit temperature suddenly dropped dramatically.

Briefing had told me the Eyrie was so well camouflaged it would be impossible to locate visually, and that I should make a mosaic of the area. Our interpreters would soon spot it on giant enlargements. So I flew to Salzburg, where my map showed a railway line and a road both running due south towards the Austrian Tyrol. After 25 miles the road turned west, then swung north-west back towards Munich, about 100 miles away. Somewhere in this loop of road lay Berchtesgaden. I made a series of parallel runs covering a ten-mile square.

Heading home I was still wary of jets from Munich, even though I'd seen no interceptors on the outward run. Some of our best PR pilots had been shot down here, and Munich was a sinister name to us all. It was obvious to the enemy why I was here, and they could have been determined at all costs to stop me getting my pictures home. I decided to keep well south of Munich, along the edge of the Alps, which had now become cloud-covered.

Through a break, after a hundred miles, I saw I was flying along a narrow lake. Immediately below, on its south bank, was a cluster of buildings with an enormous red cross on the flat roof of the largest in the centre. A quick map reference showed that I was over Lake Constance, and flying over Switzerland. There must have been a strong crosswind from the north.

I could visualise being involved in an international incident of some magnitude if the Swiss complained that an RAF plane was photographing the Red Cross Hospital of a neutral country. But I heard no more of this.

The only sequel to my trip was a jubilant report in the newspapers a day or so later that a squadron of Lancasters in a daylight raid had flattened Hitler's hide-out at Berchtesgaden.

Part Eight
Victory

18
King's Messenger

We had known for a week that Hitler was ready to throw in his hand. Our trips had grown longer as the Allied armies pressed eastwards across Europe, and interceptions by the Luftwaffe were less keen. Hanover, Hamburg and Kiel, the hot-spots for jets, now offered only half-hearted resistance. A con trail would appear five to ten miles ahead suggesting that a perfect interception was being made, then, when you were near enough for him to see you he would sheer off in quite another direction.

At first this was disturbing. Was he a decoy to distract you while his pal jumped you? Gradually it became clear that the Luftwaffe squadrons now accepted that shooting down a PR plane would no longer help their war effort.

During those last days, while waiting for a German surrender, we were planning a celebration in the Mess, that would be the party to end all parties. I was buying a book at a stationer's in Wallingford when news came through on the shop radio that Germany had downed arms.

Victory in Europe Day! After five and a half years of war and two thousand hours' flying, now, what about that party!

Curiously I found that instead of rushing back to the Mess I was still browsing in the bookshop. Finding the right book seemed more important at that moment. After all, it was only the afternoon, and beautiful weather — fellows off duty like me would be on the river at Shillingford Bridge, or with their girls in Oxford, or playing tennis at Ewelme. They'd probably not even have heard the news yet.

I paid for my book, and met John Ludman and Ron Smyth in the High Street. Yes, they'd heard. Good show, wasn't it? They were just going for tea at The George. Feel like joining us? In due course we drifted back to the Mess. Not a soul in sight! Early days, of course. Probably everyone changing. The bedrooms were very quiet, but we showered and changed into best blue and went downstairs and drank a beer.

One by one they turned up. There was forced cheerfulness everywhere. The truth of the matter was that we had all been at full stretch for so long we could not relax when the tension suddenly went. Reaction. We talked about when we were likely to be demobbed, what we would do in civvy street, whether to apply for long service commissions in the RAF and, inevitably, of the fellows who had not lived to see victory.

Then the Mess secretary came over the tannoy to tell us the Mess was going to throw open its cellars, the cost to be shared on everyone's mess bill. This was more like it. We waited expectantly for the champagne to put us in the right party spirit.

My first drink was an inch of Spanish sherry in the bottom of my pint beer glass. I had to finish this rather quickly to make room for the Ruby port that followed. Then somebody poured me a slosh of Gordon's gin. The cellar was already feeling the strain. The Mess secretary suggested we should tank up for a while with beer. This we did until as a sort of splendid finale to a very damp squib, sufficient whisky and vodka was found for everyone to have a few snifters each.

Quite suddenly I noticed that John Ludman's normally firm, well defined features, had gone quite hazy. His face seemed to be growing bigger and smaller as though alternately advancing and retiring. All this took place quite suddenly to the accompaniment of a swirling mist.

'For Pete's sake, John, stand still,' I entreated. 'What the hell are you playing at?'

'It's not me, it's you,' he accused. 'You're reeling all over the ruddy deck.' Suddenly he laughed, and flung one arm clumsily round my shoulder, spilling what was left of his vodka down my collar. Normally I would have resented this happening to my best blue. Now I grinned complacently at him.

'You know what?', he confided. 'We're pissed.'

'Ridiculous,' I protested. 'We've drunk practically bugger-all — if that.'

'Remember what mother always told you,' he said, rubbing his nose with one finger in an air of deep philosophy. 'Never mix your drinks, she used to say.' He was right. She did. And she was right. It really is fatal. This was another lessson the war was teaching me.

'Never mind,' John consoled, 'I've got just the cure.' He took my arm and led me like a lamb to the slaughter from the lounge to the wash-rooms. He put the plugs in two wash bowls and ran the cold taps till they overflowed.

'Now, put your face in there. Stay under as long as you can. I'll do the same. It'll really clear your head.' I had overlooked the fact that John Ludman's condition was probably even worse than mine. No sooner was my face in my bowl than, instead of ducking into his own, he put both arms on the back of my head as if leaning over a wall, dropped his chin on his wrists and fell asleep. He was a heavy man and I came very near to drowning before I fought my way up for air.

Fortunately my bedroom was upstairs in the Mess, and not in an adjoining building, or I would never have found it. I was grateful to reach its sanctuary and flopped on the bed. My batwoman, with more amusement than sympathy, undressed me and helped me under the sheets. But this was not the end of it. My bed would persist in tilting sideways to an angle of about 45 degrees, so that I had to go to sleep clinging tightly to one edge of the mattress to prevent myself rolling out on to the floor.

There has always been an unwritten law in the Air Force that no matter how drunk you get the night before, you fly next morning. This had never worried me, for I was never a drinker. But on the morning of VE plus one it did.

Now that our operational flying was finished some humorist at Group had thought up an amusing idea to keep the fellows interested, and not let them go to seed. We would photograph the French coastline on infra-red film. This film has great penetrative properties through mist, darkness and water. It would therefore show the high and low tide marks along the coast, whatever the state of the water together with the type of terrain, whether sand, shingle, rocks or pebbles under the water even below low tide. The photos were highly informative, for anyone who wanted that sort of information. But the experience for the pilots taking them that morning was horrendous.

My territory was the coastline round the Cherbourg peninsula, and as far east as Arromanches and the Mulberry harbour where the invasion landings were made. The weather was good, which spared me the concentration of instrument flying. But keeping a Spitfire airborne under VE plus one influence was a hazardous enterprise.

During the trip from Oxford to the south coast I turned my oxygen up to the maximum for 50,000 feet and felt slightly better. Holding up my heavy eyelids with real physical effort, I pinpointed that fat leg of land kicking out into the sea.

This was the first time in nearly six years that I had flown in peacetime. It was hard to accept that I could approach the coast of France without the drone of their radar moaning through my R/T, or welcoming bursts of flak or, if no flak, the fighters climbing to intercept.

I felt terrible. Let's get it done, and get home, and get the old head down.

Start on the west coast, going north. Must try and get the whole coastline in one run. No re-takes. Strongish wind from the north-east at this height — allow for a bit of drift by turning into the wind.

Right, cameras on, exposing at three-second intervals. After five minutes I noticed the coastline was creeping past me from under my port wing, and that I was crossing the peninsula diagonally to the opposite coast. Hell! It was a north-**west** wind, not north-east! Drunken fool! I'd doubled my drift.

Start again, with opposite drift correction.

This time it worked well enough after one or two re-takes of headlands that I'd cut off. I concentrated on the north coast. This was shorter and easier, and I went quickly round the rest of the peninsula and along the landing beaches. Then I set course for home.

The agony was far from over. A Spit XIX approaches at about 140, crosses the boundary at 110, then flattens out, holds off, and gently three-point stalls. Then, while you are blinded by the bulky engine rising ahead, this lovely monster has to be kept straight for the last half mile while gently shedding its speed from 80 mph. This can be a formidable task even for a pilot with a clear head. But when the inside of the head is enduring the clatter of hangover hammers, and wants only to lie itself gently on a cool soft pillow and shut its eyes for ever, it is not so easy.

The result was that with the best will in the world to get that Spitfire down in one piece, I found there was quite a lull between the moment I flattened out to land, and the actual landing itself. If landing is the right word. Fortunately Mr Mitchell included a strong undercarriage in his specification, making it able to withstand the crump of my arrival. Fortunately I did not drop a wing, nor therefore, a clanger.

And so to de-briefing, and bed. So much for VE day.

★   ★   ★

I was lucky to keep the best of my war until the last.

Winston Churchill, as our leader, was responsible for drafting the surrender terms, and decided to adjourn to some quiet place to consider them. He chose the fashionable pre-war holiday resort of Biarritz, on the southernmost stretch of the west coast of France, overlooking the Bay of Biscay. In spring, the weather was as kind here as in any part of Europe.

To maintain contact with his Ministers in London he appointed the pilots of 541 Squadron as King's Messengers. We were all solemnly sworn in to faithfully and loyally carry his Diplomatic Mail — including 'Jane' in his *Daily Mirror*. The Grand Old Man had organised a very efficient postal service for himself. We would fly to Bordeaux, which was a civil airport, park our Spitfires there and be ferried clutching our diplomatic bag in a light aircraft to a tiny landing ground behind Biarritz. Thus his mail reached Benson from Biarritz in well under three hours, with a further hour by fast car to London.

To maintain this service we kept two Spitfires on the ground at Bordeaux with the pilots at Biarritz. When one left for England another flew out to replace him. Thus each pilot spent two days at Biarritz.

I was fourth on the roster to fly out there. A transport pilot met me at Bordeaux and ferried me in a Dominie to the little field at Biarritz. A Humber brake drove me to the beach. Even the barbed wire barriers the Germans had built against an Allied invasion could not mar the beauty of this romantic resort.

I expected to be housed in a discarded German barrack block or billeted in a local farmhouse. Instead the car pulled up at the House of Molyneux, of world-wide perfume fame, perched on a hill above the golden sands. Inside this beautiful building there was no sign of war. High ranking Germans must have commandeered it for their own use, but they had respected it. Heavy piled carpets of exotic colours ran throughout, powder blue up the wide, curving staircase with ballustrades to tone. The walls were panelled in Louis XIV style, with ornamental mouldings. Crystal chandeliers hung from the ceilings, with softly shaded lights on the walls. The double doors in all the rooms swung both ways.

I was given a first-floor room to myself overlooking the sea. A pert little frilly-frocked chamber-maid with a dark fringe to her Peter Pan bob was proud to show off — among other things — her few words of English. My three predecessors, who shall be nameless, soon came bursting in with the news that the previous night the hotel manageress had fixed them up at a brothel.

There were three beautiful birds there, young and pretty, and they had all produced medical cards vouching for their good health and freedom from infection. They had started the evening with a piano session, then supper with plenty of wine with their 'aunt'. But soon after supper auntie went to bed leaving them, I gathered, to follow suit.

They were all virile young men to whom a French brothel had meant up to then only something in a 'hot' book. To find themselves in a real live house of sin, being treated as honoured guests — for the girls were keen to show their gratitude to the 'brave British' who had liberated them — was straight out of a fairy tale.

The fellows, I thought, seemed to have a vestige of hangover, possibly from women and wine but more likely from conscience, because they were all married. Eric — I shall call him — was rapidly becoming morose. He had been married less than a year, and had proudly brought his wife down to meet us while on leave. He loved her dearly and their first baby was due. He was terrified, despite the reassurances of medical cards, that he might have 'caught a dose' and transmit it to his wife. He was determined to visit the Station MO for injections immediately he arrived back at Benson.

Just to cheer him up we told him injections were of no avail, anyway. Surgery was the only cure.

I soon found myself mixed up with women in a different and much safer way. A Red Cross ambulance was parked outside the House of Molyneux and the two Red Cross girls who crewed it quickly introduced themselves to us all in the lounge. They told us they were taking a load of food parcels to the villages in the foothills of the Pyrenees. They were leaving for Pau, about 100 miles away, next morning and were intending to visit Lourdes and Bernadette's grotto, thirty miles further on. Would anyone like to come along?

They were lovely girls, the kind you would expect to find on a mission of mercy. Fair-haired, clear-complexioned, smiling, sturdy, competent. They were not offering a snogging session, but an invitation, with no strings, to visit Lourdes. The other three fellows had no time. Eric was going back that afternoon for an early visit to the doctor. The man whose place he had taken would leave next morning and the third had to stay as standby for an emergency. I was free providing I could get an official release.

Next morning, the Big Man himself solved my problem. A car called and the driver announced that Mr Churchill would like to meet Flight Lieutenant Holmes. I thought it had to be a legpull, but the driver was deadly serious, so I jumped in the front of the brake with him. A few minutes' drive took us to a small but beautifully laid-out country house, with white rendered walls, black half-timbering and a slate roof with tiny corner spires. The driver led me in without formality. He showed me into a downstairs bed-room. Low windows looked out on to crimson early flowering rhododendrons.

In an enormous double bed, propped up with pillows, and surrounded by newspapers and documents, sat Mr Churchill.

He beamed at me over heavy horn-rimmed glasses and extended a strong hand that looked lonely without a cigar.

'Holmes?', he said. 'Battle of Britain, they tell me?'

'Yes, sir.'

'Glad to know you. Take a seat. Make yourself comfortable. Don't worry about me, I'm not ill; I do all my correspondence in bed and get up about noon. Had any breakfast?'

I thanked him and said I had.

He asked me about 541 and our job at Benson, and said he'd be needing us again when he went to Berlin for the Potsdam confer-ence. I was relieved that he did not mention the Battle of Britain again. He said I was free for 48 hours if I wanted to make plans, and warned me if I went swimming to keep strictly to the small stretch of the beach that had been cleared of mines.

I went straight back to the House of Molyneux and claimed my seat with the girls who were just leaving in the Red Cross wagon. It was a wonderful trip. I was their messenger boy, running back and forth to houses with parcels. The girls had prepared food and drink for two days, and we picnicked in the country lanes that wound into the hills. The sun was hot and the wild flowers were out in the hedgerows.

We stayed that night at a tiny International Red Cross Hostel near Lourdes, and next morning visited the famous grotto. We had a long walk up a grassy valley with high hills each side, and a fast-flowing river below us on our right. As the valley wound to the left we saw the grotto. It was a narow, but very tall cave. It could have been a slit in the hillside made by a giant axe. There was a quiet, sacred air about it. The walls were lined with stumps of candle stuck on crags, and thickly coated with trails of wax. Most impressive of all was the display of hundreds of crutches of every shape and size that leaned against the walls or were propped on ledges, discarded by cripples whose prayers had been answered as the climax to their pilgrimage.

We arrived back at Biarritz that night to be greeted by Flying Officer Seddon, next on the roster after me. 'The Old Man was asking for you,' he grinned.

'Why, what's wrong? He said I could go. Was there some mail to go back?'

'No, but he's got his lovely daughter, Mary, with him. Can't be more than nineteen. A smasher. She wanted to spend the day on the beach with you.'

'Hell!'

'Not to worry, old boy, I took her for you. Wouldn't see you let down.'

'You did! How long did you spend with her.'

'All day. Had a super time. How did you get on?'

Suddenly Lourdes seemed deadly dull.

Flying home from Bordeaux, I came as near to writing myself off as at any time during the war. Visibility was poor, and I decided to climb above the murk and rely upon my radio to get down at Benson.

The inevitable happened. My radio went dead. I wondered if it had been sabotaged by some Nazi followers at Bordeaux. But this was no problem, northern France is as flat as a pancake, and after that came the Channel. No hills, I simply needed to let down after 50 minutes till I saw ground or water, and stay below cloud.

The cloud base was lower at the north coast, and I was just breaking through the mist at about 300 feet when something flashed past my starboard wing. Fifty feet lower in clear air, I swung round to see what I'd missed. Mont St Michel was rising sheer out of the water and capped by its spectacular towering monastery, half in cloud. It looked very, very solid. Brother! Was that close!

That's the nearest I've ever been to entering a monastery.

Two weeks later we were again King's Messengers, this time to maintain the link between London and Churchill in Berlin. He was now planning the Potsdam Conference. This status gave us Diplomatic Immunity, and priority for arrival and departure at aerodromes.

The first day three Spitfires flew to Gatow aerodrome at Berlin. Each day afterwards, as at Bordeaux, one flew home with the diplomatic bag and his replacement flew out. This gave pilots two clear days each to visit the fallen German capital before their turn came to fly home.

Part of the time there we spent in wooded land opposite the famous Brandenburg Gate, bartering for jewellery, German cameras and brandy in exchange for English coffee and cigarettes, for which there was great demand.

Flying to Berlin once the war was over was an eerie experience. It was unbelievable that it was safe simply to steer a compass course east across Germany without being attacked by enemy jets or fired at by flak. To land at Berlin's main airport was even more strange. One visualised guns spewing up lead on your approach and expected a swarm of jack-booted soldiers to rush out with fixed bayonets when you jumped down from your cockpit. Instead, when I landed, I was guided by RAF ground crews to the Officers' Mess where two very beautiful flaxen-haired German girls were singing English songs to a grand piano they played in turn in the lounge.

The German civilians were already at pains to show that none of them had ever been Nazis.

Making sure my .45 revolver was in my belt holster and loaded, I hitched a lift in a British Army lorry from the Mess to the city. With Ron Smyth, a fellow pilot from 541, we dropped off at the Brandenberg Gate, and went into the Chancellery.

The Brandenburg Gate, bomb damaged, splitting Berlin between the British and the Russian sections.

Hitler's Chancellery, with rubble on the steps and a Russian tank at the entrance — being viewed with interest by pilots of 541, who are there as King's Messengers.

The Russians had been there first. Beautiful lavender blue leather lounge suites were knife-slashed and their padding hung out. Oil paintings had been booted from their frames. A small staircase at one side led up to Hitler's medal room, where the floor was ankle deep in every type of medal and ribbon. There was even one for unmarried mothers who had played their part at stud in helping to found a future perfect race. The medals had been swept from cupboards and shelves. I scooped handfuls of them into a cardboard box to take back to Benson.

Back in Hitler's reception lounge I spotted a brass candelabra dangling by its leads from the wall. It was the only one to survive our bombing. Even so one of its three arms had been blown off. There was no electric current to the wires, so I cut them, and possessed myself of the heavy candelabra to bring home with my medals, an assortment of cameras I had bartered on the black market, and twelve dozen Bosch aircraft spark plugs which proved to be quite useless for my car. I also had a 1 hp three phase electric motor for driving my circular saw.

On my flight home I called up Benson over the R/T to say I was over the English coast, and to give them an ETA. It was a beautifully sunny, clear, June morning and as I crossed the wide mouth of the Thames six miles up I could see clearly the Dover coastline sweeping along the Channel almost as far as the Isle of Wight. It was sheer luxury to admire this view at leisure.

Imagine my amazement, then, when I was informed that visibility was nil at base and that I must continue over Benson and land at Kidlington where the weather was clear. This was a hastily devised code, to warn me that Customs officers had turned up at Benson having learned that some of our aircraft may be landing from the Continent with dutiable items such as cameras and perfume.

At Kidlington I had some difficulty explaining to the aerodrome control pilot, because of the one hour time difference, how I had left Berlin at 8 am yet was landing at his aerodrome at five to eight. Finally he covered his confusion by saying that if I had flown in from Berlin, Customs must be informed for my Spitfire to be searched.

Fortunately I had the trump card. I informed him I was a King's Messenger, with diplomatic immunity and requested an armed guard be placed on my aircraft to ensure that no one interfered with it. He was suitably impressed, and I went off for breakfast leaving three RAF Regiment Corporals with fixed bayonets on their rifles guarding my diplomatic mail, and, incidentally my brass chandelier, German medals, cameras, spark plugs, Zeiss binoculars and electric motor.

During breakfast I received a phone call from Benson saying 'the weather had now cleared' and that the fellows on the squadron who had entrusted me with their hoarded up cigarette rations were anxious to see the Leicas and Contaxes (standard exchange rate 1,000 cigarettes) I had traded for them. My personal camera was a beauty — a 3½ by 2½ inch Zeiss Ikon double-extending bellows plate camera with a 4.5 Tessar lens and Compur-Rapid shutter. This cost me 400 cigarettes and when I took up commercial photography after the war, was one of my most successful pieces of equipment. I still treasure it for its history, with Hitler's brass candelabra which is wired up on my hall wall.

I was intrigued when reading recently *The Berlin Bunker* by James P. O'Donnell, which graphically describes events leading up to Hitler's suicide in his air raid shelter below the Chancellery, to see a photograph in the book of the dictator with a group of visitors at a reception in the Chancellery in 1937. Immediately above Hitler's head, on the wall from which I tore it, was my brass candelabra. Hitler would have been furious had he known that his lamp was to lose one of its arms when the RAF bombed his beloved Chancellery and even more furious that the surviving two arms would finish up adorning the hall of an RAF pilot.

Suddenly they talked about demobilisation. The later entrants could be relied upon to finish off Japan. After all the binding, the moaning, the 'Wait till it's over,' and, 'I can't wait to get out of the mob', it came as a shock to find the links with Prestwick, Barton, Ringway, Bexhill, Sealand, 504, Russia, Montrose and 541 and all the rest were to be broken for ever.

No more Mess parties. No more sunning, or poker-playing at dispersal. An end to all the comradeship. Get a job.

No more flying!

I'd already inquired about civil flying clubs — they charged £20 an hour in a 100 hp, 100 mph toy. After 2,000 hours, free, in Hurricanes, Spitfires and the like!

We'd all talked about civvy street so longingly that we had created our own mirage. We were looking forward to the day when we could jump into a car, slip into a cafe for a coffee, or a pub for a pint, and lead the carefree existence our war had earned us. What a joy it would be. The Allies had won and the Nazis were crushed. Now we were free to sit back and enjoy the spoils.

When we found ourselves faced with the reality of the situation, the grim truth quickly became apparent. We were going back to many months of rationing, to food scarcity, to petrol restriction, coal shortage, electricity failures, strikes. Winning the war would not bring much glamour as a reward.

Like all programmes the Government launched, demobilisation plans seemed already to have been cut and dried for months. Teams of people must have worked on them long before victory ever seemed even a possibility. Suddenly the plans were launched and every Serviceman and woman was allocated a group number. Demobilisation centres were set up and stocked with civilian clothes for kitting out the hundreds of thousands who had lived in uniform for years. Length of service decided your group.

Pre-war regulars, whose pensionable age was passed during the war, were of course in the lowest groups. They were quite few, and were scattered around the country, so they were quickly demobbed. Because I had been in the VR right from the start, and served nearly three years before the war, I was in quite a low group — 21 I think.

The first blow for me was to be posted from 541 Squadron to HQ staff. This was because 541 were being re-equipped with Vampire jets, and there was no sense in me converting to jets if I would not be there to fly them. Overnight I had become obsolete.

My posting to HQ came through on 16 September. I could now rise at any time of the day, sit in the Mess reading *Flight* and *Aeroplane* or go shopping in Wallingford. I could not have home leave because my de-mob date might come through any day. It came far sooner than I could have expected. I had a week's warning to present myself at my release centre at Uxbridge, near London, on 4 October.

The emblem of the civilian was of course the bowler hat. One 'got one's Bowler'. Accordingly, at my farewell party the night before I was to quit Benson for ever, I was ceremoniously presented with my bowler hat, brimming with beer. It was a brand new hat, so we drank the beer — surprising how much beer a hat holds — and I dried it out that night over the bedroom radiator. Although it kept its shape quite well, it shrank a bit, and I looked like the thin one of Laurel and Hardy when I drove off the aerodrome in my Austin 7 with the hood down and my kitbag in the back.

I was in jaunty mood as I swung onto the A40 Oxford to London road. After all, not a lot of chaps had started the war flying and were still alive and flying at the end. I rather fancied myself in my RAF officer's uniform, topped by a black bowler at a rakish angle. I drove sedately.

People in cars quickly caught on, especially when I solemnly raised my hat and inclined my head graciously to them as they overtook. As I sauntered along in my little Austin enjoying the fresh air, the countryside and my new-found freedom, I noticed a motor coach which I could read through my mirror was bound for London, had been sitting on my tail for a mile or so.

On the long straight stretch near High Wycombe it drew abreast, with a rousing fanfare from its two-tone horns. All its nearside windows were wound fully down and the passengers from both sides of the coach were crowding the windows laughing and waving. They had understood the significance of my bowler. Somebody threw a handful of sweets, a precious commodity in those days, into the back of my car. A packet of cigarettes and a bottle of beer followed.

I had a hand throttle on my steering column so I set this, and slid up and sat on the back of my driving seat, and steered with my feet. Sounds hairy, but you steer an aeroplane with your feet. I was almost level with the coach windows and I reached out and clasped a few eager hands. There was real warmth in their brief grip. But soon we were nearing a bend, and the coach driver was taking no chances. He sounded a farewell fanfare, gave me a cheery wave and drew ahead.

My last gesture was to skim my bowler through a rear window. Someone caught it and a cheer went up and I saw my bowler being waved to me as the bus took the corner.

I slid down into my seat and shut the hand throttle. I was on Civvy Street.

Index

Note: Ranks are those that apply at the time of the individual's first appearance in this book.